I TEACH CATECHISM

I TEACH CATECHISM

A MANUAL FOR PRIESTS, TEACHERS AND NORMAL SCHOOLS. THE QUESTIONS AND ANSWERS OF THE OFFICIAL 1941 REVISED BALTIMORE CATECHISM "THE FIRST COMMUNION CATECHISM," "THE REVISED BALTIMORE CATECHISM" NOS. 1 AND 2, SELECTED, GRADED AND ARRANGED IN LESSON UNITS, ACCOMPANIED BY EXPLANATIONS, AND CORRELATED WITH BIBLE HISTORY, CHURCH HISTORY, THE ECCLESIASTICAL YEAR, THE LITURGY AND THE LIVES OF THE SAINTS

BY

RT. REV. MSGR. M. A. SCHUMACHER, M.A., LITT.D.
*Author of "How To Teach the Catechism" and
Associate Editor of "Living My Religion" Series.*

VOLUME I

GRADES I AND II

AROUCA PRESS

NIHIL OBSTAT:

REV. CHARLES R. KELLY,
Censor Librorum.

IMPRIMATUR:

MOST REVEREND JOHN J. BOYLAN, D.D.
Bishop of Rockford.

Rockford, November 11, 1945.

ACKNOWLEDGMENTS

The author and publishers make grateful acknowledgments to the following for permission to include the material specified: L. M. Wallace, for poem "When I Work for When I Play"; Sister Mary Imelda, S.L., Sisters of Loretto, Nerinx, Ky., for the poem "Jesus Dying on the Cross" from "Living in God's Love" (Book 2 of "Living My Religion Series"); Ave Maria Press, Notre Dame, Ind., for adaptation of Chapter "The Violet Stole," by Rev. Arthur Barry O'Neill, C.S.C., from his book "Clerical Colloquies"; for poem "Though Many Things" from "Petals of a Little Flower." Poems of St. Teresa. Translated from the French by Susan L. Emery, published by the Discalced Carmelites, Boston.

The text of the Questions and Answers of the "First Communion Catechism" contained in this book is reproduced by the license of the Confraternity of Christian Doctrine, Washington, D. C., the only owner of the copyright of "A Catechism of Christian Doctrine—Revised Edition of the Baltimore Catechism No. 2." Used with its permission. All rights reserved.

This Arouca Press edition is a reprint of the book originally published in 1945 by Benziger Brothers, Inc.

ISBN: 978-1-989905-52-4 (pbk) • ISBN: 978-1-989905-53-1 (hc)

All rights reserved: No part of this book may be reproduced or transmitted, in any form or by any means, without permission

Cover design by Michael Schrauzer

PREFACE

This revised edition of "How to Teach the Catechism" is now entitled "I Teach Catechism" because it contains a complete explanation of all the questions and answers in the official Revised Editions 1941 of the Baltimore Catechisms Nos. 1 and 2, as well as of the "First Communion Catechism" based on the aforestated texts. These books are offered as manuals of instruction for the use of teachers of religion in the elementary grades of Catholic parochial or private schools. The content has been organized by grades, the author having selected such questions and answers for essential learning as are suited to the capabilities of the pupils in a respective grade.

"I Teach Catechism" is the teacher's class book. It is by no means to be regarded merely as a reference book for the Community library which the members may consult at times. Daily, the teacher will take that volume written for her grade into the classroom for teaching purposes and back again to the convent for preparing the lesson for the following day. The pupil's book may be the regular Baltimore Catechism or one of the several more elaborate texts which have been especially written for child use. Plain directions at the head of the lesson and throughout each unit explain exactly just which number of the Baltimore series is to be used, and what lessons and questions of the Revised Baltimore Catechism are to be covered. These directions will be just as serviceable for more developed texts as the Baltimore is basic to practically all of them. Again—this is the daily text for each teacher.

There is no need to go into great length to explain the aim and purpose of teaching religion. The eighth-grader can supply the answer and so can the primer-pupil. One of the first answers in the Catechism informs the student that he is "to know God" and "to love and serve God" in this life. In another lesson the Catechism explains "besides believing what God has revealed, we must keep His law." In the original Baltimore Catechism, the Fathers of the Council added the motivation, "in order to be happy with Him in the next life." Knowledge of God and service to God are, therefore, the purposes of teaching religion, impelled everywhere by proper motivation. It is left, then, for the writer to explain briefly how these aims are to be gained by his method.

Knowledge: In order to teach Religion effectively, the teacher must possess a sufficient higher knowledge of Catholic doctrine, so that she may present the subject matter with the conviction that the teaching is accurate and in accordance with sound doctrine, respectively with dogmatic, moral and ascetic theology. The acquisition of knowledge in these sacred sciences cannot ordinarily and fully be obtained from the definitions of the Catechism, many of which are necessarily brief, but yet are also theologically meaningful. Sentences and phrases which occur therein are so comprehensive as to make essential instructions, particularly when principles of moral theology are concerned, most difficult of interpretation. The main object of "I Teach Catechism" therefore is to aid the teacher with a systematic presentation, fully explanatory in its character, of the doctrinal content of the new revised Baltimore Catechisms, and place at her command an ample amount of matter which will enable her to teach religion accurately and confidently and without having to resort to time-filling desk work or similar activities.

A teacher imparts knowledge in the grades through the presentation of accumulated facts; from her standpoint the material must be "teachable." The pupil, on the other hand, is not at all impressed by general or abstract statements; he learns when he listens to concrete examples that are "learnable." Because the teacher cannot be expected to conjure up examples, figures and illustrations on the spur of the moment, "I Teach Catechism" furnishes her with more than enough to make all material "teachable," and from the standpoint of the pupil "learnable."

To beget interest and ambition in the pupil to obtain knowledge, the presentation of identical subjects must be varied in the ascending grades. "I Teach Catechism" repeats all topics four times during the eight-year course, some five times, and some very important ones six times. The presentation, however, is always so different that it impresses the pupil as a new lesson, thus avoiding monotony. The composition naturally is different, and so are the introductions, the stories, the examples, the applications, the motivations. Even where a sixth repetition is deemed necessary, no line is ever repeated.

There is no short-cut to knowledge. Essential knowledge comes

Preface

only from direct study of worthwhile, informative explanations of doctrine and morals.

Service of God: Good habits, the final purpose of all religious teaching, are the resultant of many good deeds regularly practiced over a considerable period of time. "I Teach Catechism" keeps ever before the pupils, that knowledge must be followed by service today and every day. The manuals describe high ideals to move the will to religious practice; they explain how good, how necessary, how pleasant, how profitable virtue is. They also urge directly through the step of application.

The manner of presenting an explanation should carry the natural inference to be drawn therefrom, namely, service to God. The examples, stories and other matter illustrative of the subject taught must be selected with great care, keeping always in mind this learning objective. There is good reason for employing analogies relating to the airplane, the doll, the policeman and similar topics; but if these are not combined with other types that spiritualize the subject in hand, they will produce a material effect only, in the end leaving the boy pupil's imagination filled with the pictures of an airplane adventure and the girl's mind wandering into the familiar domain of her doll's house. "I Teach Catechism" therefore makes copious use of examples from Bible and Church History; nothing so impels to virtue as the sublime story of the Old and New Testament or the actual deed from Church history.

In providing applications care must be used not to overburden the pupils with too many "Do's" and "Dont's" or with too many physical acts. Religion is of the spirit too; the pupil must have faith, hope and charity in his heart, must be patient even with himself, must have contrition for his sins. Often it is more productive of results when the pupil is presented with reasons and motivations, then allowed to choose his own good deed, providing, of course, that there is no question of divine or ecclesiastical obligation.

Motivation: A potent means to beget love and service is the motivation to a better Catholic life. With this addition, the teaching of religion rises above that of the profane subjects and alone makes it worthwhile. A good teacher will know how to weave motivation into every phase of the presentation. "I Teach Catechism" goes to great length that increases as classes arrive at the "wisdom of the 'teens," in order to provide material for motivation. When our Lord enunciated so patent a fact as "Blessed are the clean of heart," He felt it necessary to add the motivation "for they shall see God."

Motivation is a play upon the will. It is a cogent reason why we should react in this or that way. The following are motivations: an example that thrills, a person who appeals, a story that moves, a picture that pleases, an incident that shocks, the consideration of the Last Things, an illustration from the life of our Lord or from the lives of the Blessed Virgin and the Saints. It is the "ah," and the "oh," the dramatic pause after even the shortest phrase. Much as we may boast of our reasoning powers, we are influenced primarily by pleasure or displeasure, by satisfaction or dissatisfaction, by joy or pain, by desire or repugnance. Thomas à Kempis said: "I would rather feel compunction than know its definition." *This is* teaching religion.

Motivation may be a concomitant step in the teaching procedure, or it may be an independent effort at the conclusion. All through the teaching procedure the teacher will find story and example occurring frequently, in order to motivate the will. Again, at the conclusion of each section she will find a paragraph presenting a particular idea for motivation as if she would say to the class, "You have *learned* something about God; now *do* something about it." The Master dogmatized little, seldom gave catechetical form to His pronouncements. If the seventy-two parables and other exhortations, which are just motivations, were removed from the Gospels, only a booklet would be left. These manuals do provide numerous appeals that should make the *knowing* Catholic also a *doing* Catholic. The pious teacher will readily discover other motivations, in answer to the question, how useful is this knowledge or practice, how necessary, how pleasant, how noble. If the Master gave such prominence to motivation, then it is surely proper to emphasize its importance in "I Teach Catechism" and in fact to assign the very first place to this important feature.

THE AUTHOR.

CONTENTS

Preface	III
The Teaching Method	XI
Introduction to Grade I	XX
Summary of Topics for Grade I	XXI
Introduction to Grade II	129
Summary of Topics for Grade II	130

GRADE ONE

page

UNIT ONE: GOD OUR FATHER. 1
  I. God Is the Father of Every Child. II. God's Home. III. You Will Always Love God.

UNIT TWO: GOD HIMSELF. 9
  I. What God Is: (1). I Cannot See God; (2). God Is a Spirit. II. The Greatness of God; (1). God Always Was; (2). God Is All-Good; (3). God Knows Everything; (4). God Is Everywhere; (5). God Can Do All Things. III. One God: (1). There Is One God; (2). The Three Persons in One God.

UNIT THREE: WHAT GOD MADE. 26
  I. God Made the Angels: (1). How God Made the Angels; (2). Some of the Angels Sinned; (3). The Bad and Good Angels. II. God Made the World: (1). How God Made All Things; (2). What God Made. III. God Made Man: (1). Adam and Eve in Paradise; (2). Adam and Eve Were Given a Test; (3). The Effects of their Sin upon Us; (4). Our Duty to God.

UNIT FOUR: GOD THE SON. 44
  I. God Promised a Saviour. II. The Mother of the Saviour. III. The Saviour Is Born.

UNIT FIVE: JESUS PRAYED: WE SHOULD PRAY. 52
  I. What Prayer Is. II. Why We Should Pray. III. How We Should Pray. IV. For Whom We Should Pray. V. Prayer Is Necessary.

UNIT SIX: JESUS OBEYED GOD'S LAWS: WE MUST OBEY THEM 62
  I. Jesus Obeyed God's Laws: (1). Why Jesus Obeyed Them; (2). The Laws of God: II. Not Obeying God's Laws Is a Sin: (1). What Sin Is; (2). Mortal Sin; (3). Venial Sin; (4). The Harm Sin Does to Us.

Contents

UNIT SEVEN: JESUS DIED FOR OUR SINS: WE MUST NEVER SIN. 71
   I. Why Jesus Suffered and Died: (1). Jesus Suffered and Died for Our Sins; (2). Jesus Bought Back Our Right to Heaven; (3). What Jesus Did for Us at the Last Supper. II. What Happened During the Passion: (1). The Agony in the Garden; (2). Jesus Before the Rulers; (3). Jesus Is Crucified.

UNIT EIGHT: JESUS ROSE FROM THE DEAD: WE SHALL RISE AGAIN. 83
   I. How Jesus Rose. II. What Jesus Did after He Arose. III. How Jesus Went to Heaven.

UNIT NINE: JESUS EARNED GRACE FOR US: WE SHOULD USE GRACE. 89
   I. Jesus Bought Grace for Us. II. Grace is a Gift. III. How We Get Grace.

UNIT TEN: JESUS GAVE US THE SACRAMENT OF PENANCE: WE MUST RECEIVE IT WORTHILY. 95
   I. What the Sacrament of Penance Is. II. What Blessings Penance Brings to Us. III. How to Prepare for the Sacrament of Penance. IV. How to Go to Confession.

TABLE OF SINS FOR A CHILD'S CONFESSION. 99

UNIT ELEVEN: JESUS GAVE HIMSELF TO US IN HOLY COMMUNION: WE SHOULD LOVE HIM ALWAYS. . . . 103
   I. What the Holy Eucharist Is. II. What the Effects of a Worthy Communion Are. III. What to Do the Day before Receiving. IV. First Communion.

MONDAY MORNING CHARACTER TALKS:
   FIRST SEMESTER. 112
   SECOND SEMESTER. 119

GRADE TWO

UNIT ONE: GOD. 132
   I. Who God Is: (1). God Is a Spirit; (2). The Perfections of God. II. Our Duty to God: (1). We Must Know, Love and Serve God; (2). Sin Offends God.

UNIT TWO: THE TEN COMMANDMENTS OF GOD. . . . 148
   I. What We Must Do to Be Saved. II. God Gave Us the Ten Commandments. III. The Particular Judgment as a Motive.

Contents

UNIT THREE: THE FIRST THREE COMMANDMENTS—OUR
DUTIES TO GOD. 154
    I. The First Commandment of God: (1). We Must Worship God; (2). We Must Honor God through His Saints and Holy Things. II. The Second Commandment of God: (1). God's Name Must Be Honored; (2). Bad Language Is Sinful. III. The Third Commandment of God: (1). The Lord's Day Is Holy; (2). We Must Avoid Unnecessary Work.

UNIT FOUR: THE FOURTH TO THE TENTH COMMANDMENT—
OUR DUTIES TO OURSELVES AND TO OTHERS. 170
    I. The Fourth Commandment of God: (1). Children Must Honor Their Parents; (2). Children Must Love and Help Parents; (3). Children Must Obey Their Parents; (4). All Must Respect and Obey Their Superiors. II. The Fifth Commandment of God: (1). Proper Care of Body and Soul; (2). Injury to Body and Soul Is Forbidden. III. The Sixth Commandment of God: (1). The Duty to Be Pure and Clean; (2). Examples of Purity. IV. The Seventh Commandment of God: (1). We Must Be Fair; (2). Stealing Is Forbidden; (3). Wrongs Must Be Righted. V. The Eighth Commandment of God: (1). The Duty to Speak the Truth; (2). What the Commandment Forbids. VI. The Ninth Commandment of God: (1). St. Stanislaus—Pure As a Pure White Lily. VII. The Tenth Commandment of God: (1). We Must Be Satisfied, Not Complain; (2). We May Try to Better Ourselves.

TABLE OF SINS FOR A CHILD'S CONFESSION. 197

UNIT FIVE: TWO LAWS OF THE CHURCH. 199
    I. The Law about Holy Mass: (1). We Must Obey the Laws of the Church; (2). The Mass on Sundays; (3). The Mass on Holydays. II. The Law about Meat: (1). How the Law Affects Children.

UNIT SIX: PRAYER HELPS US TO KEEP GOD'S LAWS. . . 206
    I. We Should Pray Sincerely and Earnestly. II. We Should Pray with Hope and Perseverance. III. Morning, Evening and Table Prayers. IV. Prayer for Special Needs.

UNIT SEVEN: GRACE. 215
    I. Grace Is a Help. II. How Grace Comes to Us. III. Kinds of Grace. IV. Using Grace.

UNIT EIGHT: GRACE THROUGH BAPTISM AND CONFIRMATION. 224
    I. What a Sacrament Is. II. The Sacrament of Baptism. III. The Sacrament of Confirmation.

Contents

UNIT NINE: THE SACRAMENT OF PENANCE HELPS US TO
KEEP GOD'S LAWS. 228
    I. The Sacrament of Penance: (1). What the Sacrament of Penance Is; (2). What the Sacrament Does. II. How to Receive Penance Worthily; (1). We Find Our Sins; (2) We Are Sorry for Our Sins; (3). We Make Up Our Minds Not to Sin Again; (4). We Tell Our Sins to the Priest; (5). We Are Willing to Do the Penance the Priest Gives Us.

UNIT TEN: THE HOLY EUCHARIST HELPS US TO KEEP
GOD'S LAWS. 243
    I. The Sacrament of the Holy Eucharist: (1). When and How It Was Instituted; (2). What the Holy Eucharist Is; (3). What Holy Communion Does for Us; (4). How to Prepare Body and Soul; (5). How to Receive Holy Communion. II. Holy Mass: (1). Our Lord's Mass; (2). The Priest's Mass.

UNIT ELEVEN: OUR BLESSED MOTHER. 258
    I. To the Time When the Angel Appeared to Her. II. From the Birth of Christ to the End.

MONDAY MORNING CHARACTER TALKS:
FIRST SEMESTER. 264
SECOND SEMESTER. 271

* * * *

BIBLIOGRAPHY XXIII
INDEX OF BIBLE HISTORY REFERENCES XXV
INDEX OF QUESTIONS AND ANSWERS FROM THE REVISED FIRST COMMUNION CATECHISM XXVII
GENERAL INDEX XXVIII

THE TEACHING METHOD

The writer takes for granted that the teacher has learned about teaching steps in her normal school course; the five steps are easily discernible in the simpler method here advised. But, neither here, nor for that matter in any subject, should there be an undue straining to carry out any step, lest the method become stilted and lifeless. The good teacher learns method in general, prepares her religion, says a prayer, teaches naturally and thinks little of steps.

The method of teaching here advised is so simple that it can be explained in one sentence—the manual is the method. It is one thing to present explanatory material, and for that we have all the books ever written on theology and catechism; it is quite another thing to teach that effectively. The practical manual will supply both matter and method, the latter indeed in so evident a manner that there will be no hesitation, no puzzling about teaching steps— the manual supplies both matter and method. The teacher has but to follow the presentations in the manual, paragraph by paragraph, direction after direction and she has the method. This does not preclude her using her own ingenuity to illustrate and amplify still further. This paragraph might suffice, but the teacher may be interested to learn why and how the writer constructed his method, so, a more detailed explanation follows.

There are two principal parts to successful teaching of religion— teacher activity and pupil activity. Teacher activity is essential for success and so is pupil activity. There is no easy way, no mechanical substitute, no magic key, in the teaching of religion. An explanation will be given of each, but it is not to be taken that the two activities are separated by distinct lines and wholly independent of each other. The good teacher strives for reaction from the pupils during teacher activity; similarly she maintains her own active interest during pupil activity.

A. Teacher Activity

Aim: The pupils must be told the aim of the lesson so that they can show interest in what follows, can grasp the sequence intelligently, and, if they be particularly bright, even anticipate parts. The Foreword preceding each grade and the outline before each unit establish the foundation for the teacher, whence she safely proceeds to the first class-contact—"What we shall learn." This paragraph introducing each unit refers briefly to what has already been learned, and then goes on to explain what is to be learned without, however, revealing too much; thus interest is maintained through curiosity of what is to come. The step "What we shall learn," composed then by the teacher, is a good beginning for any morning lesson.

Explanation: To introduce this step, the teacher finds a story, an example, or an illustration at the very beginning of the section (indicated by arabic numerals). The purpose of such introduction is twofold: first, to fix the imaginations of the pupils on something tangible and concrete; second, to give them an even broader indication of the subject to be explained, one to which in a general way they can attach the explanations which follow. The introduction is a lesson in picture.

Since the opening picture does not provide every necessary detail for full understanding of the religious truth, further explanation is provided. By the inductive method, always made understandable by numerous examples, the words, phrases and sentences are built up until they lead to the official catechism answer. The same treatment given to every question belonging to one section, shows then the unity and the relation of catechetical concepts. Before concluding the section, an appeal is made once more to child experience with a "summary by example" that displays the salient features of each answer, brings them to a practical basis for faith and human conduct; it shows the unity of and the relation between the answers of this one section. Child psychology teaches us that this "summary by example" often remains in the youthful mind much longer than the didactic explanations. Teachers in the elementary grades like to teach by mental pictures and these texts literally run over with examples, illustrations and stories.

Human nature, taking it as it is, may or may not be ready now to do what is commanded. Generally then another paragraph, called "motivation," is added to provide the pupil with a final impulse, showing him how good, how useful, how pleasant, it is to do what is commanded.

B. Pupil Activity

The pupils must now prove to the teacher that they understood her explanation from the statement of aim to the motivation. To avoid loss of time and to ensure pointed effort in pupil activity the

The Teaching Method

teacher must prompt at the beginnings. She has but to convert the first sentence of each paragraph into a question in order to draw out from the pupils the matter contained in that paragraph.

The Daily Recitation: The religion period is always divided into two parts: first, the recitation by the pupils of the matter covered the previous day; second, the explanation of the new lesson by the teacher. Regardless of whether the teacher covered a whole section or not, this recitation must be given by the pupils.

Organization: In the simplest terms, this is a review of a section. The matter for the step is supplied by the manual in considerable detail. From the second grade to the fifth inclusive it is found immediately following the section to which it refers; from the sixth to the eighth it is given at the end of the unit. It was thought better to let the teacher of the first grade make up her own questions because a personal acquaintance is necessary with beginners to get any kind of a response from them. Understand, this material is given for oral catechizing where a question must often be re-edited for a pupil who hesitates about the answer. A clever teacher will put a question in several different ways in order to get a response from such a pupil. The same questions can be used for written tests, but again the teacher must decide whether some questions need more re-editing than others to suit the mental grasp of her particular class.

Reconstruction: This is just another review, a review of a division or unit. The intermediate grades will reconstruct the smaller divisions (indicated by a Roman numeral) while the upper grades will reconstruct the whole unit. The teacher will look over the organization material and select only such questions or points which are principal; with a bright class it will be enough to take the captions. That point or question is then proposed to the pupil who is to give as complete an explanation of it as he can. The intention is to explore the comprehensive knowledge of the pupil, to find out whether he grasps the broader concepts of the lesson, to gauge his understanding of how one question is related to another. The promptings are fewer in order to give him time and opportunity to build up the larger thought; there is a more rapid progress to fundamental issues. The pupil, as it were, assumes the role of teacher; he is teaching himself to be an articulate Catholic.

The Teaching Method

C. Other Uses of this Method

1. *Monday Morning Character Talks:* They are found on the last pages for each grade and are thirty in number, fifteen for each semester. The Talk which might take up five or six minutes, is given on a Monday morning, either to point to a practical application of the catechetical lessons, or to furnish knowledge of Catholic liturgy. The introductory paragraph always gives further instructions for their use.

2. *Cycling and Combination Plans:* Naturally these manuals find their easiest adaptation in the larger schools with one grade to a room. Since many parishes are not so blessed, the following plans are offered for use of the manuals in smaller schools.

A. In schools of four to seven classrooms. Whenever two grades are in a room, establish a two-year cycle, beginning in the first year with the matter for the higher grade and going in the second year to the matter for the lower grade.

B. In schools of three classrooms. Two plans are suggested: (a) would use all three volumes covering the material for eight grades; (b) would use only two volumes covering the material for six grades.

(a) Make a temporary shift of classes during the religion period, placing grades 1 and 2 in room one, grades 3, 4 and 5 in room two, grades 6, 7 and 8 in room three.

In room one, during the first semester take grades 1 and 2 separately, using the material of each respective grade for the first semester. During the second semester, combine grades 1 and 2, using the material of the second semester of grade 2.

In room two, teach grade 3 separately, using the regular presentation for the grade. Combine grades 4 and 5 making a two-year cycle and going from the material of grade 5 in the first year to the material for grade 4 in the second year.

In room three, combine grades 6, 7 and 8. Establish a three-year cycle, using the material of grade 8 in the first year, or 7 in the second year, of 6 in the third year.

(b) This plan, which is less ambitious, uses only the first two volumes which contain material for the first six grades. Here the teacher of the first room has grades 1, 2, 3; of the second room, grades 4, 5, 6; of the third room, grades 7 and 8.

The Teaching Method   xv

In room one: First Semester.....Grade 1 is taught separately and uses the material of the first semester of grade 1. Grades 2 and 3 are combined, using the material of first semester of grade 2.

Second Semester...The First Communion class is taken separately and uses the material of the second semester of grade one.

The other two classes are combined, using the material of the second semester of grade 2.

In room two: Both Semesters....Grade 4 is taken separately, using the material regularly given for grade 3.

Grades 5 and 6 are combined in a two-year cycle, during the first year they use the material regularly given for grade 5, and in the second year the material regularly given in grade 4.

In room three: Both Semesters....Grades 7 and 8 are combined in a two-year cycle. During the first year they use the material regularly given in grade 6, and in the second year the material regularly given in grade 5.

C. In schools of two classrooms. At best this is a difficult situation when probably grades 1, 2, 3 and 4 are in the first room, and the other grades in the second room. Certainly only the first two volumes will be used, which contain material regularly used for the first six grades.

The Teaching Method

In room one: First Semester ....Grade 1 is a separate class which uses the material of the first semester of grade 1. Grades 2, 3 and 4 are combined in a two-year cycle. In the first year they use the material of the first semester of grade 3, and in the second year the first semester of grade 2.

Second Semester ...Grades 1 and 2 are combined. They use the material of the second semester of grade 1. Grades 3 and 4 are combined in a two-year cycle. In the first year they use the material of the second semester of grade 3, and in the second year the material of the second semester of grade 2.

In room three: Both Semesters ....Grades 5 and 6 are combined, making a two-year cycle. In the first year they cover the material regularly offered for grade 5, and in the second year that which is regularly offered for grade 4.

Grades 7 and 8 are combined, making a two-year cycle. In the first year they cover the material regularly offered for grade 6, and in the second year that regularly offered in grade 5.

Hence, once in four years all grades have the same material and then are combined into one class.

The Teaching Method

3. *Small High Schools:* Schools of two rooms or two classes may find it difficult to utilize courses written for the schools with a complete curriculum. It is suggested that the teacher use these manuals of the sixth, seventh and eighth grade; they are sufficiently developed to interest high school pupils placed in these circumstances.

4. *Vacation Schools:* In thousands of instances now our Sisters give a two weeks' summer course to children in parishes where there are no Catholic schools.

By using "I Teach Catechism" as suggested below, the teacher will find all necessary matter and save herself a great deal of planning in regard to supplementary branches because the manuals integrate the study of the Catechism with the kindred subjects like Bible History and the church year. The teaching matter in the manuals is of necessity more copious than she had use for, so it will be her task to condense and to select what she can cover in the short time allotted to her. The teacher is left to her own devices for pictures and activities, a very important part of this short course.

The classes are generally divided into three groups, the prayer group, the First Communion group, and the advanced group. The first two are placed in one room as they are taught by the same teacher, not too complicated an arrangement because while one class is actively taught, the other is engaged in desk work. The second teacher handles only the advanced group.

(a) Prayer Group (ages 4 to 6). The pupils use no text whatsoever. The teacher uses the Baltimore First Communion Catechism for the prayers to be learned; only one prayer, the Act of Contrition, need be changed when the pupils later arrive at the advanced class. The teacher uses "I Teach Catechism" as written for grade one. She will briefly explain the second unit, the third, the fourth, and, if there be time, also the seventh unit. The desk work will be of the picture variety, or perhaps a pupil of the advanced group can be appointed to teach the little ones their prayers during this time.

(b) First Communion Group. The pupils use the Baltimore First Communion Catechism for prayers and catechetical work. An exception is made for the Act of Contrition which is taken from the No. 1 Baltimore; better to learn the regular Act now than have to unlearn it later on.

The Teaching Method

"I Teach Catechism" is the teacher's text book. In the section written for grade two, she will find the units here referred to.

Unit One: God.

Unit Two: The story of the ten commandments. She will then, instead of explaining each commandment, have the pupils learn the table of sins for purposes of confession.
1. Have I missed my regular prayers?
2. Have I taken God's name in vain?
3. Have I missed Mass on Sundays or holydays of obligation?
4. Have I disobeyed my parents?
5. Have I quarreled?
6. Did I commit impure actions?
7. Did I steal?
8. Did I tell lies?
9. Did I eat meat on a forbidden day?

Unit Seven: Grace.

Unit Nine: The Sacrament of Penance.

Unit Ten: First Communion.

One activity suggested for the pupils in this and the next group is that they look up the Bible History stories which came up or will come up in the catechetical explanations.

(c) Advanced Group. The pupils will use the Baltimore Catechism No. 1, from which they will now learn their prayers. As to the teacher, she will make her preparation from volume two "I Teach Catechism" wherever she feels that she needs more information; but she will teach from the Catechism. Many more topics must now be covered so she can condense more easily by following this procedure; she has time only to teach the bare essentials. All the sacraments must now be taught but she will rarely ever go beyond the definition and the effects. With the sacrament of Penance she will explain only the five steps, and with the Holy Eucharist only the required disposition and method of receiving. Extreme Unction, Holy Orders, and Matrimony should take up no more than one period. The establishment of the Church is an important unit but there is no time to go into the marks and attributes of the Church. Naturally the commandments of the

Church must follow. If there is still time she will review the topic of sin and conclude with that on prayer.

5. *Catechetical Course of Sermons:* Two series may be used. The simpler one will include the material given in the manuals for grades three, four, and five. The more advanced series will cover the material given in the manuals for grades six, seven, and eight. The priest will recognize how the presentation here given is adaptable to a sermon—the introduction, the explanation, the application, the motivation.

INTRODUCTION TO GRADE I

The teacher realizes that it is utterly impossible for any manual to give her, sentence by sentence, the daily procedure in her religion class. A rather detailed procedure is offered here for classes in general; but the teacher must know the mentality of her pupils, must watch intently for reactions, and then gauge her interpretations of the manual accordingly. If an example here and there evokes no response she will have to try a simpler one. For this reason, it is absolutely necessary that she prepare the night before so that she will be able to shift her explanations if necessity calls for it on the following day.

It was thought better not to ask the first-grade teacher to attempt the step of Reconstruction because these youthful intellects cannot extend themselves that far. Probably she must rest satisfied with the daily recitation of matter covered in the previous lesson. It is left to her judgment whether or not to use the step of organization which follows and reviews each section. The few samples supplied in the manual may convince her that organization is not a too difficult step, especially when she helps with the right promptings. More samples were not supplied because each first grade is a definite psychological problem which must be solved by the particular teacher.

The unit topics are taken as much as possible from the First Communion Catechism as basis. However that Catechism in the footnotes advises the teacher to explain certain topics not contained in the text. A sentence in parentheses right under the caption of the unit informs her whenever a unit is based solely on a lesson from the First Communion Catechism. When no such direction is given, it means that the topic is not contained in the First Communion Catechism. Where the class uses a child's text especially adapted to this extraneous material, there is no difficulty. Where the class depends on the official Revised Baltimore Catechism, the matter must be taught orally. This presents no added difficulty as most of the teaching in grade one is oral.

SUMMARY OF TOPICS FOR GRADE ONE

(Lessons from the Revised Baltimore First Communion Catechism
are indicated in Parentheses)

FIRST SEMESTER OR I B

Unit One: God Our Father (Lesson 1).
  I. God Is the Father of Every Child.
  II. God's Home.
  III. You Will Always Love God.

Unit Two: God Himself (Lessons 2 and 3).
  I. What God Is.
  II. The Greatness of God.
  III. One God.

Unit Three: What God Made (Lesson 1).
  I. God Made the Angels.
  II. God Made the World.
  III. God Made Man.

Unit Four: God the Son (Lesson 4).
  I. God Promised a Saviour.
  II. The Mother of the Saviour.
  III. The Saviour Is Born.

SECOND SEMESTER OR I A

Unit Five: Jesus Prayed: We Should Pray.
  I. What Prayer Is.
  II. Why We Should Pray.
  III. How We Should Pray.
  IV. For Whom We Should Pray.
  V. Prayer Is Necessary.

Unit Six: Jesus Obeyed God's Laws: We Must Obey Them (Lesson 7).
  I. Jesus Obeyed God's Laws.
  II. Not Obeying God's Laws Is a Sin

Unit Seven: Jesus Died for Our Sins: We Must Never Sin (Lesson 5).
  I. Why Jesus Suffered and Died.
  II. What Happened During the Passion.

Summary of Topics for Grade One

UNIT EIGHT: Jesus Rose from the Dead: We Shall Rise Again.
  I. How Jesus Rose.
  II. What Jesus Did After He Arose.
  III. How Jesus Went to Heaven.

UNIT NINE: Jesus Earned Grace for Us: We Should Use Grace.
  I. Jesus Bought Grace for Us.
  II. Grace Is a Gift.
  III. How We Get Grace.

UNIT TEN: Jesus Gave Us the Sacrament of Penance: We Must Receive It Worthily (Lessons 9 and 10).
  I. What the Sacrament of Penance Is.
  II. What Blessings Penance Brings to Us.
  III. How to Prepare for the Sacrament of Penance.
  IV. How to Go to Confession.

UNIT ELEVEN: Jesus Gave Himself to Us in Holy Communion: We Should Love Him Always (Lesson 11).
  I. What the Holy Eucharist Is.
  II. What the Effects of a Worthy Communion Are.
  III. What to Do the Day before Receiving.
  IV. First Communion.

Monday Morning Character Talks.
Index of Bible History References.
Index of the Questions and Answers taken from the Revised Baltimore First Communion Catechism.
Index of Catechetical Topics.

UNIT ONE: GOD OUR FATHER

(Revised Baltimore First Communion Catechism: Lesson 1)
  I. GOD IS THE FATHER OF EVERY CHILD.
  II. GOD'S HOME.
  III. YOU WILL ALWAYS LOVE GOD.

What We Shall Learn: Dear children, this is the beginning of your school years and right away you are told about God. You often heard Mother talk about God and she told you wonderful things about Him. Now you come here to learn still more about Him. Every day in the coming school years you will learn about God because there is no one of whom so many wonderful things can be said as God. Great as He is, you will learn that He loves little "you" and you are also able to please Him by loving Him. You will therefore start the school year with a thought that will make you happy,—the great wonderful God loves you. You have all heard your sisters and brothers talking about learning the catechism and you thought it was something difficult. Well, it is not difficult because today and every day now you will learn how much God loves you and you will daily be happy to learn that you can return that love of God by being good. The Catechism just tells you how to be good, and good children are always happy children. In short, you will learn how always to be truly happy.

I. God Is the Father of Every Child

With children of this age it is above all things necessary to begin an explanation with something they can visualize; it must not be a house but *the* house, not a home but *their* home. For that very reason the personal pronouns "we" and "you" are so often employed in these first months, just to make the talk personal and second to put the teacher on a friendly level with the pupils. To begin, it will establish an atmosphere of confidence if the teacher asks the pupils, which of them has heard about God? What did Mother and Father tell you about Him? Probably only a few will give an answer but a point has been gained. The teacher may continue this line of questioning, encouraging the children to tell all they know. Even with this introduction it will scarcely be wise to launch into a catechetical explanation on the first day. It is rather suggested that the teacher show the pupils how to make the sign of the cross correctly; this activity will enable her to go amongst the pupils, helping them and thus also getting them over their first bashfulness. For directions the teacher will refer to Morning Talk Number 1 in the rear of Grade I material.

Then comes the first effort at catechesis, the concept of God the Father. The teacher begins her work with the concept of the father in the home in order to lead to the climax of God the Father. The appealing concept of mother love will be utilized later in the division.

Picture a room in your own home. Your father has been explaining how you should make the sign of the cross. He repeats all the words several times until you know them by heart. Then he goes back to the first words, "In the name of the Father." You ask him why God is called your Father, and he tells you why, tells you too that God is your Father who loves you very much.

You love your own father because he takes care of you. Father earns money to buy food and clothes for Mother and the children. He does everything to make you happy, even buying candy and little things for you to give you extra happiness. Many times during his work, he is encouraged by the thought that he is doing it for you. You feel that you could not get along without him and indeed you and Mother would have a very difficult time to get along if he were suddenly thrown out of work.

You consider your father as a big, big man, the biggest and best in all the world. He is much taller, heavier and stronger than you and fills you with admiration at the apparently wonderful things he can do. He is over you at home, directing and commanding, for a father has that right and duty. You look up to your father because he is so wise. It will not be long before you ask him for help in doing your homework; you will ask him for help with your spelling and your numbers. He has lived so much longer than you and is wiser in all things. He answers the many questions you ask him every day. He is kind to you because he knows that you need him and all his advice and direction is for your good.

God is your Father too but He is a much bigger, much wiser, and even a better Father than your own father at home. One time our Lord told His friends to pray to God, explaining that they should call Him, "Our Father." Perhaps indeed some of you know that prayer beginning with the words, "Our Father." You must not only call God, Father, but you must say, "Our Father," to show that He is the Father of every boy and girl here and of everyone in the whole world.

God is the Father of all; He is "Our Father." No little child is shut out nor any grown-up person in the whole world. He is the biggest Father imaginable because He is the Father of every child or grown-up, be he white or red or black or yellow. God is such a big Father that He can take care of the biggest family. Every child can kneel down tonight and say, "You are my Father."

Just as you belong to your father at home, so do you belong to God. You are His child, a member of His family. He desires your obedience and He has a right to it. He wishes you to be of good will so that you will be pleasant to all the other children and pleasing to Him. Like every good father of a home, God has rules for His children too and He wants them to behave well. His principal rule says, "Be good," meaning to be kind to one another and respectful to Him.

All must look up to God, respect Him. In a few days you will learn more about the greatness of this, your Father. Just now it is enough to know He is bigger and better than a thousand, thousand fathers here in your home.

Q. 1. Who made you?
A. God made me.

The teaching of the first weeks must be mostly oral as supplementary activities are hardly possible.

II. God's Home

Picture the great big world and all the beautiful things in it, the trees, the rivers, the meadows, the flowers. God owns the big, big, world and it is His home.

We say though that heaven is God's real home. In that heaven are beauties greater than are to be found in the world, so great that no man can describe them.

In that heavenly home God has other children who were good in times past and will be happy now and forever. There too are the angels, the saints and the Blessed Virgin.

My father and mother love me. Picture a humble but neat cottage on some side street. Down the street comes a man somewhat begrimed with a dinner pail in his hand. Mother with a baby in her arms stands on the verandah. A little girl sees him. It is father returning from work. With arms outstretched she runs forward to greet him.

Sometimes you meet Daddy as he comes home because you know that he loves you. All fathers love their children. You remember how he praises you sometimes, how he tells of his love, how he shows it by a kiss or an embrace. You have no idea how his love showed itself when you were a tiny babe. You were so little and so weak that sometimes he feared you would die. Then he worried about you and called the doctor. He went to church to pray for you or he prayed in his bedroom that God would make you well.

Picture your father as he goes about his daily task. Why does father work all day? Just to earn enough money to get you food, clothing and good schooling. Often his work is very difficult; or perhaps he is not feeling well but he keeps on because he loves you so much. Just think of the many beautiful things he has bought for you at various times.

God the Father loves you. You are so much smaller than this Father, yet He loves you. A violet is smaller than you, yet you love the violet. And God the Father can love you so very much more than any father on earth because God is so big and able to love so much. Your father loves you and you love your father but because he is bigger he can do so much more for you: God is able to love you even more than you can love Him.

> God gives you food. Picture your own family at dinner. You are all saying Grace because God supplies that food and you want Him to bless it.
>
> God cares for you. Picture yourself asleep in your bedroom. The hand of God is over you. God loves you and takes care of you while you sleep.

God your Father loves you in many ways. He is glad that you were born and He provided parents to care for your body and soul. He was good to give you Baptism which made you His child. He wants you all to grow up as good children, and all through life He will help you to be good. Finally he wants you to be with Him in heaven where His love will shower more gifts on you than you can even imagine.

Grade I II. God's Home

God's love for you is a special kind. Your father loves you all the time but he is not with you as much as Mother. She too shows her love much more, as you know from her extra care, kisses and embraces. A mother's heart is made for love. Now God's love is greater than Father's, than Mother's, greater than both combined. In the months to come you will learn more and more about the great love which God has for you.

God made you because He is good. He likes little children and He hopes that they will be good so that He can give them much love and care. God made you for the one reason only, that He wants to make you happy here and in eternity. A good child is always the happiest child here on earth. But the good child has a still greater happiness in store for it, namely, the happiness in heaven. God made you for heaven. Suppose you met a man, a good friend of your family, downtown who said, "Come along with me; I told your mother that I will take you to a show." Afterwards you would tell Mother about the good man you had met. And Mother would say, "Yes, he was a good man because he only wanted to make you happy." So God in His goodness made you only that He might make you happy.

Can you imagine what that means to be happy forever in heaven? There you will meet those wonderful saints about whom you have been told stories. You will meet that highest of saints, the Blessed Virgin, and she will love you as she loved Jesus when He was with her at Nazareth. But greatest joy of all, you will meet the good, the beautiful, the holy God about whom we have been talking during the last several days.

Q. 3. Why did God make you?
A. God made me to show His goodness and to make me happy with Him in heaven.

Summary by Example: The teacher will here tell the children the story of Moses found in the basket. The moral is that God the Father loved that little child Moses and protected it from the wicked Pharao. God did not want that child to be killed through the orders of the wicked ruler; so He instructed the mother and the little sister how to hide him. God took care of that child also in later years and made him a great leader of his people. You have no idea of the many dangers that surround you. Just be good and God will save you from dangers like accidents and sickness, and the greater danger of losing your soul. (Some teachers might be tempted to tell the story of Christ blessing the children but the variation of a deed of the second Person might confuse the little ones in regard to the first Person—we must keep on a straight line).

Motivation: You should therefore be very happy. Every day you should thank God for what He has done for you and especially for giving you so much love. All others will die and their love cease but God will never cease His care. The little orphan that has no parents still enjoys the love of God.

Organization of Section 2. With children of this age, always begin the organization with the opening picture or example. How did Father show his love for you when you were a tiny babe? What does Father do for you all day long? Does God the Father love you still more? Who gives you the food you eat? What does God do for you while you sleep at night? What does God want you to do all your life? Where does He want to take you when you die? Tell the story of Moses found in the basket. What does the story tell you? The learning concept is: God's love for you is greater than Father's, than Mother's. The motivation is: God's love lasts forever.

III. You Will Always Love God

You will always love God. You are entering the church. Perhaps your brother or sister is with you. You are about to attend Holy Mass where you will tell God that you will always love Him. You will show your love by keeping His laws all day.

A good child will always return the love of a father and mother. He will be pleasant about the house, greeting them with a "Good morning" and saying "Good night" before he retires. He will be cheerful all day because he appreciates what they do for him. He will try always to be good because he knows that pleases them above all. When he is able, he will even try to help them.

A good child of God returns the love of God too. He will not only say that he loves God but he will do the things that please Him. Father and especially Mother has told you often how to please Him. When you do those things you really show your love of God. You must not only say it but you must do it. A loving child not only prays to God every day but he does everything all day that God wants him to do.

God wants every child to love Him. Mother wants love, so does

Grade I   III. You Will Always Love God   7

Father and so does God. God made you and He put you on this earth just that you might love Him. And He wants you in heaven so that you will love Him forever more.

In order to get to heaven, you must be good. The little boys and girls who are in heaven now, were good and we must be like them.

You must first learn what it means to be good. Daily now you are going to study the catechism which tells you what things you must do and what you must not do so that you can get to heaven. You will learn about God and what He wants you to do. The more you get to know about God, the more you will desire to be with Him in heaven.

By and by you will study about God Himself, and you will learn such wonderful and beautiful things about Him that you will love Him. God is your best Father, worthy of your greatest love. Little Annie loves her father very much because she realizes what a great man and what a good parent he is. Little Annie is not satisfied with just saying to her father that she loves him but she will say kind words and do good deeds that please him. When you love God you will wish to serve Him. You serve God by doing what He commands, and not doing what He forbids. Annie goes to Mass every Sunday because God has commanded it, and she will never talk unkindly of a companion because God has forbidden that. You can serve God too by praying to Him. You can pray to God anywhere and everywhere. Generally, however, you will fold your hands and pray to your Father in heaven. That is what you will do tonight before you retire and again tomorrow morning when you arise. That is what you will do whenever you pray to God outside the Church. When you are in church you look at the tabernacle because God is in there.

During these first days therefore you have learned one wonderful truth. Besides having a father here on earth who is quite wonderful, you have a Father in heaven who is God and who is the most wonderful Father of all. Besides being a child of your father at home, you are a child of God the Father who is in heaven. You have learned how you can get to heaven where God your Father is.

Q. 4. What must you do to be happy with God in heaven?
A. To be happy with God in heaven I must know Him, love Him, and serve Him in this world.

Summary by Example: Two little boys were arguing, as children do, about the respective merits of their fathers. One said: "I bet my father is a thousand times stronger than your father." The other one replied: "I bet my father knows a thousand times more than your father." It was nice to show that love but a little girl spoke up: "I bet my father is the biggest and best of all, for God is my Father." Who, do you think, won the argument?

Motivation: St. Francis of Assisi gave up everything for God, even his parents. There he was without money, without decent clothes, without a home. Then the Saint said: "Now I have only one father, God my Father, who is in heaven." For the rest of his life, only God was his father. Wasn't that saint lucky after all? Wasn't he rich? He had given away so little and had received so much in return. You are rich, you have God the Father for your Friend.

You should be happy that you can love God. You should resolve right here that every day in your prayers you will tell God how much you love Him. You should resolve right here to prove your love by doing the things all day that please Him. You want to get to heaven where you can love God always and where God will always love you.

All the children have seen a bird's nest in the spring, with a mother-bird and perhaps three fledglings. Perhaps you have watched the mother-bird as she busied herself all day long finding food for the young ones. She will starve herself in order to find that food because she loves them. And the fledglings are nervous and discontented until the mother returns to the nest because they love the mother. God loves you: you love God.

UNIT TWO: GOD HIMSELF

(Revised Baltimore First Communion Catechism: Lessons 2 and 3)

I. WHAT GOD IS.
   1. I CANNOT SEE GOD.
   2. GOD IS A SPIRIT.

II. THE GREATNESS OF GOD.
   1. GOD ALWAYS WAS.
   2. GOD IS ALL-GOOD.
   3. GOD KNOWS EVERYTHING.
   4. GOD IS EVERYWHERE.
   5. GOD CAN DO ALL THINGS.

III. ONE GOD.
   1. THERE IS ONE GOD.
   2. THE THREE PERSONS IN GOD.

What We Shall Learn: We have now learned that God is our Father in heaven, that He loves us very much and wants us to love Him. We know now that we should be good so as to please God who is so good to us. It is easy to show God that we love Him. All we have to do is to speak to God and say, "Dear God, I love you"—"Dear God, I thank You"—"Dear God, let me be good." And now we want to learn still more about God. We want to know what God is. We want to know how long God has lived, how great and big He is, where He is and what He does; we want to learn wonderful things about God, how holy He is, how loving how He forgives us, how He cares for us. Here in the classroom, at home every morning and every night we shall talk to Him and tell Him how great He is and that we want His help.

I. What God Is

1. I Cannot See God

The concept of God as a simple spirit is indeed deep theology but still it is not difficult to make children see that He is a living Personality who intimately affects their lives. Through a progressive accumulation of details intelligible to children, they can ultimately grasp the idea of the Person of God and of His perfections. The use of stories, analogies and examples is an important phase and the teacher will do well to multiply, if possible, those which are given in this explanation.

We can see much with our bodily eyes. Our parents and friends can see us. As long as they are alive, they can see what we do in their presence. As long as they enjoy vision, their eyes can follow us. In the home, in the classroom, on the playground, we are generally under somebody's vision. And also we can see persons and things as long as they are within the range of our vision.

We cannot see everything because our eyes are too weak. We cannot see a man behind a tree even though we know that he is there. We cannot see Father after he has walked two miles down the road. There are many specks in the air which are so small that our eyes cannot make them out.

There are many things which we cannot see but we know that they are here. We cannot see God but He is here, He is everywhere nevertheless.

> I cannot see the wind: I cannot see God. (The teacher must supply copious details for this picture and all such that follow.) Perhaps some of these boys have flown a kite. Something took that paper kite from the ground, swept it higher and higher until it hung way up in the sky. That something was the wind, something which could not be seen yet had a force to raise the kite.

We cannot see God. We cannot see our guardian angel either but we know and oftentimes feel that he is beside us. Sometimes Mother comes into our dark bedroom: we cannot see her but we hear her moving about and we know she is there. If we had brighter eyes we could discern her. So our eyes are not bright enough to see God who is everywhere about us. Mother often tells us that we have a soul and that we must take good care of it. No one can see his own soul, yet it is within his body, giving it life to see, to hear, and power to move and do. That soul is a real spirit because it has no body and yet it has life to know and to understand. We know that God is everywhere about us because He keeps us alive. He watches the birds in the air, He takes care of the grain in the fields, He sees us, He sees everything but we cannot see Him. When we reach heaven our eyes will be brighter and we will be able to see Him.

Summary by Example: If the teacher now opens the window and lowers the curtain, all the children will observe that the curtain flaps noisily. The same wind which cannot be seen, pulls it in and out. Perhaps some fallen leaves are scurrying over the playground because they are pushed along by something which really exists but cannot be seen, the wind. Surely by now the children have sufficient courage and confidence to tell about a tree that was blown down by an invisible force, about the heat that oppressed them during the summer yet could not be seen. We cannot see God.

Motivation: Your God is not only great but He is a wonderful God because He can be everywhere yet not be seen. He is more wonderful than the wind which moves the kite, drives the leaves or vibrates the curtain. He made the invisible wind. Pray to Him tonight. You cannot see Him but He is there.

Organization of Section 1. Principal questions will naturally be followed by supplementary ones made up by the teacher. Leading sentences here will be: What can you see with your own eyes? Can your eyes see everything, for example, a man behind a tree? What can the wind do? Can you see the wind? Is there a wind? Can you see Mother in a dark bedroom? Is Mother there though? Can you see your guardian angel? Is he there though? Can you see God? Is God there though? Summarize by the example of the wind that blew down the big tree. Although you cannot see God, you can pray to Him tonight.

2. God Is a Spirit

This is not the first time the child hears the word "Spirit"; the word has been frequently used in one way or another by the teacher in the classroom and by those at home. The child knows the sound of the word. It is required only to affix it to God, a living Person.

I cannot touch the light: I cannot touch God. I cannot see God; God is a spirit. It is early morning and probably the sun's rays are shining into the room. The sunlight is there but it cannot be grasped or touched because it has no body. If the rays are very warm they can be felt, but not having body or matter they cannot be pushed about. Here we have something which is very helpful, though it is without body. Recalling the analogy of the wind we have something that is very active but cannot be seen.

We learned in the last lesson that we cannot see God. We raise our eyes to Him in prayer; we know He is before us but we cannot see Him. God is like the wind or the light but there is one important difference. The wind and the light really exist but they have no life. God really exists and has life. Anything which has no body but is nevertheless alive, is called a "spirit"—God is a spirit. The wind does not know when it is blowing because it has no life. God knows what He is doing because He is alive. We call God a "spirit," because He has no body and yet is alive.

Perhaps a child in the class has lost a father or a mother by death. The child will say that Father or Mother is in heaven now. The same child will readily agree that the body of the parent is in the grave. Then that parent is a spirit; the parent is alive in heaven but has no body. Only, God is a spirit many, many times greater and more wonderful. All who are in heaven are spirits as long as their souls are separated from their bodies. Always though, God is the greatest Spirit.

A spirit then is a being which is alive, which knows what it is doing, which can do what it wills but which has no body. God is the biggest, grandest spirit which can be imagined.

Summary by Example: God is in this classroom although you cannot see Him. At the same time He is in your home and in every home in the world. No one can see Him because He is a spirit. He sees every one in the world and is doing good for every one; He is very active. Everywhere He is, He is alive and thinks about every one; He can and does help every one because He is alive and able to help. Everyone can talk to Him and He hears every one. God is a Being who is alive yet has no body. God is a spirit.

Motivation: How wonderful is God that He can see us wherever we may be! We long for that blessed day in heaven when we shall really be able to see Him face to face. How we shall rejoice when our eyes open to behold Him for the first time! In the meantime we will talk to Him in daily prayer because He is actually right before us. We will particularly be attentive when saying the Our Father because by that prayer we speak to Him directly. Now the whole class might rise to recite the Our Father in unison.

II. The Greatness of God

1. God Always Was

The concept of the eternity of God must be conveyed to children by examples within their experience. The term "eternal" is better

II. The Greatness of God

understood when translated as "always was and always will be" or "always lived and always will live." The pupils cannot help but be affected in a general way by the explanation of each perfection of God. The term "perfection" is not used because it is beyond the pupil's vocabulary: they do understand "greatness." The "other" perfections of God are not given specific treatment; they are implied in the explanation of the principal perfections. The invisible Father is now, if the phrase is legitimate, given a personality.

Children can make comparisons between the ages of persons and things. They will tell the teacher how old they are and admit that brother is older, father still older, and grandpa very much older.

The tree is old—God always was—the man will die—**God always will be.** Picture a gnarled old tree on the corner that stood there long even before grandpa was born. That hill to the east or to the west stood there long before the tree began to grow, thousands and thousands of years before. Picture a very, very old man sitting beneath the tree and wiping his forehead. The man is old and weary and will soon die. **God above will never die.**

The pupils will point out details of the picture which show age and greater age. They will enlarge by repeating the examples given orally by the teacher. Coming back to the text they will repeat, "God always was and always will be: God always lived and always will live."

God was here long before anything we see. He was here before there were any persons, trees or mountains.

God always was and always will be. If the children could count back ever so far, they could never get to the beginning of God. He existed so long that man cannot count the years. God always was.

Q. 8. Did God have a beginning?
A. No, God had no beginning. He always was.

God is a spirit who always lived and lives now. He talks to the saints today as He talked to the saints hundreds of years ago. He talked to Adam and Eve thousands of years ago. Even before there was a world, God, the living God was. He lives today, loves all His children in the whole world and wants to be loved by them.

God is a spirit who always lived, lives now and always will live. When every child here is dead, God will still be. When all have passed away and there is no more world, God will still be. An endless number of years from now, He will still be in His heaven talking to the children who were good and who will then be with Him.

Q. 9. Will God always be?
A. Yes, God will always be.

Summary by Example: If a bird had to remove the contents of a sand box by taking away a grain of sand every thousand years, it would take the bird so long that no man could count the years. Yet God has existed still longer; He always was.

Motivation: How great is God! We are so small in comparison and yet this God concerns Himself over us and loves us. He would seem to want nothing, yet He wants our love. He was alive long before we were born and He thought of us. He knew when we would be born and He was glad. He is alive and thinks of us every minute now. He will be alive after an endless number of years and He wants us to live with Him an endless number of years. He will be here when I am ten years old, fourteen, twenty and when I am grey-haired. Never will I be alone, never away from God. Will I be with God after an endless number of years?

2. God Is All-Good

The explanation covers two points, God's lovableness in Himself, and His fatherly love towards us. The conclusion is therefore similar to that of the first division—God loves us; we love God.

Mother is good: God is all-good. Picture a mother caring for her sick child. All day long she goes back and forth to the sick bed, consoling the child, or bringing it cooling drinks. During the night she tiptoes into the bedroom to see that the child is well covered. Then picture Christ working a miracle of healing; for example, the healing of the two blind men. Just consider what a terrible affliction blindness is. These two men cried to our Lord and in His mercy He restored their sight.

Father and Mother are good. They must be good because they teach us to be good. It is a sign of goodness when they are patient with us, when they bear up under crosses, when they are kind to each other and to us. They are good because they go to Mass and receive the sacraments. Then Mother has told us about other good people, some of whom were good enough to be called saints. Perhaps Sister will tell a story about one of these saints.

II. The Greatness of God

God is so good in Himself that He could not be better. We love pretty flowers but God made them all. We wonder at the beautiful sunrises and sunsets but God paints them all. We admire and esteem the goodness of a father and mother but God is still more lovable. Mother is sweet and pleasant and father is kind, yet God surpasses them by far. A child loves the warm embrace of a parent but the loving embrace of God is still more pleasant. We believe our parents are faultless but God is perfect in Himself. The saints were so good that although many of them lived hundreds of years ago, they are still admired for their goodness; yet not even the goodness of a saint can be compared to God's. The greatest human saint, the Blessed Virgin Mary, never committed a deliberate venial sin; she was not impatient even once, yet her goodness is in no way comparable with God's goodness. God has no sin, cannot have even an imperfection; He is perfect. He has the good points of our parents, of all good parents; He has them in an unlimited degree. We say that God is all-holy, meaning that He could not be any holier. The angels in heaven sing before Him, "Holy, holy, holy!"

God is good to us. Whatever we have and whatever we hope to have comes from God. A long, long time ago He put little seeds into the ground that still grow and today furnish us with our food, the bread and vegetables. He planted other grains and placed animals into the world to give us wool, flax and cotton for our clothing. Those animals too give us milk to drink and meat to eat. He made us in the first place, then by Baptism made us His own dear children. He gave us parents and friends to rear us and guide us. He gave us a guardian angel who is ready to whisper good things in our ear all day long. He thinks always of the time when He can take us to Himself in heaven and make us happy forever.

God is good to us too because He is so forgiving. If we slip a little and just tell God sincerely that we are sorry, He will forgive us. Sometimes men commit very big sins but God is ready to forgive if they are only sincerely sorrowful.

Summary by Example: St. Francis of Assisi burned with love for this all-good God. He gathered holy followers about him, instructing them to go out and tell all men about the lovable God. He and his Franciscans did indeed bring thousands to a better love of God.

Motivation: We are beginning to learn what a wonderful God this is to whom we pray. The reasons are piling up why we should love to pray to Him and indeed always pray. He is the most lovable Being we can imagine. What is more consoling still, He wants us to pray to Him so that He can grant us thousands of favors. We say, "God, I place all my hope in You; God, I love You above all things and persons. God, I love to talk to You." *A Story:* One time a famous king was taken captive by the Romans and stripped of all his possessions. Before he was led to prison, he asked for bread, a sponge and a harp. "Why do you want these?" asked the gaoler. "I want the bread to satisfy my hunger," replied the captive. "I want the sponge to dry my tears; I want the harp to sing praises to God."

3. God Knows Everything

The explanations are becoming more important as they have a more practical bearing on the child's religious life. The reasons for avoiding evil and doing good are gradually becoming evident.

God sees everything: God knows everything. On top of Mount Wilson is a telescope so powerful that men use it to photograph the surface of the moon. They call it "The eye of the world." The real eye of the world is the eye of God that sees every deed in the darkest corner in the furthest part of the world. Picture the eye of God gazing over the world.

God knows everything about us. He knows what each little boy here did last week, whether he worked hard at school, whether he said his morning prayers devoutly, and God does not forget. He knows what each little girl is doing now, whether she is attentive, whether she is devout as she hears about God, and God remembers. He even knows how kind they will be on their way home from school and how polite they will be to Father or Mother at home this evening.

God knows everything in the whole world. He knows who planted that old tree on the corner long, long ago. He knows what all the people did who ever lived, the good deeds they performed, the kind acts they omitted, and He does not forget. In far countries are people whom we have never seen, millions of them, but God knows exactly what each one of them is doing at this moment. He knows who of all the millions will serve Him or offend Him in the years to come.

God knows hidden things. If a little boy here has an unkind thought Sister does not know of it but God does. If a little girl

Grade I II. The Greatness of God 17

goes into her dark bedroom and fails to say her night prayers, God knows. God remembers and God keeps account of everything.

God is all-wise. He knows everything that each child here is trying to learn. He knows more than Sister or the pastor or the smartest man on earth. He knows what is in every book and what will be in every one still to be written. He understands every machine, knows the purpose of every wheel in the factory. What is under the earth is known to Him and what is in the stars, the sun and the moon. His mind and will runs the earth, makes the days and the nights and tells the stars where to go.

Q. 6. Does God know all things?
A. Yes, God knows all things.

Summary by Example: Surely some time you were in a large library and you saw thousands of books. You wondered at all the knowledge contained in those books. God knows more than is contained in those books, even in all the books of the whole world.

Motivation: Nothing is wasted that is done for God because God knows everything. Children must never think that a thought, word, or action of theirs is too insignificant for God to notice. "Please God, help me," is a very short prayer indeed but it cannot escape His notice. He even knows when we think of being kind, of being polite or of saying just a two-word prayer. Perhaps Mother did not even observe how some child here tried to be particularly tidy this morning but God knows all about it. Perhaps Sister was preoccupied and failed to hear our "Good morning"; those words are not lost because God knows about them. During our whole life we should strive first to please God because He will always notice and He will always remember. When the great Cardinal Wolsey of England was removed from his high office by his king, he is reported to have said that if he had served God with half the love with which he served his king, He would not have abandoned him in his old age.

Organization of Section 3. The story of the telescope leads to the all-seeing eye of God. What does God see in our daily lives? Looking over the world what does God see and know? Explain how God knows hidden things. Now compare what all people know with what God knows. All these questions lead to the Catechism answer number 6. Now summarize with the description of the library trying to bring in all prior concepts. The Motivation here can be made very practical.

4. God Is Everywhere

The pupils have already inferred from what has gone before that God must be present everywhere. It remains only to make the fact part of their own lives.

God is here: God is everywhere. Picture a crowded boulevard where thousands of automobiles are whizzing up and down. No one would think that God is in this busy street. Yet, He is here and everywhere.

God always was: He knows everything that happened in the past; He knows everything that is going on now. In children's words He must therefore be "all-over."

A Story: The master had left home leaving two servants in charge, the one a Christian, the other an unbeliever. The latter proposed that they quit work, saying, "The Master has gone away." The Christian servant replied, "My Master has not gone away; He looks down on me. God is my Master too and He is everywhere."

God is in all places. Far from church and far from teacher, God is on that distant grassy slope where we hold our picnic. He is where every one else is. He is in every part of the United States and in every part of every other country. He is where the birds are high in the trees, where the fishes are deep in the ocean, where the snows are high on the mountain tops. He is on the earth, the moon and the stars. He is in purgatory with the Poor Souls, and in heaven with the saints. No one can go any place where God is not, on earth or in heaven.

God sees all people at all times. He sees us wherever we are whether we be in the light or in the darkness; we just cannot hide from Him. One time the first man, Adam, tried to hide from God after He had committed a sin but God knew where he was and called to him. Perhaps we do a good deed and no one sees it: God sees it. Perhaps a man does a wicked deed at night thinking that no one sees it: God sees it. Of course, we cannot see God because, as we have learned, God is a spirit who cannot be seen with our bodily eyes.

God watches over us. God did indeed give us parents to watch over us and an angel to guide us but He was not satisfied even with this tender care. He Himself wanted to watch over us. God watches over us when teacher is not present or parents are away.

He watches over us in order to help us. Often He saves children from bodily harm. Perhaps a boy is about to step into a dangerous hole in the street when something seems to warn him; actually God pulled the boy back. He sees when we are sick and if it be His will, He will cure us at the right time. Perhaps a little girl is on the point of visting some friends when she seems to hear a voice, "Don't go there"; it was really the voice of God warning her away from bad companions. God watches over children in order to help them do good. He sees when they should call on Him, say their regular prayers, help others, make a visit to the Blessed Sacrament and so He reminds them in some way or other of their need and of their duty.

Q. 5. Where is God?
A. God is everywhere.

Summary by Example: A bad man had committed a great crime. He leaped into his car and raced away from the scene. The police could not catch him any more but still the man felt that some one was looking at him. He jumped on a train and rode a thousand miles. Still he felt that Presence. He went across the ocean and still some One seemed to look straight at him. He went half-way around the world but he could not get away from that big Eye. He turned back and gave himself up. "I could get away from the police," he said, "but I could not get away from God." (Although God is everywhere, we do not see Him because He is a spirit and cannot be seen with our eyes).

Motivation: We must remember the presence of God all our life in order to avoid evil and do good. We can fight temptations better when we reflect that God is watching the fight and is ready to help us. We can do good more joyfully because it pleases God who sees everything. When we hear that little voice, "Do not do this evil" or "Do this kind act," we will know that God is beside us and is talking to us. We will fear to offend Him because He is looking right at us; we will be eager to please Him because He sees our good act instantly. To remember the presence of God is the first rule for a good life.

5. God Can Do All Things

The first idea which children associate with the bigness of God, is big power. More often than not, such power is coupled with terrifying circumstances; so it is well if the teacher explain rather about a God of benignant power.

God can do all things. Picture the scene at the marriage at Cana. Describe the miracle where Jesus turned water into wine. No man can change water into wine. Only God can do it because He can do all things.

We get an idea of the almighty power of God by studying the things He created. God gave the power to these forces of nature. Last week a wind swept over the town, bending low the trees in its path and making the windows in the houses rattle. Through our city there flows a river that pours a powerful volume of water over the dam; it sends its power into the factories making mighty wheels move. The children have watched a river in the springtime when, swollen with the melted snows, it rushes along like an uncontrollable force. The star that fell in the heavens the other night was so large that no child can imagine its size, yet God's hand was under it so that it would fall so far and no farther. God has moved mountains. God put the power into the wind and the water.

Many things which God has made and to which He gave great power, are beautiful to behold. God sends rains that give drink to the thirsty grains over millions of acres. He created the mighty Niagara Falls, one of the wonders of the world, which is visited annually by tens of thousands. Even children can observe how the mighty hand of God moves the clouds at sunset until they glow with a worshipful fire.

God uses His great power to help us. He gives us health to do our work well, even helping our mind so that we can follow our studies more easily. But what is more important, He can and wants to help us to be good. He is every ready to make us strong to fight temptations and to do good deeds. The saints prayed to Him for strength and God made them real heroes.

Q. 7. Can God do all things?
A. Yes, God can do all things.

Summary by Example: A Story: St. Gregory Thaumaturgus wished to build a church but found that the presence of a mountain did not leave enough room for the building. He prayed to God to move the mountain and when he awakened the next morning he discovered that God had actually moved the mountain just far enough to permit the construction of the church.

Motivation: We are all in the powerful hands of God. *A Story:* A little boy was asked, "Where is Chicago?" "In Illinois," he replied. "And where is Illinois?" "In the United States." "And where is the United States?" "In the world," was the quick answer. "And where is the world?" He thought for a while when the light dawned upon him, "In the hands of God." From this lesson we are inspired with greater hope in God. We will need many helps and favors as we journey through life, health of body, success in our work, health of soul. We will not fear because God is almighty and can help us. We are content to place ourselves in His almighty hand.

III. One God

1. There Is One God

The teacher will not attempt to prove the fact of "one God" to primer-children. When Mother first stated it, they believed without question and they will believe the mere statement now. It is difficult to make a lengthy explanation of the truth to children of this age; such an effort would not be beneficial at all but cause questioning wonderment instead.

There is one God. Let us hear how a great Saint spoke of God. St. Patrick was a great Bishop who lived in Ireland hundreds of years ago. He loved God very much and he wanted the people in Ireland to know about God so they also could love Him. He would go from place to place dressed in his sacred vestments and holding a staff in one hand. The people would come around him and then he would tell them about God. (If possible show a picture of St. Patrick in his Episcopal vestments, with crozier in one hand and holding up the shamrock in the other hand.)

One day St. Patrick came to a large city in which the King of the country lived. It was a beautiful day. The sun was shining brightly and a big crowd of people had come out in the green fields to hear St. Patrick. The King was there with his family, and many soldiers. These people had never heard about God. They did not know that this one true God made them. They did not know that this one true God made the world and all the beautiful things in it. St. Patrick was afraid that the people might not believe what he was going to tell them about God, so he said a prayer to God. He asked God the Father, God the Son and God the Holy Ghost to help him say the right thing so that the King and his soldiers and the people would believe in God. Then St. Patrick began to tell them all about God, how God made the world, the heavens, the angels and all the people. When St. Patrick stopped, he saw that the people liked what he told them. They even asked St. Patrick to tell them more. Then St. Patrick said, "I am going to tell you something very wonderful about God, this great, big, wonderful God." The people in that island listened to St. Patrick all day; they believed what he told them about one God and all became Catholic.

There is only one father to a family, only one teacher to a classroom, only one pastor to a parish; each one in his respective sphere has everything to say, may give every command. One God is in charge of the whole world and He has everything to say, may command every one either directly, or indirectly through others like the pope, the bishops, the priests, parents, teachers. One God always was and always will be, and He has all goodness in a limitless degree within Himself so that there really is nothing left for another God. One God knows all, sees all and is everywhere present. There is no need of a helper because this God can do everything.

All our prayers finally end with this one God. No matter to whom we pray, the prayers go to God. We may pray to many saints or to the Blessed Virgin but all these carry the prayers to God and ask the one God for the big favor.

Q. 10. Is there only one God?
A. Yes, there is only one God.

Summary by Example: A little boy once gave the best answer of all; "There is only one God because there isn't room for another."

Motivation: A missionary was talking to a learned man of India. "Do you believe it is sinful to steal and to murder?" "Yes, I do," answered the scholar. "But God never appeared to you to tell you that," proposed the priest. "No, He did not," answered the man, "but I have God in my heart. I hear Him talking in my heart."

God speaks to our hearts. If we listen to Him respectfully, we will discover that He teaches us many things. We must thank God that He is so close to us, that He talks to us and that He wishes us to talk to Him. Would we not be flattered if the President of the United States wished to talk to us! We must be devoutly thankful that this great, one God wants to talk to little children.

Grade I   III. One God

Organization of Section 1. Since this section deals with a mystery, organization can be only limited. Probably the catechism answer will be enough. More will be made of the Motivation.

2. The Three Persons in One God

Again no proof should be attempted. The teacher merely states and by analogies shows the children that there is a similitude between the Trinity and various circumstances in life and nature. She can explain until doomsday but the pupils will still picture God the Father as an old man of prophetic visage and God the Son as the Christ of the Bible story. Symbolism pictures the Holy Ghost as a dove but we know of difficulties which primer-teachers experience with this representation. Without denying the value of the symbol, we judge it better to emphasize the Holy Ghost as the Spirit of light and love.

There is only one God but there are three Persons in that one God. The Persons are the Father, the Son and the Holy Ghost.

> In God there are three Persons. St. Patrick explained this fact to an Irish chieftain, in the following manner. Taking a three-leaved shamrock, he pointed to the first leaf and asked, "Is that a shamrock?" The chieftain nodded his assent. Pointing to the second, he asked, "Is that a shamrock?" Again the chief agreed that it was a shamrock. Pointing to the third leaf, the Saint put the same question and got the same answer. The Saint paused, then asked, "Now how many shamrocks have I?" "Only one," was the answer. So explained St. Patrick, each of the three Persons is God but there is only one God.

Each of us is one person. I am one person, Mary there, is one person, Johnny over there to my right is one person. But God is three Persons: God is three Divine Persons. There is only one God, but in that one God there are three divine Persons. One of the three Divine Persons in God is the Father, the second Divine Person is the Son and the third Divine Person is the Holy Ghost. The first Divine Person, the Father is one Person and is God; the second Divine Person, the Son is one Person and is God; and the third Divine Person, the Holy Ghost is one Person and is God. God the Father is not God the Son or God the Holy Ghost. God the Holy Ghost is not God the Father or God the Son. But all three Divine Persons, each one being different and each one as being God, are nevertheless only one God. The three Divine Persons are one and the same God.

Q. 11. How many persons are there in God?
A. In God there are three Persons—the Father, the Son and the Holy Ghost.

The three Persons are in God together. The Father is God and the first Person of the Blessed Trinity. The Son is God and the second Person of the Blessed Trinity. The Holy Ghost is God and the third Person of the Blessed Trinity. "Blessed" means that they are very holy. "Trinity" means that there are three in one.

Q. 12. What do we call the three Persons in one God?
A. We call the three Persons in one God the Blessed Trinity.

These statements do strike us as very strange but they are nevertheless true. The man who has lived in a far-off country, will explain the wonderful sights there. His stories provoke our wonderment but we believe them because we know that the man always tells the truth. So do we believe these statements about the Blessed Trinity because God has told us so, and God always speaks the truth.

Q. 13. How do we know that there are three Persons in one God?
A. We know that there are three Persons in one God because we have God's word for it.

Summary by Example: The teacher will go back to the sign of the cross because it is the official prayer dedicated to the Holy Trinity. She will instruct them again, then ask several pupils to make the sign before the class. She will commend those who make a correct, a large and reverent sign. She will rehearse the Our Father because it is a prayer to the first Person; next, the Hail Mary because it makes particular mention of the second Person. She will explain that the Holy Ghost gives us light to understand. We should often begin our work in school with the little prayer, "O Holy Ghost, give me light to see."

Motivation: As from day to day, we come to know more and more about God, we see how much God cares for us. We can pray to any one of the three Persons. At home not only Mother sees our needs but Father also. It would be still better if Father could hear the special favors we ask of Mother and vice versa. Yet, the whole Trinity hears our prayers because the Three are one. We need only address our prayers to God without any particular mention of a Person, and all three Persons will hear us. To conclude this division, the whole class will rise and in unison make the sign of the cross.

UNIT THREE: WHAT GOD MADE

(Revised Baltimore First Communion Catechism: Lesson 1)

I. GOD MADE THE ANGELS.
   1. HOW GOD MADE THE ANGELS.
   2. SOME OF THE ANGELS SINNED.
   3. THE BAD AND GOOD ANGELS.

II. GOD MADE THE WORLD.
   1. HOW GOD MADE ALL THINGS.
   2. WHAT GOD MADE.

III. GOD MADE MAN.
   1. ADAM AND EVE IN PARADISE.
   2. ADAM AND EVE WERE GIVEN A TEST.
   3. THE EFFECTS OF THEIR SIN UPON US.
   4. OUR DUTY TO GOD.

What We Shall Learn: We shall now take a long, long journey. To all the parts of the earth we shall go, to the stars and even into heaven. We shall ask, who made the angels in heaven? We shall look at the sky and ask ourselves, who made it? We shall see the fishes in the waters and all kinds of birds in the air and ask ourselves, who made them, how did they get there? Finally we shall turn to ourselves with the same question. And when we have learned the answer to all those very interesting questions, we shall still have the most important one of all to answer: Why were all these things made? For what purpose are we here on earth? Let the pupils therefore prepare for a very interesting series of lessons.

To the Teacher: Divisions I and III are not contained in the *First Communion Catechism Prepared from the Revised Edition of the Baltimore Catechism.* The footnotes on page 1 of the First Communion Catechism do nevertheless suggest that these topics be taught to first-graders, the inference being that they must be taught orally.

I. God Made the Angels

1. How God Made the Angels

If the first semester begins in September, this unit should be finished by December first so that the Christmas month will be wholly taken up by a study of God the Saviour. No new material is furnished for those weeks in January which conclude the first semester but the class can review what was covered in the first four months. The pupils are then able to read and can interestedly follow whatever basic text they have in their hands. If the first semester begins later in the year the study of the first semester material continues until completed.

We now come to a topic which will be grasped more readily by the primer-pupils. The teacher should marshal her facts in an orderly manner so that she will be able to tell these stories interestingly and effectively. The word "create" is not yet used in the pupil's text as being above a child's vocabulary but there is no objection to the teacher giving an oral explanation of the term, that it means making something out of nothing.

There was a time, long, long ago, no one can tell how long ago, when the great big God, about whom we have now learned much, was all alone. There was nothing else, no spring, no summer, no autumn, no winter. There were no skies, sun, moon or stars. There were no people, animals or flowers. There was nothing at all. There was only emptiness.

Then the great big God did something wonderful. He was all alone. He was happy. He did not need anyone else to make Him more happy. But He wanted someone with whom He could share His own happiness. A good boy too will want others to share his sweets and his playthings.

God resolved first to make angels to share His happiness. They would be happy with Him and they would be happy with each other. Their home was to be heaven which is full of joys that no child can imagine. God is good.

God made the angels, so many of them that no child can count them in a lifetime. He made nine classes of angels, and each successive class was higher than the other and more beautiful than the other. Sometimes men try to paint angels, giving them the most beautiful faces, the whitest, most graceful wings, and the richest garments, but an angel is so beautiful that no man can even imagine it. Now there were millions and millions of angels. They sang songs to God and praised Him for making them. They bowed down before God and cried out that He is God. God is good.

The angels were spirits, meaning that they had no body. Sometimes angels have appeared on earth and then they took a body like ours so that they could be seen. After their work was done, however, they cast off that body again, for angels in heaven have no body. The angels were greater than the prettiest flower because they could understand who they were, how happy they were, who God was, how good God was. Also they had a free will so that they could first of all wish to praise God, then do what they wished; they could desire to be happy and next they could do what helped their happiness.

God made the angels wise, powerful and holy. The pupils here must study every day and they must attend school many years in order to learn what is necessary for life. The angels did not have to study but knew everything at once; they did not have to learn from a catechism or do home-lessons every day. While they were not almighty like God, yet they possessed power surpassed only by God's; an angel today can move a mountain or bend a tree. The angels were very holy; they had to be such because God intended to give them pleasant tasks around His own holy throne. Their leader so shone with wisdom, power and holiness that God called him Lucifer, which means Light-bearer.

Summary by Example: The children will be told of the many angels swirling in circles through the blue sky, moving about the earth and roaming through the beautiful heavens. Those angels see and understand; they go where they will. They understand everything which they see upon the earth; they are powerful to help. Perhaps the children can tell about a statue or picture of an angel in the parish church. When they describe such a statue or picture, the teacher can recall that angels are spirits and have no body but that sometimes they assumed a body for a short time when they appeared to someone on earth. Three concepts are emphasized: God is good; God made the angels; God gave them great happiness.

Motivation: We admire the goodness of God who wished others to share His happiness. He did not have to create the angels, yet He did it in order to make them happy. In all the stories which will yet be told, we will observe each time that God's intention always was to make one happy. God is good.

Organization of Section 1. The organization becomes simpler when the class deals with concrete things, with living things. Thus the paragraph, "There was a time" will resolve itself into questions like, Was there a spring, a summer? Was there a sun, a moon? Were there animals or people long, long ago? The concept of God's goodness in wishing to share his happiness is a principal one. Paragraph after paragraph will be easily turned into many interesting questions, care being taken that concrete facts and examples are brought out. The conclusion must be, God is good.

2. Some of the Angels Sinned

In this explanation the concept of hell must be brought out, though briefly. Doctrinal facts must be plainly stated and must by no means be minimized. "The fear of the Lord is the beginning of wisdom" and even children must know that there is a sanction to the laws of God. Mother Church talks of hell; the loving Christ taught the doctrine.

All of us must undergo tests if we wish greater success or happiness. Does not Mother often say, "If you are a good boy today, I'll take you with me to the show?" If your big brother wants to belong to the football team or if your big sister would like to be one of the basketball players on her school team, they will have to show the coach that they know how to play the game. The coach tries them out, tests them. He finds out whether they will do what he wants, whether they will remain true to him and the team in everything.

God also wanted to try out the angels before He would give them still more wonderful gifts. He wanted to find out whether they loved Him more than anything else. God had been so kind and good to the angels, that they should have stayed true to him.

> The test. A great temptation came upon the angels. The chief angel, Lucifer, said, "I will not obey." Other angels, very many of them, said, "We will not obey." Now picture a great battle. Right away the good angels who would not listen to the bad angels formed a big army, and took another great angel named Michael for their leader. Then they gave battle to the bad angels. It was a terrible battle but the good angels won. They drove the bad angels into a place called hell. The bad angels had failed in the test.

The bad angels disobeyed the very first law of God. They refused to worship or give honor to God who had created them. Their act was sinful, very much so. There are other sinful acts which are not nearly as serious as this one but whether grievous or not, they all break some law of God.

Q. 22. What is sin?
A. Sin is disobedience to God's laws.

The bad angels will stay in hell forever. They will never see God. The good angels who had stood the test were taken into heaven where they will be happy forever.

Q. 23. Who committed the first sin?
A. The bad angels committed the first sin.

Summary by Example: In heaven now there are millions of angels who are called good. In hell there are millions of angels but they are called bad; they are also called devils. All might be in heaven today but some were foolish enough to disobey God. Where they are now, there all will stay forever.

Motivation: The children cannot help but be impressed by the punishment which God meted out to the bad angels. They see here the terrifying results of one act of disobedience. Now the disobedient angels are shut off forever from the sight of the lovable God. How terrible! God wants to love, to reward, but God also can punish. The pupils will take their little practices of obedience to heart because they do not wish to be like the bad angels. Little acts of disobedience can lead to worse acts. Once more they will resolve to do what God commands, to do nothing which God forbids.

Organization of Section 2. This section lends itself very easily to organization because it deals with concrete facts. The Motivation in this instance is of particular importance.

3. The Bad and the Good Angels

We first explain the work of the bad angels. By contrast then the children will be more impressed by the work of the good angels, and principally of the guardian angels. Tradition favors the belief that each person has his own angel to guide and guard him through life.

The bad angels had lost God and heaven forever. They would always suffer. But they would also hate everybody. They hated God. They hated the good angels and most of all they hated men, women and children on earth. They hated us because if we are good and love God, we would some day be in heaven with God.

Two pictures tell the story. On one you see a boy reaching forth to steal an apple from a fruit stand. If you could see a spirit, you would see a bad angel tempting the boy. On the other, there is a little girl obediently going to Mass. Again if you could see a spirit, you would see a good angel urging her to be good.

The bad angels want to hurt you and keep you out of heaven. They do not want you to love God. They do not want you to be in heaven some day. If you go with bad boys and girls, it is the bad angel who is trying to make you sin. If your mother tells you to come home right after school and you do not go, but play with other boys and girls on the street, then it is the bad angel who is making you disobedient. If a boy sees a nice new baseball lying on the grass where other boys are playing ball and he feels like taking that nice new baseball, although he knows it belongs to another boy, then it is the bad angel who is trying to make him steal.

Summary by Example: In Africa the hunters place a piece of meat in a thicket as a bait for tigers. The tiger is not suspicious because the branches and leaves surrounding the meat are just what he sees every day. He sniffs the meat, approaches warily, grabs the meat and "click," his leg is caught in a steel trap. So the devil sometimes leads children into what seem to be innocent surroundings. There in the middle is a temptation that looks so attractive; it may be extra freedom to which they feel entitled; it may be a pleasure that would seem to satisfy. They reach for it; "click," the bad angel has caught them. We call these efforts of our enemy, temptations.

Children need not fear; there is an army of good angels just as strong which is fighting for them. These have, first, the pleasant task of serving God around His throne. They are ever there not unmindful of us but pray to God for us that He may send us more and more help to save our souls.

God sends good angels to protect us. God has at times sent angels in visible form to bring His message to men. Thus, the angel Gabriel brought a message from God to the Virgin Mary at Nazareth.

God has given each of us an angel to protect us from harm, both physical and spiritual. This angel is called the guardian angel. Like all other angels, he is a spirit and a spirit has no body. Our guardian angel is always with us, no matter where we are (let the teacher enlarge) at play, when we sleep, etc. He helps us to keep good. He keeps harm away from us.

Our guardian angels tell us to do good. Often they tell us that it is time to get up and get ready for school; that we should say a cheerful "Good Morning" to our parents; that we should be kind to our companions on the way to school; we should obey Sister. They remind us to say our prayers devoutly, to go to Mass, to do all our work well. *A Story:* St. Frances of Rome had lost an infant son. Shortly after his death the little one appeared to her in company with a youth of wonderful beauty. The infant spoke, "This companion is your guardian angel who watches over you day and night." Afterwards whenever St. Frances did not understand clearly what God wanted of her, she asked this angel. When she was bothered with temptations she called upon him to drive away the evil spirit.

Summary by Example: When you are good your guardian angel is happy. A teacher told the children in a classroom that she had to leave the room for a while and asked them to be good and keep quiet while she was away. A little while later the Principal of the school came in; she was happy to see that the children were so good and quiet when their teacher was away. She asked them, "How is it that you are so quiet when you have no teacher to watch you?" The children said, "Oh yes, Sister Principal, there is someone watching us, our guardian angel." Perhaps Sister can show the pupils the picture of the little girl chasing a butterfly. The guardian angel is protecting her as she tries to cross the stream on the slippery stones.

Motivation: The children will have great confidence because not only is God Himself ever present but He has given them guardian angels to protect them and to help them. On October second the Church celebrates the feast of the holy guardian angels. She reminds us to put our trust in them and to pray daily to them for help. Their guardian angel will often advise the children, "Don't do this"; then they must not perform a certain action because it is sinful. Often he will advise, "Do this"; then they must follow the order to obey Sister, to pay attention, to say the class prayers well. Because St. Frances of Rome always listened to her angel, she became a saint. Children can become saints if they always follow the advice of their guardian angel.

> Angel of God, my guardian dear,
> To whom His love commits me here,
> Ever this day be at my side,
> To light and guard, to rule and guide. Amen.

(Indulgence, 300 days. Plenary indulgence once a month, on the usual conditions if recited daily.)

When learned by heart this stanza will be a pleasing addition to the morning prayer. The hymn "Dear Angel! Ever at my side" might here be taught to the class.

II. God Made the World

1. How God Made All Things

In presenting the doctrine of the creation to these pupils, the teacher can touch only on essentials. Examples will help the children to understand, and as many as possible will be included; more may be added at the will of the teacher. Means for visualizing shall be employed, such as pictures of nature subjects, scenes, birds, animals, rivers, etc. The teacher will gradually change the terminology "made" to "create."

> God made all things out of nothing, that is, He did not need anything beforehand from which to make all things. When a boy makes a scooter he must use wood, nails and screws. When a girl makes a doll dress she must use cloth, thread, lace and needle. God did not need anything and did not use anything to make the world and all that is in it. Because He made the world out of nothing we say He "created" the world.

> God made all things just by wishing them, that is, He needed no time to make them. When a girl makes a little apron for herself she is busily engaged for a couple of days. God did not need any time for the various creations; He just wished one after the other and they were there.

Summary by Example: The children may have heard the fairy tale of Aladdin and his wonderful lamp. He rubbed the lamp, wished, and the wish was granted. When he wanted a fairy castle, he rubbed, wished and the castle was there. Of course, Aladdin never lived and no person can get things just by wishing. But God is almighty. He just said, "Let this be" and what He wished was there.

Motivation: Now we get a new note to prove the almighty power of our God. Not only can He powerfully move what is on earth but by His almighty power He made those things in the first place. As the prophet Isaias (XLV, 15) said, "There is no God like Thee" meaning there is no God like our God. This fact reassures us. Sometimes we think that God cannot and just will not grant some very big favor. God is bigger than any request which we can make. Oftentimes individuals have been afflicted with some disease which the doctor declared cannot be cured. We have many instances in which these people prayed to God and were cured instantly. It is not always easy to be good, or obedient. If we pray to Almighty God He will help us and make the act seem very easy. Perhaps Mamma is unwell and the doctors do not seem to help her. A child's prayer is powerful before God. He may not cure Mother instantly but He will help her so that she will bear her troubles patiently.

Organization of Section 1. The teacher will ask the pupils about the examples given in her oral instruction and add any that will occur to her. Next, she will ask individual pupils whether they ever made anything. Then, "How long would it take God to make that plaything?" As God becomes bigger and bigger in the child's mind and likewise gets closer and closer to the child, the Motivations take on increasing importance.

2. What God Made

It is very important that the teacher explain the creation as a result of the goodness of God; the power of God was stressed in the previous section. The teacher should not defer the class discussion or rehearsal until she has finished the oral explanation of the entire work of Creation. She will find it more profitable to let the discussion take place after the explanation of the first or the second Creation period and so on. In regard to the time period of the creation, the term "day" can be explained as a name given to a long period of time; the days are described as very long ones, much longer than our's today. When the creation deals with the birds, the fish, the animals, the teacher should enliven the class by asking them to name such.

God was happy, but because He was good He wanted others to share His happiness, first on this earth and finally in His eternal heaven. He originally made a very beautiful world in order that man living in it would be very happy—God was good.

The First Day: Out of nothing, by His own will only, God created the earth. It was so large that no child can imagine its size. If the child multiplies the biggest hill a thousand-million times it will yet have no idea of the size of this first creation. Then God said, "Be light made" and from His hands came a mass of great light and He called the light Day; He called the darkness Night.

The Second Day: Out of nothing, by His will only, God made the firmament. This was the air about us and the sky above us.

The Third Day: God separated the land from the waters, and called the land, Earth, and the waters, Seas. Between the rivers, brooks, lakes and oceans there now were hills, mountains and vast tracts of dry land. Then God created the grass, the herbs and the trees, and He set them into the valleys and on the mountain slope.

The Fourth Day: Out of nothing, by His will only, God created the sun, the moon and the stars. The grass and the plants felt the warmth of the sun and leaped in their growth.

The Fifth Day: God created the fishes and all living things that move in the water, placing them in the rivers and lakes throughout the world. He created the birds, setting them in trees low and high and they filled the air with their songs.

The Sixth Day: God created the animals, big and small, lions, horses, tigers, cows, elephants, etc. They ran for the shades of the forest; they ran up the mountain slope. Now the world was ready for its highest creation: there was air to breathe, fruit on the trees, grain in the fields, animals in the field and forest. Then God made man.

The Seventh Day: God rested and He blessed that day and called it holy.

Q. 2. Did God make all things?
A. Yes, God made all things.

Summary by Example: The class should go over the Creation of one day at a time pointing out the details of the occurrence, then learning that line of the text which indicates the particular work of the Creator. Rivers, brooks, lakes and oceans are this time to be given names; so with the fishes, the birds and the animals; cut-outs will add interest. Everything must move now so as to make a delightful panorama for the pupil. He must add names of grains, flowers and living things as he saw them perhaps on a recent auto or hiking trip through the country or to the zoo. Next teacher and pupils will try to draw the days of Creation on the blackboard. The pupils will assist by offering their cut-outs to the picture. It is a play of increasing wonders which cannot help but enlarge the pupil's admiration of the good and powerful Creator.

Motivation: We view the Creation as a whole. How good was God! He was happy in heaven and did not need any thing or any person. Yet, He wanted us in order to make us happy. He made a beautiful world for us with its babbling streams, smiling meadows, high mountains, with its luscious fruits, tasty vegetables, wholesome grains, with its birds of beautiful feathers and lilting songs, its sleek and graceful animals. God was like a good father who cannot do enough for his children. If we obey God's laws we shall be happy here and hereafter. He has indeed provided many beautiful things for our enjoyment and pleasure; if we partake of them in the right way, we will never do wrong. The angels were happy; if they had been satisfied with God's joys, they would have remained happy. We must never seek after joys which God has forbidden. Very holy people are very happy people because their desires never go beyond the joys that God has provided. God's joys are enough because they are the best joys of all.

> All things bright and beautiful,
>   All creatures great and small,
> All things wise and wonderful,
>   The Lord God made them all.
>
> Each little flower that opens,
>   Each little bird that sings
> He made their glowing colors,
>   He made their tiny wings.
>
> He gave us eyes to see them,
>   And lips that we might tell
> How great is God Almighty,
>   Who hath made all things well.
>
> —*C. Frances Alexander.*

III. God Made Man

1. Adam and Eve in Paradise

God's attribute of goodness must remain in the fore. The impression may not be so noticeable now, but it will grow with the year. It is the one concept which can solve life's joys and, strange to say, its sorrows and even its death. The intention of God is always good, even when seeming misfortunes overtake us. The teacher the evening before shall read the Bible stories related to the text so that they can be told fluently and interestingly; this manual does not attempt to give every detail.

III. God Made Man

On the sixth day God created the king and queen of all Creation, Adam and Eve. At first He created Adam, forming a body from the slime of the earth, then breathed a soul into it. Next He created Eve (the story of the Creation of the woman from a rib of Adam is not told in this grade). We call them the first parents in the world or our First Parents.

Imagine that you see that piece of the earth from which Adam was made. At first there were no hands and feet to move, no eyes to see, no life to speak. But when God breathed a soul into that form made from the earth, Adam stood up at once, walked over the ground and talked about the beautiful things in the Garden. The soul of man is wonderful. God had said that He would make the soul like Himself. We have learned that God is a spirit; now we learn that the soul is a spirit too. We cannot see God because He is a spirit and neither can we see the soul because it is a spirit. God is alive; the soul is alive and gives us life.

God placed Adam and Eve into a large, beautiful garden called Paradise. There were no storms there to frighten, no excessive heat to oppress, no sharp stones to injure, no weeds to poison. The garden was beautiful, more so than any spot on earth today. Rivers wound between green meadows and shady groves, blue lakes glistened in the sunlight, beflowered hills smiled in the distance. Fruit trees of many kinds were there, to furnish Adam and Eve food. The birds were tame and sang sweet songs; the animals obediently followed our first parents because Adam and Eve were their masters.

Our first parents were good. There was not a sin on their souls. They were kind to the birds and the animals; they were very kind to each other. They loved each other but they loved God most of all. They were cheerful, polite, truthful, thankful to God and helpful to one another. They were children of God whom God intended some day to take to heaven.

Adam and Eve were wise and happy. Their minds understood everything so well that they did not have to study. They had no accidents, no pains, no sickness and at the end of their life they were to be taken straight to heaven without first having to die. The good God gave them great happiness.

Q. 1. Who made you?
A. God made me.

The above paragraphs had better be taken one at a time with the class. The teacher's imagination will enlarge upon the pictured page. There are valleys and flowers beyond the woods, and lakes and rivers. The doves are cooing and the birds are singing; the lion does not hurt the lamb. Eve is kind and pets the lamb, while Adam with shaded eyes looks piously upward at the God Who supplied these joys. God loved Adam; God loved Eve.

Motivation: There is true happiness only with God. If we stay close to God we will learn that He always has our happiness in mind. Nothing, no one, can bring us happiness as God can.

A story: When St. Bernard and his four brothers had resolved to devote themselves to the religious life, they paid a last visit to their parents. One of them said to a very young brother, "Now you can have all the honors and all the family wealth." The young boy answered wisely, "Yes, you leave me earth but you take heaven; I am not satisfied with my share." Several years afterward this boy also entered the religious life. He preferred happiness with God rather than earthly pleasure. The Sister who is teaching this class, the pastor who has charge of the parish, left many worldly honors and joys too, because they believed that there was more happiness in following God.

Organization of Section 1. Where the step is exceedingly simple, as in this case, no directions will henceforth be given. Absence of directions always implies that it is very easy to convert the first sentences of a treatment into questions.

2. Adam and Eve Were Given a Test

The transgressions of our first parents had such dire effects upon the human race that even children must be made to realize that the test given by God was fair. The fact must constantly be repeated that God wished to make them still happier.

We are all willing to undergo tests to attain something better or to prove our love to a benefactor. A test is a kind of examination, a trial or try-out. These pupils are ready to take a test next June in order to pass into the second grade, they are, in fact, being tested daily in order to see who will head the class.

Sometimes Mother gives a little test before she leaves the home, "If you behave well while I am gone, I'll take you all for an auto ride next Sunday." Children have many little tests at home by which they can prove their love for their loving

Grade I III. God Made Man 39

parents. Little Jane would rather go out playing but instead she helps Mother dry the dishes. William hears his chum whistling for him but instead he helps Father rake the fallen leaves from the lawn. All these tests are taken gladly because they are fair.

Our good God gave Adam and Eve a test. Everything in that beautiful Paradise was theirs to use but God gave them the one commandment not to eat of the fruit of a certain tree.

Adam and Eve should have obeyed God's command. It gave them a chance to prove to God how thankful they were for all the favors already received. By remaining faithful they could continue to enjoy these favors and receive still more.

The story of the temptation and of the fall follows as narrated in any Bible history. Emphasis should be placed on the phases that the devil's approach appeared innocent; that he lied to Eve by promising wisdom; that Eve was too curious and lingered too long near the danger; that Eve disobeyed God by eating the fruit; that Adam was too easily led when at Eve's request he also ate the fruit.

Q. 24. Who committed the first sin on earth?
A. Our first parents, Adam and Eve, committed the first sin on earth.

The story of the punishment follows. In that moment of sin, Adam and Eve were no longer holy and pleasing to God but on their souls was a big sin of disobedience to God. Being no longer children of God, the right to heaven was taken from them. God drove them from Paradise into a world that had suddenly been changed into the world as we have it today with its excessive heat and cold, its thorns and its sharp stones, its hardships and its dangers. Comfort was gone and in its place came work, accident and sickness. The privilege of being taken to heaven was taken away; now they had to die before entering eternity.

Motivation: Several weeks ago we learned that the bad angels try to harm us by tempting us to sin. One bad angel tempted Adam and Eve, telling them how happy they would be if they followed his urging. They believed him and sinned against their good God. Then the truth struck them that they had been deceived. Right away they tasted sorrow instead of joy, hardship instead of comfort. We must never listen to the bad angel's temptations because they are always lies. He says, "Go out and play instead of obeying

Mother. Say a mean thing to your companion. Do not pay attention to Sister. Throw your books around carelessly." He is lying because we will surely feel bad if we do what he says. The other day a wicked man was condemned to prison for life. Before he entered his cell he said, "Sin does not pay. I believed the tempter when He promised me joy through a sinful life. Now I must spend the rest of my days in loneliness and sorrow."

> I love my God in every way.
> He guards me both by night and day.
>
> —*Helen Reuland.*

3. The Effects of Their Sin Upon Us

It is not wise to explain the exact meaning of "original," that it is so called because of our origin from Adam; just now it is called "the first sin," meaning the first sin committed on earth. As yet we do not even use the word "grace" but circumlocute with the phrase "holy to God."

We inherit Adam's sin and its consequences. "Inherit" means to be left something by someone who is dead. For example, a rich man gave a poor man a sum of money which he was to use and pass on to his children. The money eventually did pass on to them, for it was left to them when their father died; they inherited it.

The teacher will draw a word picture of a boy laboriously mowing the lawn. Why must he work and sweat? Under a tree nearby two girls are busily studying their lessons. Why must they study hard? It is because of the first sin.

Adam and Eve are our first parents. They underwent a test not only for themselves but for all of their children ever to live. Even today when our own father has steady work and earns lots of money, we, his children, can get better clothes and a better education as a consequence. If Adam and Eve had remained faithful, we their children, without any work on our part, would have received all their blessings.

Q. 25. Is this sin passed on to us from Adam?
A. Yes, this sin is passed on to us from Adam.

(The following cannot be explained with theological exactness to six-year olds.) As punishment of the sin of our first parents, we are all born in original sin. This is a state where the soul is neither holy nor pleasing to God, nor is it friendly to God.

As we grow up we find other disabilities or punishments afflicting us because we are the children of father Adam who sinned. We must study hard in order to learn; we must suffer many temptations; we have to fight hard to save our souls; we can meet with sickness and accidents. All must some day work hard to make a living. In the end we all know that we will die.

Q. 26. What is this sin called in us?
A. This sin in us is called original sin.

Summary by Example: The other day Sister said to the eighth grade, "If you all work hard this week and write a good examination paper I will give the whole school a hodiday." Those boys and girls were older and they should have used this opportunity. Actually some in the classes were lazy, so they spoiled the holiday for themselves and for every other grade.

Only one human being was, from the first instant of her existence, free of the first sin. This person was the Mother of Jesus, the Blessed Virgin Mary. Jesus wanted a mother who always was holy, so He never let the first sin fall on her soul. The Church celebrates a feast in honor of this great fact, called the Immaculate Conception. The long words just mean that Mary, alone of the race, never had the first sin. On that day, December 8, all Catholics of the United States must attend holy Mass. They tell Mary they are glad because she never had the first sin and they thank God because He gave her this high honor.

With the help of the teacher the pupils will describe the details of a picture of the Immaculate Conception. The angels at her feet are some of those who remained faithful to God. Her white dress tells of her great purity. The ring about her head tells of her great holiness.

Mary was the most beautiful lady who ever lived, but what's more she was also the most holy. The story of the apparition at Lourdes would here prove quite interesting to the children. The text begins to hint of the reason of man's creation—to know, to love and to obey God.

Q. 27. Was any one ever free from original sin?
A. The Blessed Virgin Mary was free from original sin.

Summary by Example: A new-born baby should be baptized as soon as possible. Baptism erases the first sin from its soul. Mary never had to be baptized because she never had the first sin.

Motivation: We offer ourselves to Mary as her dear children. She knows that we are the children of God but she wants us to be her children too. Jesus said one time that we are her children. We know how our mother is easily impressed when we tell of our needs. But Mary is the best mother, the greatest mother of all, has a heart more tender even than our own mother's and loves us more even than our own mother. Above all, this heavenly mother wants us to get to heaven and she is very anxious that we ask her often for her help. This very day we shall go to church, kneel before her statue, and promise that we shall always be her good children. Today we shall say our Hail Marys much more slowly and with greater love and hope.

4. Our Duty to God

The class has learned many things which they must do for God; it is their duty to know God. They have learned many ways of showing their love for God; it is their duty to love God. They have learned many things which they must do to be true children of God; it is their duty to obey God.

> Picture a boy studying his catechism; the boy is trying to know God better. Picture children marching in a Corpus Christi procession; the children are showing their love of God. Picture some altar-boys helping Sister to decorate the altar; the boys are trying to serve God.

Children must pay close attention while the teacher or the pastor explains how they can prove their love for God. They must pay particular attention as they hear what God said must be done; to disobey such a commandment is sinful. The short phrase "to know, to love, to obey God" might also be called the great commandment because it includes and colors every activity of life.

Q. 3. Why did God make you?
A. God made me to show His goodness and to make me happy with Him in heaven.

Q. 4. What must you do to be happy with God in heaven?
A. To be happy with God in heaven I must know Him, love Him, and serve Him in this world.

Motivation: God saves no one without his own effort. God will not say at the end, "You went to a Catholic school; that was enough; come, enter heaven." But God will ask, "Did you try to learn about Me, what I said, what I commanded?" It means that we must never sin because by sin we show hatred to God. It means that we must often tell God in our prayers that we love Him.

Directions for organization will henceforth be omitted. They have been given often enough to let the teacher know that the step is just a review of the section and follows each section. The method also is now well understood, namely, that the teacher prompts the class by converting the first sentence of the paragraph into a question.

UNIT FOUR: GOD THE SON

(Revised Baltimore First Communion Catechism: Lesson 4)

I. God Promised a Saviour.
II. The Mother of the Saviour.
III. The Saviour Is Born.

What We Shall Learn: Now you come to a story which all children love very much, one which you often heard at mother's knee. One of the first holy words which you learned to say was "Jesus." You will therefore learn about Jesus. You have a pretty good idea of what went before, of God the Father, of the greatness of God, of the angels, the good and the bad, of how the world was made, of your first parents and all the consequences of their fall. Towards the end, the picture got pretty gloomy because you learned that your first parents had lost everything for themselves and for you. You will learn now how that gloomy picture was turned into a bright one, how dark feelings were turned into joy. The Person who did it was Jesus and because He saved you from so much trouble you call Him, the Saviour. Now you will learn much about your Saviour, Jesus Christ.

I. God Promised a Saviour

As Christmas approaches, the class will learn Christmas hymns and prepare class posters which indicate the feast. With Sister's help the pupils will make a crib. Perhaps some of the pupils will be adept enough to make one which they can take home. The teacher will prepare herself by diligently reading the story of the Promise from the Bible history.

God is good. We know that Adam and Eve had sinned. They did something that God had told them not to do. God punished them by sending them out of the Garden. But God was good. He was sorry for Adam and Eve. Even though the human race through our first parents had offended Him, God still loved the race. He still wanted us to be happy here and happy forever in heaven. He saw how sorry Adam and Eve were and how sorry we would be. He chided Adam and Eve then, but because He was so good He told them not to lose hope for themselves and their children.

God promised some day to send His own Son upon the earth to save all men and restore to them what had been lost. This Son would be born of the Virgin Mary and His name would be Jesus. He would be called the Saviour because He would save men. He would pay the big debt men owed to God for their sins. He would reopen the gates of heaven to them and give men a second chance to gain heaven.

The teacher might show the pupils the picture of the Immaculate Conception by Murillo. She will again explain that Mary alone never inherited the first sin. Mary was placed on earth to help drive the first sin from the souls of men.

Motivation: In a way the great promise was the most hopeful message ever given to man and all should be eternally grateful for it. Children are happy when Mother forgives and gives them a second chance even though there is little at stake. How much more should they be thankful to God who gave them a second chance to attain heaven! The children will strive still harder to know God, to love Him and to obey Him. They will try particularly to prepare their hearts during the season of Advent, for that commemorates the years of waiting which followed the great promise.

Men waited long for the Saviour:—The biblical stories that follow will not be explained in detail here, so the teacher must prepare them diligently the evening before from the Bible History. One story at a time should be presented to the class with its own oral instruction and learning procedure, just as if it were a complete unit.

Adam and Eve waited:—Our first parents lived a long time, hundreds of years, but the Saviour did not come in their lifetime. Many a time did they think with sorrow how they had offended God, and besides had brought so much grief upon the children whom they were now bringing into the world. Their minds did not see God so clearly and it was difficult to be good. They even saw how temptations got the better of their children. But Adam and Eve had learned a great lesson from the Fall and both now led saintly lives. The promise of the Saviour ever filled their hearts with hope.

Cain kills his brother, Abel:—Even Adam and Eve had to see the sad effects of this fight with the enemy of man, the devil. Their own son, Cain, gave in to a temptation of jealousy, and slew his brother, Abel. What a sad day must that have been for our first parents when they found their son murdered by his own brother. Did they not realize the effects of their first sin? Cain had been weak and the devil had been strong. Truly, sin had entered the world and what a terrible sin! Here was the first death too; God had said that death would enter into the world. Even then our first parents prayed that the Saviour would come soon in order to prevent repetitions of this ghastly sin.

Noe waited:—Hundreds of years had gone by. Adam and Eve had long since died but the Saviour had not yet appeared. In the meantime the bad angels had been very busy upon the earth, leading men away from God so that God was sorry He had created man. When God said He would destroy the earth with a flood, He remembered a good man, named Noe, and He arranged a plan by which He could save Noe and his family. God is always good! The story of the flood and the Ark follows.

The teacher will go over the story with the class, pointing out moral lessons as follows: The fallen angels led those people into sin as they try to lead children today. God is all-present and He saw the good deeds of Noe even as He sees the good that children do today. God is almighty and He could cause a big flood to cover the earth. God is kind and after forty days He brought bright skies and a beautiful rainbow. After the flood God again looked forward to a people who would know, love and obey Him so that He could some day bring them to heaven and make them happy forever.

Abraham waited:—Again hundreds of years went by but the Saviour had not yet appeared. Then God chose a man named Abraham to lead His people. God told this leader many things about Himself and about the coming Saviour. Abraham did his best to keep the people good by reminding them about the great promise and telling them also about other promises which God had made. Many people listened to the holy man but others were hardhearted.

Many promptings will be necessary in order to draw these Bible stories piecemeal from the pupils. The teacher's questions must always lead to a conclusion which presents a moral lesson to the child. Thus, as Abraham refused to quarrel with Lot, so should children not quarrel with one another; as Abraham tried to save the people of Sodom, so should we try to save all people by praying for them; as Abraham remained faithful in the test, so should we remain faithful.

Grade I **II. The Mother of the Saviour** 47

Motivation: God tests our love in many ways. It is often the case that the more He loves us, the more He tests us so that He can give us a chance to show our love in return. Great saints generally had to suffer sickness, trouble and temptations, but they were glad to be afflicted because it showed how God loved them, gave them a chance to suffer for God and get higher in heaven. We should not be discouraged when we are troubled by trials and temptations but rather we should be happy. We will resolve to accept all little pains from the hands of the loving God. We will fear no temptations but look upon them as means to prove our love for God.

II. The Mother of the Saviour

The children are too young to be told about the mysteries of conception. Should a precocious youngster ask what "in the womb" means, the teacher can explain that Jesus was in Mary's heart. What follows are principally Bible stories that respond well to what might be called the "circumstance method," taking the lead from Who? What? Where? By what help? Why? How? When? Each story is to be treated as a lesson in itself.

We know that God had promised to send a Saviour, the Son of a woman, who would save the people from losing heaven. How would He come? Who would be His mother? Many a holy woman hoped that she would be the Mother of the Saviour.

The long time of waiting was at an end. The Saviour for whom the people had waited hundreds of years, was now to come. Every Jewish girl was hoping that she might become the Mother of the Saviour. But God always knew who that girl was to be. Now tell about Mary, the daughter of St. Anne, how Mary was brought to the temple school, her education and life there, how St. Joseph became her husband and how she went to live in Nazareth. It was this young girl whom God had chosen to be the Mother of the Saviour.

The Angel told Mary about the Saviour:—Yes, He will be here, here at last! The teacher will describe with all possible unction the participants of this holy drama, sinless Mary and the highest of angels at the Annunciation. She will linger over their heavenly conversation, marvel at the consequences, rejoice that the long waiting is ended. She will dwell not on the conception, but on the announcement that Jesus would appear in the world within a year. One of heaven's high angels tells

He will come and who will be His mother. Imagine if the other people at Nazareth had discovered what was happening that morning! Would they not have crowded about the house and even burst into the room, to see and hear the angel?

And how happy the angel was! How happy the Blessed Virgin was!

The children will describe the details of the picture of the Annunciation, Mary spotless, Mary praying, and the angel as the beautiful messenger of God. At the top is the dove which stands for the Holy Ghost who arranged the details of this great happening. The look on Mary's face tells that she can hardly believe the wonderful news but she does believe because the message is from God. "The angel said to Mary, 'You will be the Mother of God. You will be the mother of Jesus!'"

Q. 14 Did one of the Persons of the Blessed Trinity become man?
A. Yes, the Second Person, the Son of God, became man.

Q. 15. What is the name of the Son of God made man?
A. The name of the Son of God made man is Jesus Christ.

Motivation: We thank God the Father, God the Son and God the Holy Ghost. We are so thankful that the thousands of years of waiting are ended. We will sing for joy because Jesus is here and Jesus will save us. How terrible if He had not been promised, if He had never come! We would never have had a Christmas, never a single feast day. We will resolve again to prepare our souls by offering gifts to Jesus, to prepare our bodies for Him by being clean, our souls by doing good deeds.

Mary told Elizabeth about the Saviour:—The class makes its first attempt at learning about the mystery of the Incarnation as indicated in the Annunciation and the Visitation.

Mary was like many of us. She was so overjoyed at the good news that she could not keep it to herself. The angel had also told her about her cousin Elizabeth, who also was to have a son, so Mary hurried to her cousin. Imagine the meeting, and how their conversation just bubbled over! The words of Elizabeth testify that the Son of God had become man, and her words were true, because the Scripture says she spoke them when filled with the Holy Ghost. Elizabeth called Mary, the Mother of God.

Grade I   **III. The Saviour Is Born**   49

The journey from Nazareth to Ain-Karem where Elizabeth lived would take about four or five days. The little village was a two hours' walk west of Jerusalem. It lay on the slope of a stony hill that helped to make a beautiful valley. The white houses peeked out from the green olive and cypress trees. Vineyards lay in tiers to the valley below. The teacher must try to instill some of Mary's joy into the hearts of the children.

Q. 17. Who is the Mother of Jesus?
A. The Mother of Jesus is the Blessed Virgin Mary.

Motivation: Two great women met here, and the greater of the two was Mary. And of what did these two converse during the visit? Of the Saviour who would soon be born into the waiting world. That should be the topic for the children from now until Christmas.

III. The Saviour Is Born

The Bible story is brief but every teacher is familiar with the hundred details connected with the journey, the fruitless quest for an inn, the stable and the birth. The teacher will describe every detail with all possible unction, for the pupils must be not only interested but edified.

Jesus is born. The long wait was at an end and the hope of the sinful world was realized. To this hour men had looked forward and to it we look backward. Everything in our daily spiritual life and our hopes for eternity depend upon it. As the great promise in the garden of Paradise had been fulfilled, so will all other promises of God be carried out. The angels in the sky sang that He was God.

The angel told the shepherds that He is God. When the shepherds came they saw an Infant with tiny feet and tiny hands, with little blue eyes and smiling lips and they said, He is also man. Beside the crib stood Mary, His mother, lost in admiration and love for the sweet Child.

And standing a little further back was the saintly Joseph. He was not the father of the Child Jesus. God had placed Joseph in the holy family so that he could provide for and protect Jesus and Mary. He had guided Mary to Bethlehem and had searched for a place where they might stay and obtain food. We will learn still more how Joseph protected Jesus and His mother Mary.

Unit 4: God the Son

Q. 16. When was Jesus born?
A. Jesus was born on the first Christmas Day, more than nineteen hundred years ago.

Jesus is God. After the Fall God had promised to send His Son to save us. His Son is the second Person of the Trinity. Two months ago the question was, Is the Son God? The answer was, Yes, the Son is God and the second Person of the Blessed Trinity. The Son of God came on earth and He stayed God. When Elizabeth saw Mary she said that Jesus is God. In saying that, we mean that Jesus is the eternal God, all-knowing, all present, all-good, almighty.

Jesus is also man. We have learned that God is a Spirit. But a spirit can take a body. The angel who told Mary she was to be the mother of God was a spirit, too, but we see by the picture that he also took a body. The second Person of the Blessed Trinity, God, the Son, is a Spirit. He took a body but He kept it and has it today. That body was just like ours with face, feet and hands. Those feet and hands, those lips and ears could do what ours can do. Jesus therefore was also a real man. When He became man He took the name of Jesus Christ and that is now the name by which we know Him. Jesus is a Person who is both God and man.

Q. 18. Is Jesus Christ both God and man?
A. Yes, Jesus Christ is both God and man.

Under the teacher's guidance the children will bring out the story of the birth, of the song of the angels, the visit of the shepherds. Mary is pointed out as His real mother and Joseph as his foster father or protector. The little hands and feet say that Jesus is man; the golden halo about His head says that He is God.

Motivation: On Christmas Day the pupil will stand before the crib and pray somewhat as follows: Jesus, I am glad that You came. I see Your little face, Your tiny hands. You make me hope because You are a little child like I am. Because You loved me You became a little child like me. I am not afraid to talk to a child; I am not afraid to talk to You. I know too that You are God. You are almighty and can do anything. See, Jesus, I bring You the little gift that I have been preparing all these weeks. Will You give me a gift too.

Grade I   III. The Saviour Is Born   51

MY GIFT

What can I give Him,
  Poor as I am?
If I were a shepherd,
  I'd bring Him a lamb.
If I were a wise man,
  I would do my part.
Yet, what can I give Him?
  I'll give Him my heart.

—*Christina Rossetti.*

If the semester began in September the above lesson must be concluded before Christmas. No new material is furnished for the rest of the semester. By this time the pupils will have attained a fair proficiency in primer-reading. The entire subject in the pupil's text should be reviewed during the remainnig days of this first semester. The apportionment of work between teacher and pupils varies slightly. The oral instruction of the teacher is much briefer. The next step is a study of the picture by the pupils. The final step is the reading of the text by the pupils.

END OF FIRST SEMESTER OR I B

SECOND SEMESTER—OR 1 A—JESUS OUR TEACHER

UNIT FIVE: JESUS PRAYED: WE SHOULD PRAY

   I. WHAT PRAYER IS.
  II. WHY WE SHOULD PRAY.
 III. HOW WE SHOULD PRAY.
  IV. FOR WHOM WE SHOULD PRAY.
   V. PRAYER IS NECESSARY.

What We Shall Learn: We have already learned much about God the Father and His Son, Jesus Christ. We look upon God the Father as our Creator; from His almighty power came the world and all the things in it; from Him we came, our body and our priceless soul. He is a big God, infinite in fact, before whom we are very little indeed. God, the Son was born on the earth on the first Christmas Day and He came solely for our benefit; His act was one of exceeding great love for us. In spite of our own littleness we are in many respects very important creatures because God the Father and God the Son have a very great interest in us. They talk to us and, strange to say, they want us to talk to them. Are we not fortunate that we are allowed to talk to God? How do we do this? We do it through prayer. Therefore we shall learn about prayer, why and how we should pray, when we should pray and for whom.

To the Teacher: This unit must be taught orally because the New Baltimore First Communion Catechism does not contain a lesson on Prayer, but recommends that children in this grade be told about it.

I. What Prayer Is

What follows about prayer is introduced by presentations from the infancy and youth of Our Lord. The teacher will prepare the Bible story in advance so that she can recount it in a fluent and interesting manner. Oral instruction has better effect when it revolves around the details of a picture. The purpose of the biblical introductions is also to present Our Lord's life within a definite period. The three ensuing paragraphs are an introduction to the lesson, tell us who Jesus is and from whom we get the lesson; then the lesson about prayer follows.

Grade I **I. What Prayer Is** 53

On Christmas Day He who is called the Saviour, was born on earth. We give Him many names or titles. We call Him Jesus which means that He brought us salvation, that He saved us. We call Him Christ because He is the anointed or consecrated one; the second Person of God, because He is only one Person; the God-Man because in his natures He is both God and Man.

When we call Him the great Teacher we mean that He taught us what we must do to save our souls. When we call Him our Master we mean, for one thing, that He gave the example of all virtues to us, His children.

Jesus the Teacher, taught us how to get to heaven. *Example:* Jesus told a story about a Samaritan helping a wounded man and He said, "You shall love the Lord your God; you shall love your neighbor as yourself." At another time He told how a rich Pharisee prayed in a proud manner in the Temple and He said that we must not pray in that manner. He gave us very many beautiful instructions; we hear one or other of them in the Gospel every Sunday at Mass. He made it plain by sermons, miracles and stories what we must do.

By word and example Jesus taught us that we must pray. The teacher will tell the story of the Presentation of the Infant Jesus in the temple. The incident gives several impressive examples of prayer. Jesus offered Himself and His life's work to God in prayer. The very Presentation was a prayer, for Mary prayerfully offered the Infant Jesus to God. Not having been given a clear knowledge of this Child's future, she must have petitioned heaven most earnestly in His behalf as any mother naturally would do. She could only guess at what was still to come and like any mother she begged God to smooth the road of the Saviour as much as the divine plans permitted. Joseph prayed with her, for much of the burden of the future years would fall on his shoulders. Simeon prayed. What an immortal prayer that was! Anna prayed. All the incidents took place in a house of prayer.

The thoughts of the participants were in heaven where God is. They thought of nothing else but God; they even pictured the most lovable God the Father above them. Their hearts throbbed with love for God. Their wishes were with God. All were talking to God. Their minds and hearts were lifted up to God—this is prayer.

We can do what Jesus, Mary and Joseph did; we can lift our

minds and hearts to God by prayer. God is invisible, yet we can talk to Him. By prayer we seem to fly like a bird and stand before the most beautiful God. Children are little, but see what they can do. They can fly before the great God. They can talk to Him just as easily as Father and Mother can. Do you want to fly to heaven often? Then pray often.

Summary by Example: Prayer is like an airplane that lifts the soul to God. Straight up it goes until the soul stands, as it were, before God, able now to talk to Him and to hear Him talk to the soul. An airplane might go so high that the pilot can no longer see the earth. So, in prayer we must fly so high to God that we cannot see anything about us. Prayer is the lifting up of our minds and hearts to God.

Motivation: To lift up the mind and heart to God before a meal when we are hungry and the savor of a steaming dish is tempting us, is a meritorious act. When we do difficult things, God loves us all the more. He is pleased when we can take time out to lift our mind and heart to Him to say grace and He will be sure to bless us in a special manner. The good Catholic boy or good Catholic girl will remember God's goodness after the meal and once more raise their hearts and minds to thank God for the food. What a privilege that even a little child can in a moment fly like an airplane before God and talk to the great God!

> When I work or when I play,
> Be Thou with me through the day,
> Teach me what to do and say,
> Sweet holy Child.
>
> —*L. M. Wallace.*

II. Why We Should Pray

The three Wise Men taught us why we should pray. The teacher will tell the story of the journey of the Three Wise Men, generously filling out every detail. Their prayers and prayerful words accompanied the presentation of their gifts.

Enough had happened on their journey to convince the Three Kings that they would see God. For long hours they had kept silent, just thinking of the great privilege that would be theirs. No sooner did they behold the Babe than they fell on their knees and *adored* Him. One of their number then stepped forward and gave the Infant a golden gift such as is offered to God, for here was God, the Saviour, the second Person of the Blessed Trinity. Their hearts were full of *thanks* because He had sent a star to guide them. They thanked the divine Babe for all the favors He had ever granted them. Like children they spoke their *sorrow* for ever having been unfaithful even in little things. Before leaving, they once more knelt down and begged the Infant to *bless* them on their return journey and during the years that would follow.

We must adore God by prayer. We too must often tell God that He is the One God; that He is our God; that He is Lord of heaven and earth; that He knows all and can do everything. When we tell Him this, we are said to adore Him, that is, we tell Him who He is and we acknowledge who He is. The best way to do that is by prayer. Is it not easy, for example, to say a little prayer like this— My Lord and My God?

We must thank God by prayer. Mother and Father love us when we are thankful. We, in turn, show our love by being thankful. The Three Kings gave thanks to God. God loves us so much that He gives us everything we have. We thank God because He has done so much for us. We tell this best in our prayers. Often we should make up our own prayer and just say, "God, I thank You."

We must prayerfully express our sorrow for past sins. Little children make mistakes. They sometimes offend their parents. Then the parents feel very sad. When good children notice this they will tell Mother they are sorry; they will ask Father not to punish them. That shows the parents that the children really love them. Sometimes children offend God. Good children will tell God right away that they are sorry. They do not want anything to separate them from God. There are some special prayers in which they can tell God they are sorry; for example, the Act of Contrition.

We must ask for God's blessings through prayer. There are hundreds of special prayers in which we ask favors of God. We can also compose them ourselves. We want to be good. We want favors for ourselves, for our parents and friends. We go to God because we learned that He is all-good and will help us.

Summary by Example: Describe the event as shown in a picture of the Adoration of the Wise Men once more, soliciting the participation of the pupils. They will notice the reverent faces and the costly gifts. They will, with the help of the teacher, explain how they adored, why they thanked, how they were sorry, why they needed and asked for new blessings.

(We pray:

> FIRST, to adore God;
> SECOND, to thank Him for His favors;
> THIRD, to obtain from Him the pardon of our sins and the remission of their punishment;
> FOURTH, to ask graces and blessings for ourselves and others).

Motivation: Today the pupils, singly or in groups, will pay a visit to our Lord in the Blessed Sacrament. They are fortunate to have the same Jesus before them whom the three Wise Men visited. Surely they wish that they could have a chance to visit Jesus as the three Kings did. But they can visit Him in their own parish church. They will do as the Wise Men did. They will tell Jesus that He is their God, that they thank Him for all the favors He has given them. They will tell Him how sorry they are for their little faults and sins. They will tell Jesus that they have a long journey to make even as the Kings had. They must pass safely through the journey of life and they want Jesus to give them all the graces they need.

III. How We Should Pray

To use a biblical incident for a presentation, means that the teacher will often have to invent details that probably were present but are not given in the story-text. Broad sweeps of the brush will not satisfy children; they have a livelier appreciation when they see the little bird flying over the landscape.

Once more, Mary and Joseph teach us a lesson, namely, how we should pray. The teacher will narrate the story of the Flight into Egypt. Mary and Joseph had been given a trying task to carry this tiny, precious Saviour to a place of safety; they kept their minds on the God who could direct them safely. As they passed through the strange country they saw how helpless they were and that help could come from God only. Never were there two people who prayed more earnestly. But some time before the journey the angel had spoken to Mary as he had also spoken to Joseph, so now they had good reason to place all their hope in God. The journey was long, was tiring, was dangerous; but day after day, yes, hour after hour, they continued to pray to God.

When we pray we must keep our mind on God, that is, pray with attention. God sees us; God knows all things; God is present everywhere. If we are not attentive, we tell God that we are not interested in Him or in our own requests.

We must remember our own weakness and we must understand that strength comes only from God. We are but children and we do not tell God what He must do; rather, we ask whether He would please grant the favor.

We pray with great hope, knowing that God is all-good and will help, if it is for our own good. We know that He is almighty and can help.

"If at first you don't succeed, try, try again." We persevere in prayer to prove to God that our love and hope is lasting. We love Him not only for a moment, not only when He showers us with blessings but we are true friends who continue to love Him even when blessings seem to be withheld for a time.

Sometimes distractions persist. Thoughts of the last ball game bother the boy; a race around the corners bothers the little girl. Such bothersome thoughts are not sinful as long as the boy and girl try to put them out of their minds. Children must not be discouraged if they are disturbed thus, all through their prayer. Perhaps their prayers do not seem to amount to much; but if they try hard to get the thoughts out of their mind, God sees their good effort and He will call it a good prayer. To play with these thoughts, however, makes the prayer useless.

Summary by Example: A boy wants a pair of roller skates. Does he scrape his feet and chew gum when he asks Mother? No, he keeps his eyes on her and gives her his whole attention. Does he hint that he could get the skates in some other way? No, he tells her that he doesn't have a cent and that she has all the money. Does he express his wish merely in a low voice? No, he gets earnest, he makes gestures, his eyes glitter at the possibility of owning the skates. Does he throw up his hands as if the case were hopeless? No, he is so full of hope that he knows his favor will be granted by his loving mother. Does he give up right away? No, if Mother does not give him the money today, he will come back tomorrow with the same request, and the day after, and the day after that. "Thus shall you pray."

Motivation: We must make a real effort in order to pray well. An old sailor showed a young man his boat with its two paddles.

On one paddle was printed the word, "Pray"; on the other, the word "Work." The youth laughed, "What need is there of prayer if one works?" "Come, I'll show you that both are necessary," said the old sailor. He rowed with one paddle named "Work" but the boat only went around in a circle. Then he rowed with the paddle, "Pray" and again the boat only went round in a circle and got nowhere. When the old man rowed with both paddles, the boat went straight to sea. To work only is like depending on one paddle; we must sanctify work, make it pleasing to God, confirm it with prayer and our little boat of life will go straight to God. Holy persons begin and end their work with prayer. They even find time for short prayers in the course of their labor. And because they sanctify their work in the beginning, the work itself becomes a prayer to God. He who does this earnestly day after day, is doing all that is needed to pray well. He is attentive, humble, eager, hopeful and persevering.

IV. For Whom We Should Pray

The example set by the Holy Family shows us for whom we should pray. The story of the Return from Egypt serves as presentation. The Holy Family was surrounded by the same dangers as on the journey into this strange country. Once more Mary and Joseph had the difficult task of bringing the Holy Child back to safety. They did not just jog along day-dreaming and when they reached a shady spot of palm trees, they did not just sit down for a rest. They had too much to pray for. They prayed for themselves that they might pass safely through the dangers. They prayed for the friends whom they would soon see in Nazareth. They even prayed for the enemies round about that God would lead them to better lives. Often at night they knelt down together and prayed for their priests and their country.

We must pray for ourselves because without prayer we cannot be saved. The greatest work we have is to save our own souls and we must give this our very first attention.

Prayer must be offered for others, parents, relatives, friends, all in fact, for all are our neighbors whom we must love as ourselves. Prayers can help parents in their daily needs and can even help them to save their souls. We owe our parents so much that we should want to repay them. Our relatives and friends are closer to us than other people; God said that we must love all men but especially these friends. We love them and help them by prayer. There are other friends in purgatory who appreciate assistance very much. If we pray for them now, they will pray for us when they get to heaven.

The Church must be remembered. She is our Mother. The Church wants to do much good for souls, wants all to love God. When we pray for her she can do those things better. Perhaps our prayers will save a soul; perhaps they will bring Baptism to a little Chinese baby. We must not forget our priests and sisters.

We should pray for our own country, for its rulers. Our rulers have a difficult task because this is a large country. By our prayers we help them to rule wisely and well.

After the pupils have repeated what the teacher has explained orally, they might rise and say the Our Father for themselves, for their parents and friends, and a Hail Mary for the President and their country. (We should pray especially for ourselves, for our parents, relatives, friends and enemies, for the souls in purgatory, for the Pope, bishops, and priests of the Church, and for the officials of our country.)

Summary by Example: There is one radio station "H-E-A-V-E-N," which is the greatest in the world, for it gives service every minute of the day and night. It not only broadcasts all the time, but it receives our messages all the time and everywhere. Another great station is "Y-O-U," because you can get messages to and from heaven instantly. When the two stations are connected, prayer is the only language used.

Motivation: By this time the class has undoubtedly learned several beautiful hymns. These also are prayers, very sweet prayers. God is pleased when we use our lips to say prayers to Him. He is pleased when we use lips and voice to sing prayers to Him. The angels sing sweet songs of praise to Him in heaven. We try to be little angels when we sing hymns. We are happy when we sing and God loves the happy, joyous, prayers of children.

A story: A convict had attended Mass in the prison chapel for the first time. One of the inmates had sung a beautiful "Ave Maria." The prisoner met the chaplain afterwards. "Father," he said, "I am coming back again to my Church. I did not think that religion could be so beautiful." A hymn had converted him.

V. Prayer Is Necessary

Prayer is necessary. In this life a child can do without shows or games but it cannot get along without food. So, in the journey to heaven, no child can get along without prayer. He needs so many extra graces and the only way to get them is by prayer.

A story: In 1787, George Washington, the Father of our Country, and fifty-five companions met to make an important decision for the United States. Then that wise man, Benjamin Franklin, stood up, "Let us pray," he said. "I am an old man and know that God directs the affairs of men. If God watches the sparrow on the housetop, He certainly watches us and is willing to guide us."

Convinced of the necessity of prayer the pupils will be eager to learn many prayers. They will review the sign of the cross, the Our Father, the Hail Mary, the grace before and after meals, and the Glory Be to the Father. We generally conclude other prayers with the Glory Be to the Father. The prayer is: Glory be to the Father, and to the Son and to the Holy Ghost, as it was in the beginning, is now, and ever shall be, world without end. Amen.

The recital of The Apostles' Creed may have to be delayed until a little later in the year. For that same reason the official Acts of Faith, Hope, Charity and Contrition cannot be learned now in their entirety. The *Revised Baltimore First Communion Catechism* offers shorter forms which the class might memorize.

Summary by Example: Heaven is like our home on this earth where we can talk to any one whom we wish. Sometimes the child talks to Mother, then to Father, then to brother and sister. He talks to entertain himself or to interest those about him; he addresses a paricular member because that one is able and willing to grant a favor. He can talk to God in heaven with the Our Father; he can pray to Mary with the Hail Mary; he can ask the saints through short prayers which he makes up himself. As long as the child is good, any one in the home is eager to listen and to help. So heaven is listening always. God listens especially when class prayers are said. Does not Sister listen more closely when two or three pupils meet her after school and ask for something? Jesus said that a prayer by a group is very powerful.

Motivation: A Story: One day while St. Bernard and his priests were praying, the Saint had a vision. Over each one stood an angel who wrote down the prayers. Some were written in gold, some in silver, some with ink and some with ordinary water. God explained that the prayers written in gold were the perfect prayers. Others were more or less imperfect until they came to those written in water which were prayers of the lips only and were worthless. Does each pupil in this classroom try to help with the golden prayers?

UNIT SIX: JESUS OBEYED GOD'S LAWS: WE MUST OBEY THEM

(Revised Baltimore First Communion Catechism: Lesson 7)

I. JESUS OBEYED GOD'S LAWS.
 1. WHY JESUS OBEYED THEM.
 2. THE LAWS OF GOD.
II. NOT OBEYING GOD IS A SIN.
 1. WHAT SIN IS.
 2. MORTAL SIN.
 3. VENIAL SIN.
 4. THE HARM SIN DOES TO US.

What We Shall Learn: Thus far we have taken up quite pleasant topics, but there is another possibility in life which is not so pleasant —namely, sin. Every child here has resolved always to love God: to love God means obeying God's laws. But we wish to be warned against anything which shows lack of love and destroys that love. So first we shall learn what the laws are which we must obey. Next we shall learn that disobedience to those laws is a sin. We shall learn about big, big sins which we resolve never to commit and we shall learn about lesser sins, lesser indeed as in comparison with the big sins but still so serious that we will likewise promise God never to commit them. Our resolve will be strengthened when finally we learn what harm such sin does to us.

I. Jesus Obeyed God's Laws

1. Why Jesus Obeyed Them

The instructions are now taking a more serious turn as we slowly lead the children to the preparation for Confession and Communion whether they are to receive those sacraments in this grade or in the next.

Jesus Obeyed. The teacher will tell the story of the Finding of the Child Jesus in the Temple. His stay in the House of God is to be explained as follows: For the time Jesus heard a greater voice even than that of Mary and Joseph. His Father in heaven was calling and He owed the Father obedience above any one on earth. Hence He stayed in the Temple and explained heavenly truths to the wise men there. Jesus always did look upon the voice of Mary or Joseph as that of His Father but at this time His Father spoke directly to Him and He obeyed even though it brought sorrow to His two best friends on earth. When Jesus came on earth He had said, "I have come to do My Father's will"; when He was leaving the earth He said, "I have done Thy will."

We are here on earth to know God and His holy will; we are also here to obey God, that is, to do His holy will. God through Abraham, Moses, Noe and other prophets has told us what His holy will is. Jesus spent three years in His public life explaining the will of God. If a person never became rich or great but spent his whole life in doing the will of God, he would lead a life that is far more precious in God's sight than gold or silver.

The pupils must understand their two principal duties: to study their religion now in order to find out what are the laws of God; to study reasons now why they should obey the laws of God.

Motivation: Our faith is lively when we practice what it teaches; that is knowing and doing. These boys run foot races sometimes. A boy must know where the finish line is; besides, he must run as fast as he can in order to win. Do you believe that your finish line is heaven? Are you running towards it with all your might?

When you die, God will ask you two questions: What did you believe? What did you do?

2. The Laws of God

To prepare for the first Confession is quite a task. Not to crowd later on, we now explain in a round-about-way the first step,—the examination of conscience. Pupils of this age commit few, if any, sins. It would be unnecessary and unwise to explain all the commandments of God or all the parts of any particular one. Even if some teacher should decide to have the pupils memorize the ten commandments of God, she should immediately explain that several of them refer only to adults. Since the following division deals with the topic of sin, it is well to know beforehand what the sinful acts or omissions can be.

The teacher will tell the story: Moses Receives the Ten Commandments. God surrounded the incident with circumstances intended to instill fear into the people. There was thunder and lightning to show the power of God. His words were serious, "Thou shalt: thou shalt not."

Unit 6: Jesus Obeyed God's Laws

Our Saviour several times talked about the commandments given to Moses, telling the people that they must keep them. The children want to know what to obey and how to obey. They must not yet try to memorize the schedule that follows.

(The commandments of God are these ten:

1. I am the Lord thy God; thou shalt not have strange gods before Me.
2. Thou shalt not take the name of the Lord thy God in vain.
3. Remember thou keep holy the Lord's day.
4. Honor thy father and thy mother.
5. Thou shalt not kill.
6. Thou shalt not commit adultery.
7. Thou shalt not steal.
8. Thou shalt not bear false witness against thy neighbor.
9. Thou shalt not covet thy neighbor's wife.
10. Thou shalt not covet thy neighbor's goods.)

Motivation: All the people from the time of Moses were judged accordingly as they kept or did not keep the commandments. Many obeyed and saved their souls: many did not and lost their souls forever. Will the children save their souls? Will they lose their souls? Of course children of this age can hardly commit big, big sins, but in later life they will be tempted by the big, big sins. Then it all depends whether they fight the big temptation or give in to it. Yes, so much depends on it that they must begin now to obey God's laws. A child is like a young tree. If the young tree grows straight, it will generally stay straight. If it grows crooked, it will be hard to straighten later.

II. Not Obeying God's Laws Is a Sin

1. What Sin Is

Children are to be told the truth about sin without exaggerating circumstances. It is a figment of the imagination that the guardian angel folds his wings or the Blessed Virgin cries when the child commits a sin. There are enough reasons to hate sin without drawing unduly on the imagination.

The story of the Baptism of Jesus will first be told. St. John preached against sin, then baptized the people who were converted by his words. Our Lord asked to be baptized in order to show his approval of St. John's work and to give the good example to the Jewish people.

Our Saviour wanted to give us a good example because we must be baptized in order to be freed from original sin. Original sin is the one we get from Adam; we inherit it. *Examples:* A boy born of Chinese parents inherits a yellow skin. When a boy's rich father dies, the boy inherits or receives his money. We get or inherit what our parents leave us; we inherit original sin from our father, Adam.

Q. 28. Is original sin the only kind of sin?
A. No, there is another kind of sin, called **actual sin**.

Actual sin is so called because we actually commit it; because it is done by our own act. In contrast, the child is born with original sin, but it never had the intelligence to commit it, or even to know of it. Now this child grows up and commits an act of disobedience or an act of theft. For this the child is entirely to blame, and because he did it by his own act, this is called an actual sin.

With an actual sin, the act must be wilful. *Examples:* Wilful thought—to think you are better than others and to despise them. Wilful desire—to desire sinfully to take a bicycle that belongs to another boy. Wilful word—to call a boy names. Wilful deed—to steal a lead pencil from a companion. Wilful omission—to miss Mass.

The teacher will draw a word picture of a boy stealing a scooter, and of a girl pushing a companion into the mud. She will explain that both acts being wilful constitute actual sins.

An involuntary sin is no sin at all. Oftentimes people do things which they cannot prevent or of which they do not realize the sinfulness. *Example:* A boy turns around quickly, not knowing that there is an expensive vase on the table behind him and he smashes the vase. The act was not sinful because he did not intend to break the vase.

Q. 29. What is actual sin?
A. Actual sin is any sin which we ourselves commit.

Summary by Example: Two little mischiefs, a boy and a girl, sneak into the pantry where they know there is a jar of cookies. They had an evil thought, then a desire, then they grabbed for the cookies. Their sin was wilful.

Unit 6: Jesus Obeyed God's Laws — Grade I

Motivation: St. John the Baptist kept himself free from sin by doing penance and leading a very holy life. He would have died rather than do the slightest thing which offended God. St. John understood what a terrible thing it is to break the laws of God. He preached so boldly against sin that a wicked king chopped off his head. Priests preach constantly against sin. Sometimes missionaries come from afar off to give us special sermons against sin.

A Story: St. Andrew Corsini (February 4) had committed many sins in his youth. When he turned to God, he could not forget those misspent years. He read long prayers every day, he did penance for his sins, he took care of the poor, he made peace between enemies, he was kind to all. Tonight every pupil will pray earnestly, "Please God, give me more help that I may never commit a sin."

2. Mortal Sin

Though children of this age hardly commit mortal sins, some explanation will have to be made showing them the difference between the various kinds of sin. They can easily see the difference between stealing a writing pad and stealing a thousand dollars. For the moment they are told that some sins are lesser and some are big, big sins. Nothing is said of "sanctifying grace" or "supernatural life" because the pupils have not yet studied these topics. The explanation of other effects, too, is reserved until a later month.

Q. 30. How many kinds of actual sin are there?
A. There are two kinds of actual sin: mortal sin and venial sin.

The teacher will narrate the story, Jesus is Tempted by the devil. The story fits in appropriately for our lesson. Here Jesus endured temptation, because all people must suffer temptations to actual sins. The devil tried vainly to lead Him into mortal sin.

Mortal sin is a very bad hurt or injury. No one wants to be hurt or insulted. When some one hurts a man's good name or injures his property, he displeases that man very much, and he offends God who made the laws. In the case of a mortal sin this is a very big sin. It produces a great hurt, is a great insult, causes grave injury, or shows deep contempt.

Examples: Spreading very bad gossip about another causes a great hurt to that other person. When a man calls his friend a

Grade I   II. Not Obeying God's Laws Is a Sin   67

vile name, it is a great insult. When a man burns down someone's home, he inflicts a grave injury upon him. When a man wilfully stays away from Mass, he shows contempt for God, who is worshiped in the Mass.

Mortal sin is an offense against the law of God.—The first laws of God are the ten commandments. But God has also given full authority to the Church to make laws, such as the six commandments of the Church.

We gain an idea of the effects of mortal sin from its very name. "Mortal" means deadly because this sin kills the holiness in the soul. When a soldier has received a mortal wound, it means that he has died or will die from the effects of that wound.

Q. 31. What is mortal sin?
A. Mortal sin is a deadly sin.

The beauty of the soul comes from its goodness or holiness. It is then like a tree loaded with fruit. Every one likes to look at the tree now because it is rich with fruit, green and beautiful. When the soul is good, God and His saints love to look at it. When mortal sin enters the soul it is just like a wintry blast which strips the tree of all its beauty, its fruit, its green leaves and there remain only the trunk and the branches. Mortal sin kills the holiness of the soul.

Q. 32. What does mortal sin do to us?
A. Mortal sin makes us enemies of God and robs our souls of His grace.

This morning Father was reading his daily paper and he remarked that a man had robbed the bank downtown. That act was wilful, so it was a sin. It gravely injured the owners of the bank. It offended God who forbids theft. It put a big sin on the robber's soul. It was a deadly, a mortal sin because it killed whatever holiness the robber had in his soul. If the robber dies unrepentant he will lose his soul.

Q. 33. What happens to those who die in mortal sin?
A. Those who die in mortal sin are punished forever in the fire of hell.

Summary by Example: In a war with his neighbor, Emperor Rudolf and his army suffered extremely from thirst. All the wells were dried up, so a party of his soldiers rode several miles where they came across a party of reapers who had a jug of water. At the point of the sword, they made the reapers give them the water. Joyfully they brought the water to their Emperor explaining how they had obtained it. But Rudolf was proof against the temptation. "I will not satisfy my thirst with water of which the poor have been robbed," he said. "Go and take it back to the poor reapers." Rudolf had a noble soul; temptations show whether our soul is noble or not.

Motivation: The way to prove our love for God is not to commit a mortal sin. This is really very solid proof, because temptations to mortal sin are very severe. The greater our resistance, the greater is the proof of our love. We must expect temptations to sin and in later life temptations to commit even mortal sins. Life is a time of trial during which our love for God is tested by temptations big and small. We can show love, too, by avoiding occasions which cause these serious temptations. Such are bad companions and bad movies. When temptations assail us we should have recourse to prayer, especially to the Blessed Virgin. We must always be devout clients of Mary. It is said that those who love her, cannot be lost. Ask her often to plead for you, too. No one who daily asks the intercession of Mary need fear mortal sins or the temptations thereto. The explanation of sin naturally fills these little souls with a nervous dread that is not at all to be recommended. We reassure them at once with motives of confidence. The power of Mary's prayer was illustrated at the Marriage at Cana. The teacher will tell the story, concluding that, as Mary helped then, she will help now.

3. Venial Sin

Do we not make a mistake in overemphasizing the word "little" when explaining venial sin? Actually and truly no sin is little. The teacher makes it clear that venial sins do not entirely separate from God nor kill the holy life of the soul but she will not make them appear as of no consequence. Are our imprudent explanations not the reason why children often make so little of lying? Just now it will only prove a waste of time to explain that even in matters of great importance, the sin is venial if committed without sufficient reflection or full consent. The distinctions are too subtle for these minds and besides, we do not want them to spend too much time even thinking of mortal sin.

All sins, even venial sins, are hateful to God. *Example:* A dead man strikes us as a calamity, but a wounded man can be a very pitiful spectacle. Draw a picture of a man covered with wounds, and explain that he resembles a soul wounded by venial sin. A little girl whispering during class does not kill the holiness in her soul but she lessens it; so also boys who are quarreling over the use of a baseball glove, are not so pleasing to God.

Examples of a big fault and a lesser fault. A son may become so wicked that his father expels him from the house; that is like the effect of mortal sin. A son may be so disobedient that he is a perpetual cross to his parents; they do still let him sit at table with them but he receives very little love from them; that is like the effect of venial sin. The soul in venial sin is still tolerated by God the Father, but receives less affection from Him.

Q. 34. What is venial sin?
A. Venial sin is a lesser sin.

Summary by Example: To give your brother a little slap offends venially against the commandments of God. Your little brother was not seriously hurt, and so the slap was not of grave importance.

Motivation: We must be faithful to God also in little things. Look at the clock on the wall. If the clock loses a second, it does not seem to make much difference. Nevertheless it proves that the clock is not running right. If it loses a second every little while, it has little worth as a timepiece and it must be taken to the repair shop. One venial sin does not seem to matter much but it shows that our soul is not working in the right way. When we commit many venial sins it is time to look into our soul and see what has gone wrong; it is steadily losing something, the love of God. The temptation to venial sin is a test for the soul. A true soldier fights bravely not only in the big battles but also in the little ones. We prove our love for God by fighting even the smallest thing that offends Him. We want His whole love. We are not satisfied just to sit at God's table and pout but we want to be happy there and we want God to smile at us. He smiles at the children who are faithful to Him even in little things.

4. The Harm Sin Does to Us

For obvious reasons the injury done by mortal sin is not considered. The point now is to teach children to avoid venial sins.

Unit 6: Jesus Obeyed God's Laws

At this time the pupils should hear stories of holy souls who excelled in a hatred for venial sins: such are Blessed Imelda, St. Aloysius, St. John Berchmans, St. Stanislaus Kostka, the Little Flower, and Blessed Guy. One of these stories will make the presentation for the ensuing explanation.

Venial sins show a falling off in our love for God. A man may be a fair soldier but he does not think much of his officer if he appears before him with dirty shoes, baggy trousers or a shabby coat. Venial sins lessen our love for God by lessening our fervor when we talk to God in prayer. A whistle with a hole in the mouthpiece, does not make a clear, sweet sound. A soul with a venial sin cannot say such a sweet prayer. Venial sins make us lazy in God's service.

Q. 35. Does venial sin make us enemies of God or rob our souls of His grace?

A. No, venial sin does not make us enemies of God or rob our souls of His grace.

Many venial sins lead to mortal sins. Dropping water will wear away even the hardest stone.

Venial sin brings punishment both here and hereafter. God sends us little disappointments, little aches now. In the next life He will make us suffer the pains of purgatory.

Summary by Example: A venial sin is an obstacle in our holy life. Two boys apparently sound and of equal ability started a race. They had not run far when one began to lose ground and eventually was badly beaten in the race. He explained his defeat by saying that his little toe was sore and chafed him so much that he had to favor it and consequently lose the race—a little toe did that. A boy with a sore toe cannot run as far or as fast as a boy with healthy feet. Neither can a boy who commits venial sins serve God as well as a boy who avoids them.

Motivation: A venial sin may seem small but it is like that sore toe. It does not wholly incapacitate a person but it does make his soul just a little lame so that he cannot perform his Christian duties so well. St. Paul compared a Christian to a man in a race. Well, the runner with one or more venial sins will have a harder time in running the race to heaven.

UNIT SEVEN: JESUS DIED FOR OUR SINS: WE MUST NEVER SIN

(Revised Baltimore First Communion Catechism: Lesson 5)

I. WHY JESUS SUFFERED AND DIED.
   1. JESUS SUFFERED AND DIED FOR OUR SINS.
   2. JESUS BOUGHT BACK OUR RIGHT TO HEAVEN.
   3. WHAT JESUS DID FOR US AT THE LAST SUPPER.
II. WHAT HAPPENED DURING THE PASSION.
   1. THE AGONY IN THE GARDEN.
   2. JESUS BEFORE THE RULERS.
   3. JESUS IS CRUCIFIED.

What We Shall Learn: When a person says that he loves us, we are pleased. When he does something for us, we are convinced of his love. Our Saviour has said that He loves us and He has proved His love. But in His case love is all the more remarkable because He did it after we had sinned; in fact, He suffered and died for us because we sinned. When we had lost all right to heaven, He could not bear to consider us as forever locked out of heaven but wanted us to regain that right. When we had turned away from Him by sin, He could not bear to see us forever turned away. Therefore in this important lesson we shall learn why He suffered and died. We shall learn what He suffered and how He died. Our resolve shall be that never, never shall we sin.

I. Why Jesus Suffered and Died

1. Jesus Suffered and Died for Our Sins

Children are governed to a great extent by their imagination which often can picture details more vividly than the same faculty in the adult. More time must be given to descriptive details of the sacred Passion than to deep moral conclusions. The pupils need only be reminded here and there of the reason why the Saviour died. Sin, they realize, hurt Jesus. Terms like "justice of God" or "satisfaction" or even "redemption" are hardly to be used with first-graders; the teacher will have to use circumlocutions.

Sin had brought damage to our souls and Jesus came down to repair that damage.

A vandal breaks into a church and smears paint over the walls. The beautiful edifice has been damaged and the damage is righted only when a skilful painter removes the blotches and makes the walls as good as new. Men had smeared sins all over their souls, and Jesus by His sufferings wiped out the smears.

We had offended God by sin so that His face was turned away from us. Our Saviour offered His life to the Father, for our serious offense. God the Father was pleased with this offering and smiled at us again. *Example:* Mother is so hurt by the disobedience of her son that she just cannot look at him. The boy regrets his act, picks a sweet-smelling rose from the garden and tells his brother to give it to Mother. She is pleased with the offering even though it came to her in a roundabout way; she forgets the past and smiles on her boy again.

By sinning we had insulted God and some one had to pay for those insults. Jesus paid for those insults with His precious life. *Example:* Suppose the President of the United States would be publicly insulted. The offender would be arrested, brought to the civil court and forced to make good the wrong. Suppose now, a noble man stepped forth in the court and publicly apologized for the man. So Jesus blotted out our insult to God.

Jesus made the payment for us. Sin is so terrible that we could never have made enough payment to God, no more than a little boy could pay a fine of one thousand dollars. Jesus was good and He could make such a large payment that it could satisfy for everything. *Example:* Because of pure carelessness, James ran his chum's bicycle into a tree and smashed it to bits. Now his chum naturally demands that James pay for the bicycle. James has not the money and he really fears the anger of the boy's father. Luckily James has a big brother who is very kind to him. The brother gets James out of trouble by paying the chum $31.00 for a new bicycle. We were too poor to pay the debt of sin. Jesus, our Brother, made the payment for us.

The practical conclusion of the lesson is a sense of appreciation for the sufferings of the Saviour. The very first lesson in the Primer days was—God loves me. Now must come a firmer resolve to carry out the second lesson—I love God— and the reason is, because God has done so much for me. In every subsequent step of

I. Why Jesus Suffered and Died

this theme on the sacred Passion, the pupils must revert to the phrase—God loves me: I love God.

Q. 19. Why did God the Son become man?
A. God the Son became man to satisfy for the sins of all men and to help everybody to gain heaven.

Motivation: Our Lord once said that the greatest act of love is to lay down one's life for a friend. He laid down His life for us. A missionary in Africa told this story: One Good Friday the natives came running with the news that a man was dying on the seashore. The priest hurried down and because he still noticed a spark of life in the man, had him brought to the camp. When he had revived him a little, the priest told the dying man the story of Good Friday. The man asked, "And did Jesus also die for colored people?" "Yes," answered the missionary, "for all people." "And did He die for big sinners like me?" "Yes," again replied the priest. "He died especially for sinners." The Negro was much moved. "O Father," he said, "please baptize me. If Jesus died for me, I want to die for Him." The missionary did as he was asked and shortly afterwards this wondering soul passed into eternity.—Jesus loved us so much that He gave up His life for us. We must love Him in return and be ready to do anything and everything that proves our love.

2. Jesus Bought Back Our Right to Heaven

The teacher must constantly revert to the concept that the human race is one large family even though the members are born at different times. By repeated statement of this fact the pupils will learn an important doctrine.

The red Ticket. A very brief review is to be made of the story of Adam's sin and its effects upon the human race; this time emphasis is to be put upon the fact that it closed the gates of heaven. The added personal sins of men closed the gates even tighter. Jesus purchased a ticket for each person by which he could gain admission into heaven. It was a red ticket because it was colored with His precious blood. Or, picture a boy trying to open a heavy door; the door remains shut until a strong man opens it for him. Men too were unable to open the door of heaven but Jesus came along and opened it for them. Now they gain admission to heaven by the red ticket.

Through the sufferings of Jesus the gates of heaven were reopened. No man could open them because no one could fly there. No man could open them because he was too weak. No man had a right to reopen them because he had sinned. But God who lived also in heaven, was there. He could open them because He is the almighty God. To bring out the concept of opening the gates of heaven, the teacher can add examples showing how a strong man can do things which a weak man cannot do, how Father can move objects which his little son cannot budge. The Saviour offered His sufferings to the offended Father who then by His almighty power opened the gates of heaven. The Saviour paid the price.

Jesus bought back the right to heaven which we had lost through Adam's sin and through our own sins. *Example:* If a girl wants to go to a movie theatre, she must have the money for a ticket. Jesus bought for us a ticket to heaven. He alone could buy it because the ticket to heaven costs very much. He paid for all our tickets with His blood.

Summary by Example: A Story: The passenger ship, the Swallow, was a mile and a half from Buffalo when the cry broke out, "Fire, Fire!" The Captain called to John Maynard the helmsman, "Try to hold on for a half hour and run her up to the beach." "With God's help, I will"; replied Maynard, although the flames were already licking at his feet. The brave man stuck to his post and brought the ship to land. All the passengers were saved, but John Maynard fell over dead. The hair was burned from his head, his body horribly burned, his steering arm was a black coal. He had died to bring the passengers to safety.

Motivation: The red ticket. Will we ever lose that ticket to heaven which Jesus bought with so great a price? Will we soil it even with venial sins? No, we will hold it tight and let no force of earth or hell take it away from us. No ticket ever cost so much. It is red because it was bought with the blood of our Saviour.

3. What Jesus Did for Us at the Last Supper

This division does not explain but describes only three great mysteries—the institution of the Holy Eucharist, of the Priesthood and of the Mass. Children are not puzzled by mysteries and would be surprised were any one to attempt an explanation of truths taught them by the pastor and the Sister. Just now, the purpose is to prepare them remotely for the reception of the Holy Eucharist and also to maintain the chronological sequence of the sacred Passion.

I. Why Jesus Suffered and Died

The Last Supper. The night before Our Saviour died, He ordered His apostles to meet Him in the large upper room of a certain house so as to have supper with them. While they were at supper He took bread and blessed it. Then He gave it to His apostles saying, "Take and eat; this is My body." Next He took wine and blessed it. Again He gave it to His apostles saying, "All of you drink of this; for this is My blood." By His words our Lord had changed bread into His body and wine into His blood.

Jesus Gave Us Holy Communion.—The apostles received His body and blood; in other words, they received Holy Communion. Jesus could do this because He was almighty. The apostles believed what their almighty Master had said; they believed that they had received the body and blood of Jesus Christ in Holy Communion. Jesus had said; "Take and eat; this is My body. All of your drink of this; for this is My blood." Jesus made Holy Communion for us.

Jesus Gave Us Priests.—Then Jesus turned to His apostles and He gave them power to do just what He had done. He said to them "Do this." Then and there He made them priests to change bread into His body and to change wine into His blood as He had just done. Then and there He gave all priests the power to change bread and wine into His body and blood. Our priests now give us Holy Communion.

Jesus Gave Us the Mass.—Our Saviour did yet another thing. Before He gave His body to the apostles, He held it up to His heavenly Father and offered His body to Him. Before He gave His blood to the apostles, He likewise held it up for a moment and offered His blood to Him. That is just what the priest does in Holy Mass. Well, this was the first Mass—the offering of the body and blood of Christ to His Father. Here is where the priests learned how to offer up the Mass and also got the power to offer it. Jesus said to those first priests, the apostles and to all priests, "Do what I have done." Now the priests in the Mass offer up Christ's body to God as Jesus had done at the Last Supper; they offer up Christ's blood to God as He had done at the Last Supper.

The Mass is the holiest act which man can offer to God. It is better than any prayer which even a saint can compose. In the Mass the Redeemer is present on the altar, takes our place and offers Himself to God to erase our sins and to scatter His graces over us. He takes our place in that church and prays in our place to God His Father.

Our Mass has three principal parts. The first is called the Offertory and begins when the priest uncovers the chalice and offers the bread to God. During that time those present ask God to bless them and make them clean so that they will be worthy to take part in the Mass and to share in its graces. The second principal part is called the Consecration and occurs about the middle of the Mass. Here the priest does what Christ told him to do, changes bread into Christ's body and wine into Christ's blood. During this period, those present offer Christ as a gift of adoration, of thanksgiving and of penance to God the Father. The third part occurs near the end and is called the Communion. Here the people ask God to give them graces for soul and body and many receive Holy Communion in order to obtain God's favor.

All Catholics, unless reasonably excused, must attend Mass every Sunday under pain of mortal sin. Under like conditions they must also attend Mass on every holyday of obligation.

Summary by Example: The teacher will ask such questions as: Do we have priests today? What do they offer to God every morning? What does the priest do at the Elevation? Who gave priests the power? Why do people towards the end of Mass come to the railing? Whom do they receive? Is it the same Jesus whom the apostles received? Will the pupils here ever be able to receive the body and blood of Jesus Christ as the apostles did?

Motivation: On Holy Thursday the Church recalls what Christ did at the Last Supper. First, a Mass is sung in which the Gospel tells the story of how Christ instituted the Holy Eucharist. At the end of the Mass, the Blessed Sacrament is removed to an altar decorated beautifully because it is a day of rejoicing that we have received so great a gift. All day long the Blessed Sacrament is kept there while the people stream in to adore and thank our Lord for His great favor. They bend on both knees to tell Him that He is their God. Sister brings the pupils to the church in relays and they sing and pray to Jesus in the tabernacle.

II. What Happened during the Passion

1. The Agony in the Garden

It will be necessary for the teacher to prepare herself the evening before by a diligent reading of the scriptural story that will come

Grade I — II. What Happened during the Passion

up the following day. Not all phases of the sacred Passion are covered here; the teacher may use her judgment about adding others.

Now we learn how Jesus died for our sins and how the gates of heaven were reopened through Him. The great physical and mental tortures of Christ's Passion begin now. Jesus had a human nature which was just as sensitive to pain as ours and more so because His body was more delicately formed. He needed extra strength that He could endure the suffering to come, so He prayed.

At the agony in the Garden, He had a vision of all the sins of the world and He tried to offer to His Father a satisfactory act of sorrow for them. He said that He was sorrowful unto death over them. How terrible must sin be! What a deep and heartfelt contrition it must demand! The painful sorrow could scarcely be endured and Jesus prayed with all the power of His Sacred Heart.

Perhaps His apostles would help Him to pray. He went to them and found them asleep. Sadly He said, "Watch and pray." If Peter had only watched and prayed!

Our Saviour returned to pray. He needed strength to endure the sufferings that would shortly begin. He foresaw them; they seemed already to be upon Him. He fell down beneath the pain. He prayed but always He finished by saying, "yet not My will but Thine be done." He made up His mind to suffer for us. Again He got no consolation from the apostles for they were asleep. "Watch and pray," He said. If Peter had only done so!

Again Jesus returned to pray. This time the thought of the ingratitude of men struck Him to earth. It was the hardest blow and His sweat was like drops of blood, falling upon the ground. After all His sufferings, men would still sin. Perhaps some of the pupils here will commit sins.

But the prayer of our Lord was answered. God always answers prayer. An angel came from heaven to strengthen our Saviour.

Then Jesus went back to His apostles saying that He was ready to begin His sacred Passion. When the soldiers approached Him and asked Him whether He was Jesus, He answered "I am He" and immediately the words caused the soldiers to fall on the ground. Jesus had the almighty power to kill them all but He wanted to suffer for all men, so He let them take Him away.

Much should be made of the conduct of Peter who did not pray with our Lord but slept instead. Peter did not know that a dark temptation was coming nearer and nearer. Had he only prayed!

We learn two principal lessons from the words and actions of our Lord—to watch and pray. The apostles, not having obeyed His admonition, fled when danger appeared. Our Saviour Himself prayed during His trouble and gained the strength that enabled Him to go on with His sacred Passion.

Motivation: We are surrounded by trials and troubles but none need ever crush us if we pray. We must especially be on the watch against temptation; we must not enter into the occasion of it. We will watch that we do not run into the occasion. If two children are quarreling, we will walk away from them; when tempted we will go before the crucifix and pray. Jesus wanted the apostles to pray with Him but they fell asleep; we will tell Jesus that we will pray with Him. We want strength to be given to us from heaven so that we can remain faithful in all our trials. If we pray, strength will come from heaven.

2. Jesus before the Rulers

It is better to select one moral lesson from each story rather than many.

Our Saviour was dragged before the Jewish High Priest, Annas. How calm Jesus was in the presence of His unjust accusers! Then a rude soldier struck that beautiful, kindly, kingly face, leaving on it a livid mark from his fist.

Did Jesus cause the earth to open up and swallow the wretch? No, when He recovered from the blow, Jesus calmly gave an answer of such wisdom that for a moment all were speechless. The lies of the witnesses were so self-evident that it was beneath His dignity to deign further reply. The moral is that we must not flare up immediately when some real or apparent offense is given. If we answer calmly, we answer strongly; and what is of more worth, we imitate the patience of Jesus.

Jesus could have struck the rude soldier dead. We recall how His words threw to the ground the first soldiers who had come to seize Him. He would not free Himself because He wanted to suffer for us. In the Garden He had resolved to take on Himself the punishment which we deserved for our sins. He would go through with the sacred Passion.

Jesus Forgave Peter.—The teacher will first tell the story of Peter's temptation, how he denied Jesus three times. She will draw a parallel with the case of Judas who also had denied and even sold His Master.

But the action of each, after the fall into sin, was different. Judas ran away from his Lord; Peter still lingered near the Master. And of a sudden the eye of Our Lord caught Peter. It held him spellbound, transfixed him, and the face of Jesus showed a hurt unto death at the denial. The steady eye reproved and yet invited; it showed abysmal sorrow, yet lured to hope. Peter's heart was laid bare, and he saw his sin. He grasped at grace, and an immeasurable sorrow filled his heart, so that he went out and wept bitterly. And pious legend has it that every night at this hour the apostle went out into the night and wept bitterly, so that, as he grew older, two deep furrows showed on his face where the tears had run down so often.

Jesus in the Court of Pilate.—It is strange that the few times Jesus spoke during the Passion, He did so in answer to questions about His divinity. He wanted to tell us all that a God was suffering, that His sufferings were very great and precious and that He was offering His precious Self to satisfy God the Father for us who had offended the Father.

In this incident, do we not feel indignant at the cowardice of Pilate? This Roman governor was well educated and saw through the scheming of the Jews, knew that the Man was innocent, yet he had not the courage to release Him; he had the power to free Him, yet he could not make up his mind. Are we sometimes too cowardly to do what is right?

Our Lord Is Scourged.—The devilish purpose of this punishment was so to lacerate Him, that the mob, being moved to pity, might release Him. How a whip hurts that is wound around our legs! Now imagine leather thongs with hooks of bone at the end, swishing and winding around the white delicate body of our Lord. They lashed Him and cut Him until the executioners' arms grew tired, and they left Him sunken to earth and weltering in His own blood. We will bear pains patiently.

Jesus Is Crowned with Thorns.—They pick up the wounded body of Jesus and drag Him to a broken pillar. His head had not yet been hurt, so they must inflict pain on that delicate member. After placing a ragged purple garment over His shoulders, they laid a crown of thorns upon His sacred head. Then soldier after soldier came up, and striking the crown with a stick, forced the thorns deep into the tender skin. If a thorn in our finger hurts, a thorn in the head causes excruciating pain. But Jesus' face is still untouched, so they spit into it.

Behold the Man! Pilate took the abject Figure to an elevated platform and showing Him to the people said: "Behold the Man." What a sight! What a sorrow! What a picture of pain! Do they say, "It is enough." No, they cry: "Crucify Him! Crucify Him!" And Pilate said, "Crucify Him." Sympathy is called for here. How could they do it? What would you have answered? Why did Jesus let them do it? For whom did He do it? We despise Pilate for his cowardice. We see what the cruel Jews and the soldiers did. We will never be like them.

Motivation: I wish I had been an angel while You suffered so terribly, my Saviour! I would have tried to stop the hand that held the whip; and if it fell, I would have tended the wound and poured in soothing oil. I would have tried to take the crown of thorns from Your head and replace it with a wreath of bright flowers; but if I could not, I would have wiped away the blood that trickled into Your eyes and over Your Face. I would have pushed aside the soldiers who gave You mock adoration. Instead, I would have knelt before You sincerely and told You again and again that You are my King and my God, that You are Christ the King. Thus would I have loved You who loved me so much.

3. Jesus Is Crucified

Cruel men nailed Jesus to the cross.—The teacher will narrate the story of the painful Way of the Cross and of the crucifixion.

Throughout the recital of these incidents we have been wondering why Our Lord did not use His almighty power to kill His torturers, why, most of all, He endured these indescribable pains. The answer is, He suffered and died for our sins. He let the soldiers nail Him to the cross. He had power to free Himself but He wanted to save us from sin. He wanted to take our punishments upon Himself. The reason for this suffering was a love that men can never fathom. No friend, no father, no mother could endure such sufferings for the best child. How He must have loved us! We must pray every day that we may understand more and more how He loves us. We must take Him to our hearts and promise to love Him, too, forever and ever.

The children are still too young to be taught the short way of

Grade I **II. What Happened during the Passion** 81

making the Way of the Cross, but they might be asked what they remember of the pictures of the Stations. This lesson can be drawn out by attention to details and by recitations from pupils. The teacher will briefly tell the story of the Burial of Jesus.

Q. 20. How did Jesus satisfy for the sins of all men?

A. Jesus satisfied for the sins of all men by His sufferings and death on the cross.

Motivation: The Church recalls the death of the Saviour by her Good Friday observance. The statues and crosses are still veiled, for we think now only of the cross of Calvary. The priest enters the sanctuary vested in black because it is a time of sorrow. He prostrates himself on the floor and makes an act of sorrow for the sins of the world. A little later the people come up to the railing to kiss the image of the crucified One. The Mass in black is a strange one; there are long silences; the choir sings only in sorrowful tones. It is the remembrance of the death of our Lord.

Jesus suffered for sin, for everybody's sins, even for the sins the children have committed and may still commit. Sin must be an evil thing so to offend the majesty of God. Sin is, in fact, the worst evil in the world. No other misfortunes of any kind could have made the Saviour take upon Himself this terrible punishment for us. Sin is worse than any calamity. We will forestall temptations by watching and praying.

Who condemned Jesus? Was it Pilate? Was it the Jews? They spoke for us; they spoke for our sins. Our sins cried "Crucify Him!" We will here make an act of sorrow because our sins caused the death of Jesus. The whole class should repeat the Act of Contrition in unison.

Can we ever sin again? Dare we ever sin again? We kneel down in spirit at the foot of the cross. We ask Mother Mary to give our prayers to her divine Son. We tell Him, we promise Him that we will never offend Him. Tonight, every night, as we kneel at our bedside, we will repeat this promise. Every morning as we rise we will ask Mother Mary to help us carry out the promise.

A POEM

Jesus, dying on the cross,
  Tell me, was it I?
There are great big tear drops, Lord.
  Did I make you cry?
I have been a naughty child,
  Naughty as can be.
Now I am so sorry, Lord.
  Won't you pardon me?

—*Sister M. Imelda, S.L.*

UNIT EIGHT: JESUS ROSE FROM THE DEAD: WE SHALL RISE AGAIN

I. How Jesus Rose.
II. What Jesus Did After He Arose.
III. How Jesus Went to Heaven.

What We Shall Learn: The last few periods have indeed been gloomy while we followed the sufferings of our Saviour and came to realize what terrible injury and loss was caused by sin. Because of sin God had closed the gates of heaven against us. Now come the glorious events in our Saviour's life, which showed that He really had bought back our chance for heaven. We see Him rise again from the dead and it gives us the firm hope that we shall rise again. We see Him ascend into heaven and it gives us the firm hope that we can get to heaven if we obey God's laws. We shall therefore study that great event of the first Easter Sunday and again we shall learn that our Saviour is God. We shall study that great event on the mountain when He went up to heaven and it shall fill our souls with a burning desire to get to heaven too. Jesus is our Saviour; we wish to be saved.

To the Teacher: Since this lesson is not contained in the Revised Baltimore First Communion Catechism, it must be taught orally.

I. How Jesus Rose

The section is actually an explanation of how, when and why Jesus rose from the dead. We are concerned more with the circumstances of the story than trying to make it an apologetical treatise on the divinity of Christ. The mystery of the rising of Christ from death after having been three days in the grave, is not explained by the teacher unless some pupil asks the question. The pupils will grasp the fact that Christ rose because He is almighty.

The Resurrection story is the one narrated in the Gospel of Easter Sunday. Jesus, glorious and immortal, rose from the dead. Scripture states it as a fact through the words of the angel, "He is risen; He is not here." The door of the grave had been sealed and Pilate had even stationed guards to prevent the Resurrection; yet on Easter morning the heavy stone fell outward and the guards were struck to the ground. No more did Pilate and the soldiers have power over the Risen One; they were utterly defeated.

Jesus had come forth from the grave, glorious and never to die again. His garments were white as snow and His whole body shone like the sun. It was a glorified body now; men could not hurt it any more nor kill it. The body could pass through stone walls; it could go from place to place quicker than an airplane, in an instant.

The teacher will perhaps bring pictures of the Resurrection into the classroom. She will point out the fear of the soldiers as depicted by their attitude and in their faces. She will also point out the joy and glory of the scene. She will draw attention to the eagerness, love and anticipation expressed by the holy women who had come to visit the tomb. She will describe their surprise and hope. All these sentiments the children must be made to feel. Then isn't it often true of life in general that a huge stone blocks the way? And who can roll it back but one of God's angels? (Revised Baltimore Catechism No. 1 Q. 49. When did Christ rise from the dead? A. Christ rose from the dead, glorious and immortal, on Easter Sunday, the third day after His death.)

Motivation: We must rejoice over the final triumph of Our Saviour, just as good children would be happy for a father who had been unjustly imprisoned and is finally freed. Remember how during the Passion of our Lord His enemies had bound Him; now He is free. Remember how His enemies had disfigured Him; now He shines gloriously. They thought they had killed Him forever; now He rises immortal, full of life. They denied He was God; now He strikes them senseless with His divine power.

The Church recalls this great mystery by the Feast of Easter Sunday. There is no sorrow now, only gladness that Jesus has risen. The vestments of the priest are white and the most beautiful in His possession; the altar is gaily decorated with flowers; the choir renders its best music. Many churches place a statue of the risen Saviour in the sanctuary; our Lord points upward; He carries a banner of victory to show that He has triumphed over death.

II. What Jesus Did after He Arose

The apparition of our Lord to Mary Magdalen after He had risen appeals to children and is easily understood by them. In order to make the pupils grasp the idea that our Lord remained on earth forty days after His Resurrection, the teacher might add the story of the apparition of Jesus on the shore of the lake of Tiberius or in the upper room in which the apostles were gathered.

The story of the apparition to Mary Magdalen is surpassingly sweet. This woman, once a great sinner, had shown a great love and fidelity to our Lord. Undoubtedly, she was with Mary when she met her Son on the Way of the Cross. We know that she followed Jesus to Calvary, and was one of the faithful few who stood at the foot of the cross when He died. And now He came to her amongst the first, to reward and console her. The passages of affection between our Lord and Mary Magdalen are most touching.

In Mary Magdalen, we see a result of the Redemption. She had deserved punishment for her past life but the Master had taken her punishment upon Himself; He canceled her punishment and made her now the object of His tender love. She had sinned but the Master had paid for her sins so that now she had only love for Him in her heart. Jesus told her about heaven where His Father would be her Father too. He spoke of the love in heaven that would know no bounds.

During these forty days our Saviour appeared, according to the Gospels eleven times, He wished to reassure His apostles who acted like distraught children seeking for a lost friend whom they loved very dearly. He also wished to prove to all the world that He had risen from the dead.

The teacher may tell the story of the apparition in the upper room where Christ gave the apostles the power to forgive sins. During these forty days, our Redeemer organized our own Catholic Church. He told His apostles how they were to proceed with this great task when He should leave them. The old Jewish Church had been rejected on the day of the Crucifixion when the veil of the Temple was rent. The Redeemer had been slowly building up His new Church. In this period He spent some time with the apostles telling them what kind of a Church it must be.

Motivation: We too shall rise some day. Our souls will rise immediately after death. Our soul really never dies but just as soon as it separates from the body, it goes straight into eternity. Will our soul be glorious as Christ's was when He arose from the dead? It all depends on how we use our time now.

Even children have a great task before them. They must begin now to earn the great reward which Jesus has promised. They must begin now to make themselves worthy to enter the golden gates of that beautiful heaven.

Often during life they will be subjected to the Big Test of mortal sin. If they can pass that, they will prove themselves faithful and God will give them a glorious resurrection as reward. If they want to make absolutely sure that they will attain heaven, they must try to be faithful even in the Lesser Test of venial sin.

The best way is to try hard not to sin; to try to spend their lives in doing good deeds. If they want a glorious body some day, they must train the body to be good now: the hands must help others; the feet must go to holy places; the eyes must see holy pictures; the voice must say pious prayers; the mind and heart must love God.

> Lord Jesus, King of Paradise,
> Oh, keep me in Thy love,
> And guide me to that happy land
> Of perfect rest above.
>
> —*Father Faber.*

III. How Jesus Went to Heaven

The biblical narrative will supply the details for the Ascension of our Lord. A note of rejoicing should permeate the description that our Lord's task on earth was now happily ended. In spite of every obstacle He had completed His work. As we see Him ascending into heaven and slowly taking on the glories of immortality, we know that He is the Victor.

The Feast of the Ascension is a holyday of obligation in the United States. The pupils have noticed the Paschal candle which has been standing beside the altar since Easter day. This candle represents the risen Saviour. They will also notice that the server extinguishes the candle after the Gospel on Ascension Day. The candle represents Christ; it is removed now as a sign that He has gone to heaven. Christ ascended, body and soul, into heaven on Ascension Day, forty days after His Resurrection.

Christ has gone to heaven. This is the heaven of which He talked to His friends. This is the heaven whose gates He caused to be opened. This is the heaven He has promised to good children. It is our home.

Heaven is an abode of everlasting joy, where we see God face to face. Does not the very sight of a dear friend gladden our hearts here on earth? We recognize him by some familiar movement while He is yet a block away, and with joyful expectation we run to meet him. The moment we enter heaven, we will see the God we tried to picture to ourselves all our life, and the reality will far surpass our fondest imaginings. Thrilled to the bottom of our soul we will run towards Him. He will let us nestle against His Sacred Heart, and tell us that never again shall we be separated from Him.

The greatest joy of all is love, and in heaven we shall love God above all measure. To love is to be thrilled through and through. So great is the power of love that it makes heroes of men and women. We can forget everything else when we love, can forget to eat or drink. A father will rush into a burning building to save the child he loves; any mother will give her life for her boy. And the instant we enter heaven we will see God, the most lovable of all that is lovable, and all the love we have ever had on earth will be as nothing to the love we feel toward God. They call it heaven: the joys shall last forever. The happiness of the blessed varies according to their merits. Heaven is won by suffering and self-denial.

When Jesus ascended into heaven, He left behind Him a Church which would carry on the great work of saving the souls whom He had redeemed by His sufferings and death on the cross. He Himself had founded this Church. He had brought faith to it on Pentecost Day when the Holy Ghost descended upon the apostles. These latter were the first men who took up the task. The Holy Ghost gave them strength and light to carry on the great, but difficult work.

This is our Church, our Catholic Church, of which we became members by holy Baptism. By the Church is meant all the Catholics who believe and practice what Jesus Christ taught. It is a very large Church, the largest in the world, numbering over 300,000,000 people. The Catholic is distinguished from other religionists because he is ruled by the Pope who takes the place of Christ on earth, because he receives the sacraments made by Christ, and because he believes in the Mass and all the other truths taught by Jesus Christ. The Catholic believes in everything taught and commanded by the Saviour in contrast with non-Catholics who believe only in part and who therefore follow an incomplete and wrong religion.

The Catholic Church now gives out the graces which our Redeemer earned on the cross. She does this principally through the sacraments instituted by the Redeemer for this very purpose. She teaches men what is the road to heaven and how it is possible to attain heaven. As a ruler she helps men to stay on the road to heaven. Since all these means were instituted or begun by Jesus Christ, it is really then through Jesus Christ that we save our souls.

Q. 21. How does Jesus help all men to gain heaven?
A. Jesus helps all men to gain heaven through the Catholic Church.

Summary by Example: A certain man had by dint of hard work and excellent management accumulated great riches. He was a great lover of the poor, so he now wanted to do something for them. He himself could not do it because he was called to a far country, so he appointed a committee of men, left with them a great sum in gold and ordered them daily to feed 10,000 poor people.— Jesus loved us and on the sacred cross He had earned an unlimited number of graces. But He ascended into heaven. Then He left behind Him the Catholic Church to which He gave the graces and to which He gave orders to dispense the graces to us.

Motivation: We have learned much of our heavenly home and we all want to get there. All today we will think of this and we will often say, "O Jesus, take me to your beautiful home!" We will be especially kind today to our playmates. God wants them to come to heaven too. If they are good they will one day be beautiful saints in heaven. We will therefore enlarge our prayer and say, "O Jesus, take us all to heaven with you."

Daily we are learning to love God more. We love Him so much now that we have great confidence in Him. We are not afraid of the Little Test and we do not even fear the Big Test because our loving Jesus will help. We are sure even that we can do many good deeds with His help. We will be faithful because we earnestly desire to get a very high place in heaven.

UNIT NINE: JESUS EARNED GRACE FOR US: WE SHOULD USE GRACE

I. Jesus Bought Grace for Us.
II. Grace Is a Gift.
III. How We Get Grace.

What We Shall Learn: We often heard mention of the word, "grace." The priest uses the word many times in his sermons. Sister uses it often in the classroom. Every time we recite the Hail Mary we say, "full of grace." It seems to be quite an important word; it seems to have a lot to do with saving our soul. So, we shall learn what grace is.

We spent several weeks in studying the sacred Passion and death of our Saviour. We learned that the crucifixion has everything to do with reopening the gates of heaven and giving us a chance to get there. Surely we still wondered how we could get there. In this lesson we shall learn that we can get to heaven with the help of grace. We shall learn how to get grace and how it will save our soul.

This unit must be taught orally as the First Communion Catechism has only one question on grace (Question 39).

I. Jesus Bought Grace for Us

Grace can be taught to six-year olds only through examples and illustrations within their own experience. Children accept mysteries with no wonderment at all. What is a mystery to elders, is passed over without questioning by children. The First Communion Catechism defines neither actual nor sanctifying grace; question 39 mentions one effect of the latter. Actual grace can easily be understood by first-graders. The subject of sanctifying grace is more difficult and so will be given only brief mention using the words of the First Communion Catechism.

A Brother Helps.—Mary Lou is trying to make her way against the strong wind but can advance very little. Mary Lou needs help. Her brother sees her from the window; so he goes out, takes her hand and pulls her along. When some one else helps, we can do many things which we could not do alone.

Grace is a big, big help from God to save our souls (actual grace). We could not save our souls without it because we are not strong enough, we do not see well enough. Of ourselves we are often too lazy to do good, we do not fight temptations strongly enough. *Example:* The pastor says, "You all have permission to go to the big Fair in New York." Then the pupils look at each other and think, "But we need help to get to New York. We have no money, no food. We just have old clothes and we need new clothes. We cannot walk there because it is too far and we cannot fly there because we have no airplane." All together they shout, "We need help, Father."

We need help to get to heaven. It is sometimes quite difficult to avoid sin which can rob us of heaven. For example, it will be hard for Mr. Turner to go to eight o'clock Sunday Mass when he worked in the factory all night. We need light to see how horrible sin is, how it offends God. The devil paints sin in beautiful colors in order to lead us into it. God says, "I want to help these little children. I will give them grace so that they will be smart when the devil tempts them to sin; I will give them light so that they will see how horrible sin is and how it offends Me."

We must do many good deeds to get to heaven. Sometimes we are lazy or afraid. We may feel lazy when it is time to go to school or we may be afraid to tell the truth. Left to ourselves, we perhaps would stay in bed too long, or perhaps we just would keep quiet and say nothing. We must be brave, must have courage. God says, "I want to help these little children. I will give them grace so that they will be brave to do what is right and to do good deeds." Grace is a help from God.

Grace (sanctifying) makes the soul beautiful.—Sunlight in the classroom. The sky had been overcast during the first hour of class. The walls were dark, there were dark shadows everywhere, the pupils could hardly see the printed page. Then suddenly the sun came out and bright rays flooded the room. The color of the pictures on the wall came out brilliantly. Sister and the pupils looked up and smiled gratefully. All were happy.

God also puts grace into the soul (sanctifying grace). It is like the sunlight making the soul beautiful. That grace makes the soul holy. God is pleased with a soul that is holy. When there is a big, big sin on the soul, it is like the dark classroom, and God does not love it. Then the sinner is very, very sorry. God forgives the sin and right away He puts grace in that soul. That grace stays as long as the soul is good. Grace makes the soul holy and pleasing to God. (Sanctifying grace makes the soul holy and pleasing to God).

Q. 39. What does grace do to the soul?
A. Grace makes the soul holy and pleasing to God.

Jesus bought the graces for all men. Jesus suffered much during His sacred Passion and crucifixion. The question is, What did the sacred Passion mean for us? What did it do for us? What did we get out of it? Did the Father give His Son something for His sufferings? Did the Son offer His sufferings to His Father and buy something with them? Yes, Jesus bought grace for us. Yes, Jesus offered all His sufferings to His heavenly Father in order to buy something. He had suffered very much and He bought something very valuable. Sometimes when Father does extra good work at the shop, the boss gives him extra good pay. *Jesus bought grace for us* with His sufferings.

Summary by Example: When Jesus suffered He had us all in His mind. He had little Joan in His mind. He foresaw how yesterday she was surrounded by the other little girls who made fun of her Catholic religion. Jesus said to His Father, "I offer My sufferings also for little Joan to buy grace for her on that day. She is a little weak, a little bit afraid of those other little girls and I want her to have the grace of strength." It worked just as Jesus hoped it would. Joan received grace and she said: "What you girls say about the Catholic Church is untrue. I am proud to be a Catholic." Joan by means of grace did one more good deed by which she hoped to gain heaven. She did not do it alone; God helped her with grace He had bought with His sufferings.—Joan's soul has grace. That grace makes her soul holy and pleasing to God.

Motivation: First, we should thank God that He supplies us with these big, big helps. Next, we should thank our Saviour that He bought these big, big helps for us. We should think very much of them because He bought them with His blood. Nothing else in the world ever cost so much as grace. Because Jesus paid so much for it, we know that He wants us to use it well.—We must always keep grace in our soul because we want our soul to be pleasing to God.

II. Grace Is a Gift

(The Catechism uses the term "merited grace." This is more correct theologically; nevertheless, the writer uses the verbs "earned" and "bought" as being better understood by children.)

Father gives us gifts. When Father works hard all week, we know that he will get a paycheck and that we often receive a gift from him on that day. Father may take us downtown on payday and buy us a new suit or a new dress. Perhaps after he has done this, he will even take us to the corner drugstore and buy us an ice-cream soda. But we did not earn that suit and we did not pay for the soda. Father worked hard for his money and now we who did not work, get something out of it; we get gifts. Grace is a gift.

Jesus earned the graces and bought them for us. He alone suffered; we did not. He suffered the scourging, the crowning with thorns and death on the cross; we were not even there to see His sacred Passion. We did not see Him offering His precious blood to His Father nor did we see the Father giving Him oceans and oceans of graces for our benefit.

Grace is a gift from God. When we receive something for which we did not pay, we call it a gift. When on Christmas Day, Johnny finds amongst his presents a ship which will float around the bathtub, he calls it a gift. He did not buy the ship, did not in fact know that he was going to get it. So we get graces every day which we do not earn. With grace, every day is Christmas day. When a boy has to mow the lawn, that is his job and he is supposed to finish it. If the boy from next door comes over and helps, that boy gives his help freely; his help is a gift. So God's help, namely grace, is a gift. When the lawn mower is heavy, the neighbor's boy teams up with his friend and both shove the machine. So we have a heavy job to save our souls but God teams up with us. We have no real right to expect God's help. He freely offers it. God's help, namely grace, is a free gift that helps us get to heaven.

Summary by Example: It was Ralph's seventh birthday. He was very much surprised to receive an envelope on which was written, "To Ralph from his grandfather." Little Ralph was puzzled. "But I never knew grandfather; he died a year after I was born. I do not deserve a gift from him because I never did a thing for him." Ralph opened the envelope to find $50.00 in bills. His mother explained: "Grandfather gave that envelope into my keeping before he died, with instructions that I was to give you the money on your seventh birthday. You never knew grandfather; you never did a thing to gain his favor, yet six years after his death you receive a birthday gift from him." Then Ralph thought for a while: "It makes me think of what Sister told us about grace. Jesus died a long time ago and after much suffering He earned a lot of graces. Now every day I receive what Jesus earned long ago; I can get grace. With this heavenly gift, I can get to heaven."

Motivation: We are just little children but we will have no fear. Little boys and girls have often become very great saints because they used grace when God offered it to them. One time Our Lord picked up a little boy and set him before the people. That was a very good boy who had used God's help; he had stayed away from sin and he had been very good to his parents and kind to his playmates. In that crowd were people who were perhaps fifty or sixty years old; those people were strong and they thought they were very wise. Yet, Jesus told them that they had to become like that little boy before they could get to heaven.

III. How We Get Grace

We have learned that Jesus offered His sufferings to God, and God in turn made up piles and piles of grace which could be used by man in saving their souls. But, there is a third Person of the Blessed Trinity, namely God the Holy Ghost and now we shall learn what part He has in this matter of grace.

Illustration: Three men lived near a gold mine. The first worked hard for many years, digging and drilling. His brother, the second person, owned the mine and after ten years he gave him a large, very large pile of money for his reward. Now what was to be done with all this money? It was to be used to buy food and clothes for thousands of poor children. Then the third brother stepped up and said that he wanted to give out the food and clothing as the poor children needed them and asked for them. So it was agreed and all three men then had a part in the kind work.

All Persons of the Blessed Trinity had part in the holy work of getting and giving grace to people. In our way of talking, the Holy Ghost said, "I wish to give out the graces when the people need them and ask for them." The work of distributing the graces is attributed especially to the Holy Ghost; it is a work of love and the Holy Ghost is the Spirit of Love. (The Holy Ghost sanctifies souls through the gift of grace).

The Holy Ghost gives us thousands of graces which we do not ask for and thousands more when we request them in prayer. Very often we do not even know when a grace comes and we do not know that we are using it. The Holy Ghost watches over us every minute of the day and supplies graces as we need them. *Examples:* A little boy has a temptation to play hookey. Right away he sees that it would be mean and he marches straight to school. Or, a little girl all of a sudden feels it would be very holy to go to Mass on a weekday and off she marches. Actually, the Holy Ghost had helped them without their knowing of it. Everybody gets enough graces to save his soul even though he may not know of their presence all the time. But we can increase the number of our graces. We can pray for graces and the Holy Ghost will give us still more. Or we can ask God the Father, Our Lord, the Blessed Virgin or any saint. They will tell the Holy Ghost. In the end it is the Holy Ghost that sends the helps or the graces. There are times when we feel the need of more graces; for example, when we are sick or troubled. Then we will be wise to kneel down and ask for more graces.

The Holy Ghost gives grace in many ways. Sometimes He uses a holy picture to put a good thought into the mind; that holy thought will help to a better life. Sometimes it is the reading of a good book, the kind remark of a friend, a direction from Sister, a sermon by the pastor. Very, very often the Holy Ghost works through our guardian angel admonishing us, "Do this; do not do that." All these helps are graces which the Holy Ghost sends.

Summary by Example: Betty and Lou were going to the class picnic. Mother had packed a lunch for them which she considered ample. Betty looked at it, then spoke up: "Mother, we are going to play a lot of games and perhaps we will get extra hungry. You better add another sandwich for each of us." So, when we need more grace, we should ask for it and the Holy Ghost will supply it.

UNIT TEN: JESUS GAVE US THE SACRAMENT OF PENANCE: WE MUST RECEIVE IT WORTHILY

(Revised Baltimore First Communion Catechism:
Lessons 9 and 10)

I. What the Sacrament of Penance Is.
II. What Blessings Penance Brings to Us.
III. How to Prepare for the Sacrament of Penance.
IV. How to Go to Confession.

What We Shall Learn: If a man has a dangerous sickness, would he not be happy to hear of some doctor or some treatment that could cure him? We have learned in the past weeks that sin can be the most dangerous sickness in the world; it can not injure only the soul but can even kill the beautiful life of the soul. Now we shall learn about a doctor who can cure this sickness; it is the priest who acts for Jesus Christ. We shall learn of a treatment which can drive out this sickness; it is going to confession. We want to learn therefore who gave us this wonderful sacrament of Penance and what are the effects of the sacrament. We want to learn how to get ready for it so that we can receive it in the right way. We ourselves want to go to confession so we shall learn what we must do when we want to have our sins taken away.

I. What the Sacrament of Penance Is

Children in some schools make their First Confession in the first school year, perhaps during Advent; in other schools the reception of the Sacrament is postponed to the second year. The difference of custom arises from a different interpretation of the age of reason. The bare essentials are explained here because those who do receive the sacrament now are so innocent that confession is hardly necessary. Those who do not go this year will profit by learning a minimum which will be enlarged for them next year.

Our Lord suddenly appeared to the apostles in an upper room after His Resurrection. He breathed on them, meaning that He was giving them a very great power. He said, "Receive the Holy Ghost," meaning that they would use this great power with and through the third Person of the Blessed

Trinity. Then He said, "Whose sins you shall forgive, they are forgiven them and whose sins you shall retain, they are retained." By those words He gave them power to free men from sin; He also gave them the right to refuse forgiveness.

Jesus gave the apostles power to forgive all sins committed after Baptism. Original sin is taken away by Baptism as also any other sins which an older person may have committed before his baptism.

Our priests today can forgive sins. They take the place of the first priests, the apostles to whom Jesus Christ gave the power. The first priests died and other priests came to continue their work. Today the priests whom we see, carry on the work of forgiving sins as the apostles did in their day. *Example:* While the pastor of the parish lives, he rules the parish; when he dies, another pastor will come to do exactly the same work. So the priests today do the same work as the apostles, the first priests did; one part of that work is to forgive sins.

The actions of the priest and of the one who seeks forgiveness go to make up the sacrament of Penance. A sacrament, we know, is a very holy thing given to us by Our Lord Himself. Penance first removes sin which is very unholy and next it makes the soul holy and friendly to the all-holy God. The act by which the priest forgives is called absolution which means a "loosening," like loosening a rope that is choking a person, or it means a "freeing" like freeing one of a sickness. The priest uses the power which Christ gave him to forgive sins; after he has heard the sins committed after Baptism, he says, "I forgive your sins," that is, "I absolve you."

Q. 44. What is the sacrament of Penance?
A. The sacrament of Penance is the sacrament by which sins committed after Baptism are forgiven.

Summary by Example: The big Picture. Christ spoke to all priests. While instituting the sacrament of Penance Christ had, as it were, a vision of all the priests yet to live and He addressed them all. Draw this picture for the minds of the pupils. The pupils bring the picture down finally to their own priest, Father————. Then when and where does the local pastor use this power? The formula of absolution tells them how.

II. What Blessings Penance Brings Us

Only a few effects of Penance are explained here because first-graders can hardly understand more.

II. What Blessings Penance Brings Us

The parable of the Prodigal Son with its appealing details will interest the children. The father ordered a new garment to be given to the son; he placed his own ring on his son's finger. The son was once more presentable before his father. So, God gives grace to a repentant soul, making it holy and pleasing to Him.

Grace.—The sacrament of Penance gives the soul a beauty or grace which makes it holy and pleasing to God; if the soul already has it, the sacrament gives an increase of beauty or grace.

God rejoices when the soul returns to His arms, is happy when He finds a new friend. As the father of the Prodigal decorated his returned son, so does God decorate the soul of the returned sinner with grace. If grace has not been entirely driven out, He adds more, making it holier still, more pleasing to Him.—As the father in the parable once more gave the Prodigal the place of a son, so does God take the sinner back in His family making him a child of God, or if grace is still there, a more friendly child of God.—As the father of the Prodigal kept the son near him and spent many joyful hours with him, so does the Holy Ghost love that soul and makes his home in it.—As the father promised to leave his possessions to the returned son, so does God promise that He will give heaven to the repentant one. God, as it were, gives the ring of friendship to him, perhaps an even better one because it had enjoyed His friendship before.

Sin.—By the sacrament of Penance sins are forgiven. A man in mortal sin has a deadly sin on his soul. It has driven out grace, has killed the friendship of God, has expelled the Holy Ghost. The soul is dark as the classroom that has no sunlight. A person in venial sin has lesser guilt. Grace in this latter case is dimmed or blurred as gold that has lost its shine; there is a cooling friendship between God and the soul. These sins are remitted by Penance.

Punishment.—Penance takes away punishment. When people commit a mortal sin, they deserve the punishment of hell but when they receive the sacrament of Penance, God says, "I will not send them to hell." When people commit venial sins they deserve to be punished in this life or in purgatory. God says to them, "I will take away punishment."

Help.—Penance gives grace to avoid sin in the future. Our Lord once forgave a very sinful woman, then said to her, "Go now and sin no more." He surely, too, gave her light so that she could understand how much better it was to lead a good life. He gave her

98 Unit 10: Jesus Gave Us the Sacrament of Penance Grade I

new strength so that she could fight temptation in the future. When we receive the sacrament of Penance, God says to us, "Sin no more" and He gives us graces to fight temptation and do deeds that please Him.

Advice.—The one going to confession receives also another benefit, as it were, on the side. The priest is very much interested in his welfare, so he encourages him, gives him advice how to avoid sin in the future and how to do good works to show his love for God.

The practical application will be a review of the Act of Contrition, the purpose being to make easier each of the steps of confession which must still be explained.

Summary by Example: Picture Jesus in the confessional, for the priest represents Him. Then describe an actual confession, that is, the steps in the confessional, always in relation to the Divine Figure. Explain what blessings accrue to the penitent. The pupils now need a picture of their own confession.

Motivation: We must thank Jesus for giving us this great sacrament of Penance to take away our sins. How terrible it would be if people had to carry all their sins on their souls all through life! Just think if a big sinner wanted to return to God and he had no way of doing it! How many, many big sinners have thanked God on their knees for this wonderful opportunity! There is no joy like that of the penitent who has been freed of his burden and returns to God. Jesus once said that even the angels in heaven are happy over such repentance.

A Story: It seemed to be an accident but it must have been the Providence of God. A young priest rapped at a door intending to ask the parents to send their children to the Catholic school. An alarmed woman admitted him. "O Father," she said, "I am so glad you came. My brother is dying and he has not been to church for ten years." The priest heard the man's confession and within fifteen minutes the man was dead. Imagine what confession meant to that poor sinner who was literally snatched from hell!

III. How to Prepare for the Sacrament of Penance

Confession for souls that are next to sinless should be made very simple; details not given here should be added only after very careful consideration.

In going to confession we ask God to have mercy on us and to give us the necessary light to understand how to do everything well. One day Jesus was going along the road to Jeru-

Grade I   III. How to Prepare for the Sacrament   99

salem. Two blind men sat by the roadside. When these men heard of the approach of Jesus, they cried, "Have mercy on us." Jesus came to them and asked, "What do you want?" They both cried aloud, "Lord, that we may see." He had pity on them and restored their sight. We want mercy: we want to see.

I must find out my Sins.—We must tell the priest what sins we have committed so that He can forgive them. We wish to do this as God wishes it to be done, so we ask God for help to see the sins, "Lord, that I may see." We wish to see our sins, so we go through the table of sins, asking ourselves:

Did I say my prayers well?
Did I miss Mass through my own fault?
Did I disobey my parents?
Did I quarrel?
Did I steal?
Did I tell lies?
Did I eat meat on Friday?

It will help if the pupils memorize the above table even though it must be amplified when later they learn the ten commandments. If they find that they have sinned on one point or another, they must try also to find the number of times they have failed.

It is most important that the pupils repeat the rhyme frequently—"I must find my sins: I must find the number of times." When they have found them and the number of times they should memorize them so that none be omitted when they enter the confessional.

I must be sorry for my sins.—For a presentation we return to the reunion of the father and his prodigal son. The son was really sorry for his misdeeds because he said, "Father, I have sinned against heaven and against you." The sinner must be sorry for all big sins. If only venial sins are to be confessed he must be sorry for some of them, still better for all of them. Venial sins displease God too and our Saviour had to suffer many pains because of them. God is so displeased by any kind of a sin that He would rather let the whole world burn than permit even the smallest venial sin to be committed. The penitent is sorry for venial sins because they offend his good God. He is sorry for venial sins because they have deserved punishment either in this life or in purgatory. He is sorry because he does not wish to suffer and because he does not wish to be lukewarm to God even for one minute. He loves God and wants to see Him the moment he passes into eternity. I must be sorry for my sins.

For the act of sorrow the First Communion Catechism gives the following: "O my God, I am sorry for all my sins, because they displease Thee, who art all-good and deserving of all my love. With Thy help, I will sin no more" (an indulgence of 3 years). It is well to repeat the act of sorrow several times to make sure that it comes from the heart.

I make up my mind not to sin again.—The sorrow of the Prodigal Son was true because he sincerely promised to lead a good life, to be obedient, to cheer his father in his old age. So sincere was he that he expressed his willingness to take the place of a servant because he was not worthy to be called a son. His love for his father, his true sorrow brought about this sincere resolve to do better.

God wants us to do better. He told the woman who was caught in sin, "Go now and sin no more." Sorrow is sincere only when it is supported by such a resolution. *Example:* A boy has offended his mother by not going to the store when told. He realizes how good his mother is, how kind, and he feels ashamed for his disobedience. He goes to her and says, "Mother, do you want me to go to the store now? I will go whenever you ask me."—I must make up my mind not to sin again.

The pupils have progressed sufficiently now to memorize the five steps of preparation. It is to be made very clear that the first three steps are to be carried out before confession, that is, while they are still in their seats.

Q. 45. What must you do to receive the sacrament of Penance?

A. To receive the sacrament of Penance I must:

1. Find out my sins.
2. Be sorry for my sins.
3. Make up my mind not to sin again.
4. Tell my sins to the priest.
5. Do the penance the priest gives me.

Summary by Example: The Supplicant.—A workingman had been dismissed from his job because of certain deficiencies in his work and this afternoon he was to see his boss in order to be reinstated. Many times during the morning he rehearsed what faults he had to admit and what words he would use to regain his place.

The sincere penitent will prepare himself too before he approaches God in the confessional.

IV. How to Go to Confession

God wants us to go to the priest.—One time Our Lord met ten lepers. These men were afflicted with a dirty disease that ate away their fingers, toes and often even their arms and legs. They cried to Him to make them clean. Our Lord could have made them clean right away because He is almighty. Instead, He told them to show themselves to the priest. When they ran joyfully to the priest, they were made clean.

Our Saviour always made much of priests and He makes very much of them today. When we are sorry for our sins and cry to Him to make our souls clean, He tells us to go to the priest and tell him our sins.

We enter the confessional.—That is the name of the box-like little room where we go to tell our sins. We kneel on the little step and when it is out turn we say, "Bless me, Father, for I have sinned. This is my first confession.'

I tell my sins to the priest.—We go slowly, not the least bit excited, because the priest is kind, loves us and is eager to help us if we seem to be puzzled for a minute. He is the good shepherd who is looking for his little sheep in order to carry them back to Jesus. After every sin that we confess we tell the priest how many times we committed it. When we are finished telling the sins and the number of times, we say, "That's all."

I listen to what the priest tells me.—The priest talks to us just for a minute. He tells us perhaps to say our prayers well or to guard against a certain temptation.

I do the penance the priest gives me.—Then he gives us a penance telling us to say the Our Father or the Hail Mary or some other prayers a certain number of times to make up in some way for our sins.

The priest says a prayer by which he takes away our sins.—Sometimes he says first, "Now repeat your Act of Contrition" but whether he does or not, we should at this time respect the act of sorrow saying it just loud enough for him to hear.

Q. 46. How do you make your confession?

A. I make my confession in this way:

1. I go into the confessional and kneel.

Unit 10: Jesus Gave Us the Sacrament of Penance Grade I

2. I make the sign of the cross and say: "Bless me, Father, for I have sinned."
3. I say: "This is my first confession" (or, "it has been one week, or one month, since my last confession").
4. I confess my sins.
5. I listen to what the priest tells me.
6. I say the Act of Contrition loud enough for the priest to hear me.

When the priest closes the little slide or says, "God bless you," we leave the confessional and return to our pew.

Q. 47. What do you do after leaving the confessional?
A. After leaving the confessional, I say the penance the priest has given me and thank God for forgiving my sins.

Summary by Example: The best summary is to go from pupil to pupil to see that each one knows the order of confession.

Motivation: We must never be in a hurry when we are about to receive a sacrament. The very word "sacrament" means that it is something very holy. Jesus Christ, our dear Friend, gave us the sacraments, bought them with His precious blood and we must not waste the graces by too much hurry. *A Story:* The penitent with bowed head was preparing for confession when a boy touched him on the shoulder, saying, "A lady in the vestibule wants to speak to you." The man replied: "The lady can wait but I cannot. After I have finished my more important talk with God, I'll talk to the lady. Perhaps she wants to hurry me but I may not hurry God."

UNIT ELEVEN: JESUS GAVE HIMSELF TO US IN HOLY COMMUNION: WE SHOULD LOVE HIM ALWAYS

(Revised Baltimore First Communion Catechism: Lesson 11)

I. WHAT THE HOLY EUCHARIST IS.
II. WHAT THE EFFECTS OF A WORTHY COMMUNION ARE.
III. WHAT TO DO THE DAY BEFORE RECEIVING.
IV. FIRST COMMUNION.

What We Shall Learn: We are coming to the end of a school period. We have learned much; in fact, it has been like climbing a hill where every step gave us a wider view of our beloved Church. In another sense it has been like a journey to the home of a dear friend. Every study was like getting a mile nearer and now we are on the last mile. A traveler looks at his clothes, as it were; or he sees if his hair is combed as he approaches the house of his dear friend. But ours is a special friend, Jesus Christ, and we see whether our soul is in order to meet Him, for we are going to meet Him in first Holy Communion. Therefore we shall learn about first Communion, what it is and what blessings it can bring to us. We shall learn what we must do to receive it worthily and to get the greatest possible benefits from it.

I. What the Holy Eucharist Is

The children learned something about the Holy Eucharist under the division "What Happened at the Last Supper." We are now concerned with the phase leading to Holy Communion. The explanation for First Communion should be made very simple remembering what Pope Pius X said, that the children need only be able to distinguish between common bread and the Eucharistic Bread. Most probably they gained that knowledge while studying about the institution of the Holy Eucharist.

The story of the institution of the Holy Eucharist will be briefly recalled. At the Last Supper Our Lord took common bread and blessed it. Then He said, "This is My body." It was then no longer bread but it was His body because He said

Unit 11: Jesus Gave Himself to Us in Holy Communion   Grade I

so. Jesus gave the apostles His body in Holy Communion. Our Lord took common wine and blessed it. Then He said, "This is My blood." It was then no longer wine but it was His blood because He said so. Jesus gave the apostles His blood in Holy Communion.

By those words and actions, Jesus gave us a sacrament, the holiest one of them all because it contains Jesus Christ Himself. At the Last Supper He turned bread into His body, and wine into His blood. This sacrament which contains Jesus Christ, body and blood, is called the Holy Eucharist.

Q. 48. What is the sacrament of the Holy Eucharist?
A. The Holy Eucharist is the sacrament of the body and blood of Our Lord Jesus Christ.

Our Lord turned to His apostles telling them to do what He had just done, to change bread into His body and wine into His blood. He made them priests, giving them power to do during their Mass what He Himself had done. Jesus told all priests to do this. Every morning our priests do what Christ did at the Last Supper. Every morning then the people can receive the Holy Eucharist.

Q. 49. When does Jesus Christ become present in the Holy Eucharist?
A. Jesus Christ becomes present in the Holy Eucharist during the Sacrifice of the Mass.

The whole Jesus Christ is in Holy Communion. Here He is as the people knew Him when He was on earth, kind, forgiving, helpful, wise. Here is His body that men beheld, handsome and strong; here is the blood that was within that body. He is a living Jesus. Here is Jesus who is God, who can do everything, who is all-wise and all-merciful. Jesus, the God-man, is in Holy Communion.

Q. 50. Do you receive Jesus Christ in the sacrament of the Holy Eucharist?
A. I do receive Jesus Christ in the sacrament of the Holy Eucharist when I receive Holy Communion.

The appearances of bread and wine remain, meaning something appears to be there but it is not really there. *Example:* A man a mile down the road appears to be very small but really he is the same size as when we see him near us. He is not smaller at all.

When Our Lord gave the apostles His body, the body looked like bread and even tasted like bread but it was not bread; it was His body for so He said. When Our Lord gave the apostles His blood, the blood appeared to be wine and even tasted like wine but it was not wine; it was His blood for He said so. Our holy sacrament looks like bread and tastes like bread but it is not bread; it is Jesus. Jesus is so bright, so mighty that we could not look at Him. He therefore covers Himself with the appearances.

Q. 51. Do you see Jesus Christ in the Holy Eucharist?

A. No, I do not see Jesus Christ in the Holy Eucharist because He is hidden under the appearances of bread and wine.

Summary by Example: We cannot understand everything about the Holy Eucharist, as for example—the appearances, but we take the word of the all-wise God that so it is. *Example:* Jimmy's father was a professor in a big school. One day he told Jimmy that there were yellow people in the world. Now Jimmy had never seen a Japanese or a Chinese but he had such confidence in his father's wisdom that he accepted the statement without hesitation. We have such trust in God who is all-truthful that we take God's word that all He said about the Holy Eucharist is true.

For a practical application the pupils can recite the Acts of Faith, Hope and Love. They believe what Jesus said about His body; they hope to get much grace through Holy Communion; they love Jesus who did so much for them. The pupils will answer again and again that Jesus gave the apostles what appeared to be bread but it was not bread. Coming to Holy Communion they will do the same, repeating, "Holy Communion looks like bread but it is Jesus."

Motivation: Children should try to love Our Lord as Blessed Imelda did. She was a very holy child who seemed more angel than human. Even while she was a babe that had to be carried, she liked nothing better than to be taken to the church by her mother. Often later while playing with her companions, she would disappear to be found later before a little altar that she had erected in her bedroom. When she went to church she could not take her eyes from the tabernacle where she know that Jesus was. Her visits to the Blessed Sacrament increased as she got older and often she had almost to be carried away from her divine Friend. Her preparation for her First Communion seemed to put her into a holy dream. She thought of it all day and it was her last thought at night. She received like an angel but her love for her Master was so great that her heart could not endure it and she died right after her first Holy Communion.

II. What the Effects of a Worthy Communion Are

No attempt is made to explain all the effects as tabulated in the larger catechism, only those which children can understand. Here there is mention of sanctifying grace but it is explained as the grace that stays with the soul; the term "sanctifying" is not employed.

The teacher will narrate the story of the Multiplication of the Loaves. This vast crowd was hungry because they had stayed with the Master a long time without partaking of food. They needed the strength that comes from bread so that they could return safely to their homes; in their weakened condition they might as Our Lord said, faint on the way. They needed the warmth that comes from food so that they could go home praising God instead of shivering with the cold. Our Lord worked this great miracle, multiplying a few loaves to feed 5,000 people. The effect was that they felt an increase of strength. Their hearts were warm now and they praised God, they were preserved from sickness, they forgot their temptations, and went home loving God.

Holy Communion has effects on our soul similar to what the bread had on the 5,000 people. Jesus becomes united with the soul in a union, closer even than the embrace of two dear friends, or even the union of bread with the body. A mother will embrace her babe so tightly that she seems to desire to make it a part of herself. Jesus in Communion actually enters the soul and takes complete possession of it.

Holy Communion gives grace. God gives a grace that stays right in the soul. This grace refreshes the soul so that it is now a healthier, better and more beautiful soul. It gives beauty to the soul so that God likes to look at it. It gives holiness to the soul so that it can now enter heaven, for only holy souls can go to heaven. *Example:* The soul in grace is like a newly decorated church. The artist has painted brilliant pictures on the walls. The sunlight streams through the stained-glass windows. God more than ever loves to live in that grand church. God likes to live in the soul after Holy Communion. His grace like sunlight streams into it. He decorates the soul with virtues. He wants to stay in that soul always, and finally to take it to His home in heaven.

Holy Communion also gives the soul those graces that help. When the people in the desert ate the bread they became strong, did not mind the coolness of the evening hour, were not at all tired on their journey homeward. The graces of Communion make the soul strong too so that it does not mind doing difficult things for God, in fact, is eager to do them. They give courage so that the soul fights off temptations more easily. Those people in the desert were enlightened and they grasped better what Our Lord had said; they saw how sensible His words were and determined to follow them. Holy Communion makes the soul wiser too, so that it understands how wicked sin is and how much nobler it is to do good deeds. And the more often a person receives Holy Communion worthily, the greater will be all these effects.

Summary by Example: The best comparison is that of bread. Whatever bread does for the body, that the Holy Eucharist does for the soul. The children have a real background of experience from which they can develop the comparison. Bread gives warmth,—Holy Communion gives fervor. Bread gives strength,—Holy Communion gives the soul strength to do good deeds. Bread preserves from sickness,—Holy Communion preserves us from sin. Bread becomes part of the body,—the Eucharistic God takes possession of the soul.

Motivation: During one of the persecutions in China, the rulers (mandarins) were very much surprised at the bravery of the Christian martyrs who could suffer beatings, fire and death without a murmur. They said, "These Christians have been eating of that strange bread." That strange bread was the Holy Eucharist.— Some generals of the great Napoleon asked him one day what had been the happiest day of his life. "The day of my First Communion was the happiest day of my life," answered Napoleon, "for then I was brought nearest to my God."—Children should be very happy to realize that they will soon be able to receive their beloved Jesus in Holy Communion. They wonder at the great happiness of the Blessed Virgin to have Him with her in the home at Nazareth but their own union with Jesus will be still closer. Their own heart will be a little home of Nazareth for Him and He will do wonderful things in that heart. He will set up His throne there. He will decorate it like a new church with sweet-smelling virtues and merits. He will make a little heaven of each little soul.

III. What to Do the Day before Receiving

Near Jerusalem lived two holy women, Martha and Mary, who were great friends of Our Lord. Perhaps He had sent word to them, anyway Jesus came to their home one evening to have supper with them. If they knew of his visit beforehand they surely spent many hours cleaning the house and making it presentable for the holy Guest. There was a feverish anxiety the last hour putting this and that in order and talking over what might be done to entertain Him. Both were at the door to welcome Him. Martha set to work in the kitchen preparing the supper while Mary entertained her Master in the front room.

Due preparation must be made for the holy Guest when He comes to us in Holy Communion. We must make the home of our heart spic and span by sweeping out the dirt and dust of sin.

The first step in the immediate preparation is the confession of the children. If this particular class is to receive First Communion they are to be instructed again on the method of confession. If not, this instruction may be omitted.

Martha and Mary let no one enter the front room after they had cleaned it; they wanted their Master to be the first One. We want Jesus to be the first One to enter our clean heart; we do not eat or drink anything except plain water from the midnight before.

Q. 52. What must you do to receive Holy Communion?

A. To receive Holy Communion I must:

1. Have my soul free from mortal sin.
2. Not eat or drink any liquid, except water, after midnight.

The pupils must carry out the preparations explained above. A word should be added about personal cleanliness, that, for example, all should take a bath the evening before, clean their teeth and their finger nails. The beautiful dress or First Communion suit is not a personal reward but a form of preparation for the divine Guest.

Summary by Example: The great Party. When you go to the party of a little friend, you put on your best clothes and your best manners. You even prepare a gift. Communion is the holy party given by Jesus Christ Himself. Do not do less; do more.

IV. First Communion

Rather than use a biblical story we now use a picture, often seen by the pupils, of Jesus Christ holding the sacred Host before Him; about His head is the golden halo of divinity. The picture tells whom the children will receive. The Host is Christ Himself. They will receive Jesus who is God, as the divine halo tells. They will receive Jesus who is Man, as the whole figure tells. There are the eyes that searched for the lost sheep; there, the hands that blessed children; there, the heart that loves them so much. They will recall—Holy Communion looks like bread; it is not bread; it is Jesus.

On the great day the children will assemble quietly in the place appointed. They walk reverently into the church, genuflecting to Jesus in the tabernacle before they enter their seats.

The Mass begins. In the early part, the children will occupy themselves with saying the Acts of Faith, Hope and Love and any other prayers which they know by heart or make up themselves. Towards the middle, the server rings the bell, for the priest is about to change the bread and wine into the body and blood of Jesus Christ. He changes them and holds them high above his head for the children to adore. They say in their hearts, "My Lord and My God." Only a few minutes remain before the First Communion and the children make acts of desire for Jesus, "O come to me, Jesus; I want You; I love You; Come into my heart."

Q. 53. What should you do before Holy Communion?
A. Before Holy Communion I should:

1. Think of Jesus.
2. Say the prayers I have learned.
3. Ask Jesus to come to me.

The children walk to the railing and the priest places Jesus on their tongue. Yes, it is Jesus, mighty God. Holy Communion looks like bread but it is Jesus. They walk slowly back to their seats where they bow their head and say, "Jesus is really in my heart." They believe it is God who made the world, God who died for them, God so wise, so holy, so powerful. They hope in God, that today He will bless them and every day, that they will be able to save their souls. They love God because He is so good in Himself and so good to them. He died on the cross to save their soul, and every day He gives them new favors for soul and body. They

110 Unit 11: Jesus Gave Himself to Us in Holy Communion   Grade I

thank Jesus because He came to them, giving Himself to them, the greatest gift any one can imagine, God Himself. They pray for themselves, for their parents, relatives and friends, for their teacher, for their pastor, for the Holy Father. And perhaps on this day of their First Communion they will do something altogether special for Jesus.

Q. 54. What should you do after Holy Communion?
A. After Holy Communion I should:

1. Thank Jesus for coming to me.
2. Tell Him how much I love Him.
3. Ask Him to help me.
4. Pray for others.

The pupils must learn what to do during the three stages,—before Communion, during and after Communion.

First communicants should be urged to receive on several successive Sundays. They have to accustom themselves to the right procedure while still under the teacher's direction, otherwise they enter vacation with still a little of that fear or strangeness which might keep them from the sacraments all summer. In some churches there is a practice, praiseworthy indeed, of having them go on six successive Sundays in honor of St. Aloysius with the intention that they persevere in their Faith. For the first few times these children should be given a special hour in which to make their confession because they must accustom themselves also to the right procedure for the sacrament of Penance.

Summary by Example: A Seat at the Banquet Table.—When you were very young, you generally had to eat in the kitchen when important company came for dinner. Then one day Mamma thought you had sufficient good manners to eat in the dining-room with a noble guest. Up to now you have been a child of God who was never permitted to go to the banquet table of God with other grown-ups. Today and always now you go to the Table of Jesus Christ with all, even the noblest people.

Motivation: One day St. Therese, the Little Flower, was walking to the church with her nurse. On the way it began to rain, so the nurse hurried back to the house with the little child. St. Therese tried to run away, saying that she had not yet visited Jesus that day. When she was nevertheless kept indoors she cried bitterly because she had not seen Jesus. The children preparing for

First Communion will daily make acts of desire for Jesus. They want Him as Martha and Mary wanted Him, as the little children once did. They want to lay their little heads on His breast near to His Sacred Heart. And Jesus will be happy and He will press them to His heart, telling them how he especially loves little children.

> Come to me, sweet Saviour,
> Come to me and stay,
> For I love Thee, Jesus,
> More than I can say.

In the week or two remaining before dismissal the teacher will repeat matter previously covered in this semester, without however going into too much detail. The repetition will be more of a reading lesson.

MONDAY MORNING CHARACTER TALKS
GRADE I

A Morning Talk is one intended to build Christian character. It is not expected to accomplish this in mighty leaps and bounds, but slowly as a mason builds a brick wall, layer upon layer. Each Monday morning the teacher will select one here given, amplifying it to take up the time she deems necessary. She will point to a practice which crystallizes the Talk, and which the pupils should endeavor to carry out in the ensuing week. To beget a willing response from her pupils, she is to remember that motivation is of equal importance with explanation.

The Morning Talks, wherever possible, are made to harmonize with the progression of catechetical topics and also with the ecclesiastical year. This double relation naturally cannot be maintained in very large schools where pupils begin a grade after New Year's. The teacher will make a rearrangement whenever necessary. In the first year, three Morning Talks relate to Advent and three relate to the sacred Passion of Our Lord. The three former are appropriate only in the Advent season, the three latter in the Lenten period.

Fifteen morning talks are supplied for each semester. The teacher will therefore arrange to introduce a new one each Monday. The stories and examples here given are brief indeed; so, to make them interesting, the teacher must supply details, action, interesting descriptions of place and environment. To aid her in the task of amplification, she may consult:

For liturgy:

>The Ecclesiastical Year, by Rev. Andreas Petz.
>The Externals of the Catholic Church, by Rt. Rev. J. F. Sullivan, D.D.
>Catholic Ceremonies, by Abbe Durand.

For lives of the Saints:

>Little Pictorial Lives of the Saints. Miniature Lives of the Saints, by H. S. Bowden. Follow the Saints, by Rev. W. Herbst, S.D.S. God's Heroes, by Rev. Thomas A. Lahey, C.S.S.

First Semester

1. The Sign of the Cross. For many reasons Catholics make the sign of the cross proudly and devoutly. It recalls to their mind the fact that the Redeemer died on a cross to save them, that in God there are three divine Persons. By it the Christian salutes his God as a soldier salutes his superior officer; by it he puts a wall between himself and the devil.

The teacher will tell the story of the crucifixion of the Saviour. St. Helen found the True Cross on which the Saviour died; three crosses were discovered but the True Cross was distinguished through the miracle of curing a sick person when it was applied to the sore body.

The pupils will now be taught how to make the sign of the cross. Individual work is necessary with first-graders as much depends on their first training. It must be made slowly, reverently and correctly. The pupils must practice, on every occasion during the week, what they learn.

2. The Our Father (Unit One). A good child knows its father well and speaks to him pleasantly many times a day. But the great Father of all is God the Father, of whom you want to know more every day now and to whom you wish to talk many times a day. Your speech to God is a prayer; every prayer is a talk with God.

Our Lord Himself gave you the words of the Our Father, often called the best prayer because He included all needs of soul and body. No child in this room could make up such a wonderful prayer. So right now you will learn the Our Father and train yourself to say it slowly and devoutly.

This week and next week you will learn wonderful things about God, how holy He is, how loving, how He forgives you, how He cares for you. You will wish right away to tell Him that He is your great Father and to ask Him for favors so that you can love Him still more. Here in the classroom, every morning, every night you will talk to Him in the Our Father.

3. Repeat the instruction on the Sign of the Cross. The apostle, St. Andrew, also died on a cross. When he first saw this cross, he hailed it with open arms, "O good cross! Receive me into thy arms." So consoled was the Saint to die on a cross like his Master that he preached from that cross for two days before he died.

Let it always be a proud moment when you sign yourself with

that cross. Did you follow this practice faithfully? What will you do this week?

4. Do everything well (*Unit One*). Try hard to pay attention because what you learn now will make you happy here on earth and it can also bring you to heaven where you will be happy with God forever. When you say your prayers tonight, be sure to say, "Please God, help me to learn all about You." And often during the day you will recall the beautiful things you learned about God.

Right from the beginning you must do everything well. You must pay close attention while the teacher instructs you and you must be diligent in the tasks which follow. The saints and even famous men in the world became great, just because they did even little tasks well.

The Little Flower of Jesus did principally little things because she was no missionary who went from country to country converting the heathen. She became a saint by doing the little things well. If you want to become a saint, you must start now to do the little things well. For many years that's all you'll be able to do and you must be a pretty good boy or girl before the big things come. The boy who exercises his arm just a little bit every day, will be able to lift quite a heavy weight ten months from now.

5. The Hail Mary. Sure, Mother taught you the Hail Mary; but perhaps Sister can tell you how to say it more exactly and devoutly. Sister will tell the story of the Annunciation, when the Angel composed the first part, then the Visitation when St. Elizabeth composed the second part; the Church added the rest of it.

Don't you often say, "Ma, will you ask Pa for me?" Here you ask the Blessed Mother to talk to God for you because you feel you will get your request a little more quickly.

On October 7, the Church celebrates the Feast of the Holy Rosary which is a series of very many Hail Marys. On that day many years ago the Christians fought the Turks at sea. During the battle the Catholics in Rome marched up and down the streets saying the rosary, that prayer composed of many Hail Marys. The Pope always said that the victory was gained through those prayers.

This week you will learn how to recite the Hail Mary and then every day you will say it slowly and devoutly. You are saying, "Please, Blessed Virgin, talk to God for me."

6. Obedience (*Unit Two*). By obedience we do what is told us by our parents, our teacher and our pastor, because God wants it; it may be a command to do something or a command not to do something. When Mother sent the child to school she said, "Now, be obedient to your teacher." When the pastor sent this teacher to the classroom, he meant that all children should obey her. What is more impressive still, is that God wants the children to obey their teacher. When they obey her, it is the same as if they obeyed God.

On October 8 the Church celebrates the Feast of St. Bridget, born of a Swedish royal family. The Saint was the mother of eight children; so well did she instruct them in the love of God and in the necessity of obedience that one of the children was later canonized a saint, St. Catherine of Sweden. Just imagine what an obedient daughter Catherine must have been!

The children have learned so much about their great God that they should be eager to obey Him in the person of their teacher. Because God loves them so much, they should be overjoyed to return His love by obeying Him. God knows everything that goes on in this classroom and He keeps exact account of the little acts of obedience. He is present in the room; they should be happy to act obediently while He is looking at them. The resolutions are: They will do whatever teacher tells them to do; they will do nothing that teacher forbids.

7. *The Glory to to the Father* (*Unit Two*). The greatest idea in your mind is that of God. Then right away you think of the three Persons in God, the Father, the Son and the Holy Ghost. You have already studied something about the three holy Persons and now as a good child you would like to give honor to them. You have learned that you can give honor to them by making the sign of the cross but you can give further and frequent honor to them by reciting a special prayer called "The Glory to the Father." When you say "Glory be to the Father, etc." you mean that you give each of the three Persons of the Blessed Trinity honor and pray that every one will give them honor.

On November 1, the Church celebrates the Feast of All Saints. These millions of saints are with God today because in their lifetime they honored God by a life of prayer and good deeds. Their life was like a long prayer "Glory be to the Father, etc." You were created to give glory to God; you must do this by good deeds but you can do it too by reciting this prayer of Glory.

8. *The Morning Offerings* (*Unit Two*). One of the first truths Sister told you was that you were created by God in order

that you might serve Him. When you talk, your speech must be so good that it pleases God; when you do anything, it must be right and good. By all these words and actions you gain heaven, in fact, buy heaven. Now you want to offer God as many good words and actions as possible. Therefore offer Him everything that you say and do during the whole day. That would be grand because you say and do so many things all day long. If you could do this you would certainly make a hundred offerings a day. Well, you can do this by making a single offering every morning of all the things you will do during that day. The day then belongs to God and with every thought, word or action you are buying heaven.

St. Ursula (October 21) was rather a young saint and so were the Sisters under her authority. This Saint and her companions gave every hour to God as they instructed little children They could not give God enough and finally they all offered up their lives to God in holy martyrdom.

The pupils can scarcely learn the long, official "Morning Offering." Perhaps they can learn it as far as the words, "Sacred Heart of Jesus." Perhaps it must be enough to say, "All for Thee, sweet Jesus!"

9. Helping others (Unit Two). This is a good deed which you can do very often at home, in the classroom and on the playground. God is pleased when you help others and are kind to them. St. Martin of Tours one time met a beggar who was shivering with cold. St. Martin was a soldier and therefore carried a cloak about his shoulders. He seized his sword, slit his cloak in two and gave one part to the poor man. That night Our Lord appeared to St. Martin and He wore the other half of the cloak which had been given to the beggar. He showed Martin that when he gave the cloak to the shivering man, it was the same as giving it to Him.

Isn't that a beautiful thought, that what you do to others, you do to our Lord! You too want to do things for Jesus; do them to others. You can help a little sister or brother at home; you can help Mother with her work. Often you can help a companion in the classroom or on the playground. Will you be kind today and helpful?

10. Be Careful (Unit Two). God loves a cheerful face because He has given us so much to make us cheerful. Everything which can make us happy, comes from God. God hates a sour, dour face.

Just about this time occurs the Feast of St. Francis of Assisi who though extremely poor and burdened with cares, was continually cheerful. Francis had a beautiful voice; he often joined in the songs of the wandering singers who went from place to place. He was the happiest one in his group of friends. His face shone when he could render help to others, particularly the poor and sick. In a war between Assisi and a nearby city, Francis was taken prisoner but the confinement and the dark of his cell could not curb his cheerful spirit. The sunshine of his smile even made the other prisoners forget their misery. He could be so happy because he had his mind set on giving his whole service to the good God who loved Him so much.

These pupils can be cheerful and bring cheer to others. There is no greater happiness than bringing happiness to others by the kind word and the helpful deed. When children foster only pleasant and kind thoughts, their faces will beam with cheerfulness. All love a cheerful face and are themselves cheered by it. Let each child resolve daily to say or do something which cheers others.

11. Grace before Meals (*Unit Three*). God wants little children to grow up in a healthy manner so that they will be strong and able to do much for Him. No boy or girl here wants to be sickly and weak. They get much of their health from the things they eat.

Good children look to God for all future blessings. The pupils have learned that God made all things from the beginning and that even now He preserves all things by His Providence and His almighty power. In the beginning God made the grain and the vegetables which are their daily food; He created the animals which furnish them with meat. Today He makes the grains grow and He gives life to the animals. Catholic children will ask God to bless the food they eat in order that it give them such health of mind and body that they can serve Him better. That great, that grand, sign of the cross must precede their prayer and must conclude it.

God can put even more health into food by giving it his special blessings. The teacher will instruct the pupils on the Grace before meals.

St. Elizabeth of Hungary understood this and she spent her life feeding the poor. One time she was carrying some food in her gathered-up apron. When she opened the apron, she found that God had turned the food into flowers just to show how He loved her good work.

12. Grace after Meals (Unit Three). Good children are thankful for the blessings they have received from God. The food which they eat three times a day is a blessing from God. He made it in the first place and by His power He preserves it today. He gives them food to satisfy their appetites and to make them strong. They should always remember that many a little boy or girl in this world has not such good food as they have; many indeed are starving. Therefore after every meal they should make that glorious sign of the cross and follow with the prayer after meals. The teacher will instruct the pupils on the Grace after meals.

Santa Claus owes his name to St. Nicholas (December 6). This great saint understood that everything he had, came from God. In thankfulness for his own gifts, he gave much food to the poor, naturally also urging the poor to be thankful to God for the alms thus given them.

13. Prepare for Christmas. We are coming to the section which leads us to the Feast of Christmas. During this time we will hear our pastor tell the people to get ready for the great feast of the birth of our Saviour by going to confession and Communion. The children are too young to receive these sacraments now, so they must prepare in another way. They all know how people bring gifts to one another on Christmas Day. What gift will they bring to Jesus? They can eat less candy; perhaps they wish to do without candy altogether. When they go to the crib on Christmas Day they can say, "Jesus, I did this as a little gift-offering to You." And Jesus will be pleased and He will show His love by giving them many gifts in return.

How do you think the Blessed Virgin prepared for Christmas? On December 8, the Church celebrates the great Feast of the Immaculate Conception of the Blessed Virgin Mary. Of course, all the children will go to Mass on this day because it is a holyday of obligation but the feast also begins the preparation for Christmas. Mary was holy from the beginning but she certainly increased her prayers as the first Christmas, in which she had such a great part, drew near. She, too, offered up many an act of self-denial to make her holier still. The children will pray more and they too will make their little acts of self-denial.

14. A Visit to Jesus (Unit Four). By now you are talking often about Jesus who comes on Christmas Day, but do you know that Jesus is in church all the time? Right there in that little tabernacle is Jesus, as real as when He lay in the crib at Bethlehem.

This week the children will pay a visit to the Blessed Sacrament. One visit is enough and again that should not be protracted unduly. They will tell Jesus again and again that they firmly believe He is in the little tabernacle. He is their Saviour, their God, and they love Him from the bottom of their heart. Of all the buildings in the parish there is none so important as the church. Of all the rooms there is none so wonderful as the little room of the tabernacle. That church is the palace of the King; that tabernacle is His throne-room where He receives His little guests, the children.

One time three Kings came from afar to visit the Infant. When they arrived they gave Him gifts. You should bring Jesus a gift every time you visit Him, a nice little prayer, a good resolution, a kind act. And, of course, you will always tell Jesus how much you love Him.

15. Repeat all prayers. You have learned five prayers thus far. That is pretty good, but do you still remember them and do you still say them in the right way?

On the fifteenth of January occurs the Feast of St. Paul the Hermit. This holy man just could not find enough time for prayer so he retired to the desert where he could pray undisturbed. You must always be regular in your time for prayer. You will learn these prayers even better now and use them morning and evening.

Second Semester

16. Exterior devotion in prayer (Unit Five). The very first rule for a perfect prayer is to observe exterior devotion. *A Story:* Emperor Charles V. had just finished hearing Mass when he was informed that a noble stranger wished to talk to him. The Emperor replied "Tell the nobleman that I myself am now busy talking with God." If you wish to hear a speaker in a hall you must shut the doors so that the noise from the street will not drown out the voice of the speaker. If you were to speak to a king you would have to be dressed in the proper way, advance slowly and bow or curtsy as you come before him. Throughout the conversation you would have to preserve the most respectful position. When you pray to God you must shut out the noise of the world, must practice exterior devotion, for God is the King of Kings. Your body must be in a respectful position, that is, you may not lounge lazily. Your hands must be folded. Your eyes must be cast either to the ground or towards heaven.

Another good example of exterior devotion can be taken from the Feast of the Purification or Presentation (February 2). The teacher will tell the class that story, describing the devotion of each of the participants. Their every act was a prayer: the scene was one of prayer.

On February 14, we celebrate the Feast of St. Valentine, a holy priest of Rome who brought comfort and help to the marytrs awaiting their death. Catholic children will commemorate the feast by trying to make some one happy. A card or a visit to a sick chum is much appreciated.

17. Interior devotion in prayer (*Unit Five*). The children must practice what they learn when they learn it. For the next few days they will try to pray earnestly and with attention, that is, with interior devotion. Their mind must remain on God and they must pray with a great desire, just as if they had to have an answer right away. They must think of what they are saying. For example, when they say the "Hail Mary" they must picture Mary as right before them or they can recall the picture when the angel said to her, "Hail, full of grace!" When they come to the "pray for us sinners" they will say it so earnestly that it seems to mean "do pray for us, please pray for us." The practice of interior devotion can best be carried out if they say their prayers slowly.

On February 11, the Church celebrates the Feast of the Apparition of the Blessed Virgin to St. Bernadette at Lourdes. The teacher will briefly tell the story. Whenever the Blessed Virgin appeared to the little shepherd girl, Bernadette knelt down in prayer and became entirely unconscious of anything going on about her. Her hands were piously folded, her head was bent eagerly forward and her eyes were fixed steadily on the figure of the Blessed Virgin Mary above her.

18. Learn the Apostles' Creed (*Unit Five*). Probably the class is now studying the unit on prayer and it is fitting that they add another important prayer to those they already know. This very important prayer is supposed to have come from the apostles themselves. (The Catholic Encyclopedia considers this theory probable). The legend has it: Before they left Jerusalem to go "into the whole world" the apostles met to decide upon a common list of beliefs which they were to teach the people. The "Apostles' Creed" was the result. Before a man can serve God, he must believe that there is a God. So the apostles made up a short catechism of the things a man must believe; the word "Creed" means a list of truths to be believed. The Apostles' Creed tells us the main things which we must believe in order to be called Catholics.

Little Child, do you know that about six years ago the Church demanded that you recite this creed and insisted too that you believe every part of it? No, you could not then recite it yourself, so the Church asked two very responsible people to recite it for you. That was at the time of your Baptism. In order to be admitted into this holy Catholic Church you had to declare that you believed everything in the Apostles' Creed. It is a most important prayer in the Church.

19. Politeness (Unit Six). Children of God must excel in politeness. If we expect politeness in the children of a king, we have much more reason to expect it in Catholics who are children of God. Their God is greater than any king because He is a spirit and because He always was and always will be. He is indeed the King of kings and by words and actions they must show that they belong to this noblest family of all.

The words and actions of the children must prove that they belong to the royal family of God. During the school hours they must be mannerly towards one another, remembering the golden rule, "Do unto others as you would have them do unto you." Both at school and at home they must know when to say, "Please" or "Thank you." Sister must always be addressed by her title and the priest must always be addressed as "Father." Entering the classroom they will say, "Good morning, Sister." When Father visits the room they will all rise and say, "Good morning, Father." Children of God are little ladies and little gentlemen.

St. Francis de Sales (January 29) left a grand worldly career to become a missionary for Christ. After many hardships, success came to him and he converted 72,000 heretics. Next to the grace of God it was the Saint's gentleness and politeness which brought so many back to God. The people could not resist one who was respectful and gentle in his admonitions, always careful that he offend no one and ever ready to concede a right to any one. St. Francis said, "I would rather account to God for too great gentleness than for too great severity." Is not God all love? God the Father is the Father of mercy." People are always influenced to think better of the Catholic religion when they meet a polite Catholic.

20. Take corrections kindly (Unit Seven). It is always difficult to take corrections at home or at school but it is necessary if you would make progress in learning and virtue. Your parents or Sister give them in the best spirit knowing that they are for your good.

Many a person can tell the same story as this priest. "Since my days at college," he said, "the only teacher I really remember and esteem above all others, is the one who gave me a severe correction just when I needed it. I resented it at the time, but in later years I came to know how good his motives were and how much his words benefited me. I wish I had been oftener told the truth about myself."

21. Suffering patiently (Unit Seven). All must suffer some pain and sorrow whether they be young or old. Every child has aches, pains, sicknesses, rebuffs and disappointments. The consideration of the sacred Passion of Jesus will teach the pupils the great lesson of suffering patiently. Their Saviour suffered more than they will ever be called upon to suffer. He never cried, never screamed, never tried to run away, but endured all patiently for love of His Father and for love of us. Even little children can make some return to Jesus for all that He suffered for them. Perhaps Father says that the tonsils must come out or perhaps the child falls and hurts its knee; sometimes a child even suffers when the weather gets too hot. Then the child will say, "I will suffer like Jesus did." To suffer for Jesus is the greatest proof of love. Jesus first suffered, then went to heaven. If little children suffer they will go to heaven too.

Consider the Martyrdom of the Seven Brothers and their Mother, St. Felicitas (July 10). Publius, the prefect of Rome, was enraged at this mother because she had converted many pagans to the Faith. He brought her and the sons before him and threatened them with death if they would not adore the false gods. Felicitas turned to the seven. "My sons," she said, "look up to heaven where Jesus Christ with His saints expects you. Be faithful and fight courageously for your souls." Arguments and promises of honors and wealth were in vain, so one by one they were subjected to the most cruel tortures and finally martyred. St. Felicitas never flinched and last of all she also gained the crown of martyrdom.

22. Kindness to dumb animals (Unit Seven). The pupils have learned how the good God made everything, even the smallest animal. He placed the birds and animals upon this world for our use but not for our abuse. They are His creations set here to serve us, to give us delight but never to be mistreated.

Children love animal pets, dogs, rabbits, kittens, canaries, pigeons. A boy without a dog is lonely. St. Francis called the birds and animals his brothers and sisters. When he prayed they hovered around him as around a dear friend. Once the Saint called to them to listen to a sermon and the fish stuck their noses out of the water and the birds gathered on the branches overhead. St. Therese, the Little Flower, almost invariably was followed by her dog, Tom. One day Tom pointed to something in the grass. It was a wounded bird and the Little Flower picked it up tenderly and took it to her home.

An animal must be made to mind but cruelty will only destroy its spirit. If your dog, Jack, misbehaves it is quite enough to give him a little slap on his snout with a newspaper. He knows what the slap means; he has not to be beaten.

Children who are kind to animals, will be kind to one another. So the children will play cheerily with their pets. If it is a dog they will comb his hair when burrs or fleas bother him. They will bathe him too, although not too often. They will see that their pets get fresh water and the proper kind of food.

> He prayeth best who loveth best,
> All things both great and small,
> For the great Lord Who loveth us,
> He made and loveth all.
>
> —*Alfred Tennyson.*

23. The Act of Faith (Unit Eight). We do not teach much about the divine virtue of faith. Children feel the divine virtues; they do not learn them or understand them. It is necessary though to give some formal prayer by which they "feel" them, so we give them the one in the Revised Baltimore First Communion Catechism.—O my God, I believe all the truths which the Holy Catholic Church teaches, because Thou hast made them known (an indulgence of 3 years.)

A long, long time ago God taught many things through Moses and other holy men. When Jesus came on earth, He told other truths. On Pentecost God gave the Catholic Church the right to teach truths. Whatever truths the children learn in these years, come from one of these sources. So the children will say the Act of Faith daily this week.

St. Patrick (March 17) brought the faith to Ireland. The teacher will tell about the Saint. As He does with all His friends, so God also tested the faith of St. Patrick. As a boy of sixteen Patrick had been carried into slavery in Ireland. One day, God told the boy in a dream that a ship was ready to take him back home. Trustingly, Patrick made his way to the coast, found the ship but could not obtain passage. He prayed and believed and after a while the sailors called him back and took him on board. St. Patrick had some ingenious ways for teaching the rough tribesmen of Ireland even the most difficult truths as when he presented the doctrine of three Persons in one God through the example of the shamrock. The people of Ireland have ever since clung to the Faith given them by St. Patrick, and neither starvation nor persecution has been able to take it from them.

24. The Act of Hope (*Unit Eight*). The children are hopefully approaching the sacraments that bring hope to the fallen race, so very appropriately they now learn the Act of Hope. They hope to receive a big inflow of grace to make them as fruitful trees in God's orchard, to make their souls still more pleasing and holy to God. They hope to receive forgiveness for any sins they may have committed, so that once more their souls are as clean as when they came from the baptismal font. They hope that God will reduce or erase entirely any punishment which they have deserved for this life or for the next. They hope to obtain many graces to avoid sin in the future and to perform deeds worthy of merit.

By the Act of Hope they tell God that they trust Him in Himself and that they trust His word that He will do everything that He has promised them. He has promised to give them enough grace to avoid sin and do good; He has promised to give them the reward of heaven. The pupils will learn the brief act in the First Communion Catechism and recite it daily.—O my God, because Thou art all-powerful, merciful, and faithful to Thy promises, I hope to be happy with Thee in heaven (an indulgence of 3 years).

Blessed Herman Joseph (April 7) placed all his hope and trust in God; he just felt that there was nothing for him to worry about. When he prayed to the Blessed Virgin he was absolutely sure that she was in front of him and heard him. The story is told that he once tendered an apple to a statue of Mary and the statue reached down and took the gift from his hand. The Blessed Virgin really was there and heard him.

About this time Ash Wednesday occurs. Its meaning will be explained the day before its incidence. The Church through the priest puts ashes on our foreheads to remind us that we will some day return to ashes and that therefore we should use the present to do penance for our sins. It should be explained in a way to be a motivation for the nearest Morning Talk.

25. An Act of Love (*Unit Nine*). What is more appropriate than to have the children who love easily, learn the Act of Love? The pupils will learn the brief official act as given in the Revised Baltimore First Communion Catechism and add it to their daily prayers.—O my God, because Thou art all-good, I love Thee with my whole heart and soul (an indulgence of 3 years).

The children love God for His own sake because He is so grand, so holy, so beautiful. They love Him because He has been so good to them. He gave them a soul that was after His own image. He made the world in which they live and He gives life and growth to the things that sustain them and clothe them. The Saviour died for them on the cross to wipe out their sins and in so doing earned graces which can bring them to heaven.

St. Joseph (March 19) loved God so he was chosen as the foster-father of the Infant Jesus. He loved the divine Infant so much that he risked his very life in guarding Jesus against danger. The teacher will tell the story of the Journey to Bethlehem, the Flight into Egypt, the Return from Egypt, the Finding of the Child in the Temple. Just imagine the feelings of Joseph's heart as he carried the Infant Jesus about in his arms! Tell God often this week how you love Him.

26. The Act of Contrition (*Unit Ten*). The pupils have learned many reasons why they should hate sin and be sorry for any they might have committed. In the units that follow they will learn about more powerful motives to produce sorrow. It is time therefore to learn a formal Act of Contrition. The Revised First Communion Catechism gives a brief form.—O my God, I am sorry for all my sins, because they displease Thee, Who art all-good and deserving of all my love. With Thy help, I will sin no more (an indulgence of 3 years).

St. Peter (June 29). What, do you think, saved St. Peter? He had denied Our Lord and you would judge that he was expelled from the band of the apostles, cast out of the Church and eventually would lose his soul in hell. Yet none of these things happened. Instead, he was made the first apostle and the first pope of the

Catholic Church. What had saved him? Just a sincere, perfect Act of Contrition.

27. *The Examination of Conscience* (*Unit Ten*). In their night prayer the children will examine themselves on the table of sins. The best way to make confession easy is to ask ourselves every evening whether we have committed any sins and, if so, how many times. A little child going to bed would be unhappy to know that Mother remained hurt over some misdeed. The child may be so troubled that it might softly go down the back stairs to tell Mother of its sorrow. So, we must never go to sleep with the knowledge that we have hurt God by some sin. We should kneel down, tell God that we are sorry, and then go to sleep. What if God would call us during the night! How glad we would be to look into God's face and know that we had made our peace with Him before we retired.

St. Aloysius (June 21) on the authority of his confessor never committed a mortal sin. The Saint offered up long prayers and undertook severe penances to prevent ever falling into sin. Avoid further sin by recognizing your past mistakes in the nightly examination of conscience and by taking measures against their repetition.

28. *A Visit to the Blessed Sacrament* (*Unit Eleven*). By now the pupils should know that the first One to visit with their troubles and their joys is Jesus in the Blessed Sacrament. Jesus has a right to learn of their rewards and blessings because He gave them; He wants to be asked in their troubles so that He will help them. It is almost a guarantee that the child who learns the habit of making visits, will never lose his faith. The visits of children must not be long; let them prattle a few minutes because Jesus loves the speech of a child.

St. Paschal Baylon (May 17) was a shepherd boy who was distinguished by his love for the Blessed Sacrament. As a young man he was frequently in great danger, and four times in danger of death; but a short visit to the Blessed Sacrament always seemed to bring him out safely. Do you go before the tabernacle when you are in trouble or danger?

29. *Cleanliness* (*Unit Eleven*). All put on their best clothes when they have a birthday or when Mother or Father has one. Children should be clean because every day with them is a day with God. The Blessed Virgin Mary and St. Joseph, who were with Jesus, were very clean. Children will resolve to wash their hands

whenever necessary, to take frequent baths, to clean their teeth every day. Not only does cleanliness become a child of God, but it also promotes health of body. Sickness can come through dirt; unclean teeth wear out quickly and cause disease. Black nails show an untidy person.

It is related of several saints that at their death a fragrance came from their body; their bodies were sweet-smelling temples of the Holy Ghost.

Keep your body clean because it is a temple of the Holy Ghost.

30. Repeat all prayers (*Unit Eleven*). Probably vacation is in the offing. It is of deep concern to the teacher that during this vacation period the pupils retain the things they have learned, especially the pious practices. First amongst these are the prayers. All week then the class will rehearse the prayers learned during the school year and ever and ever the teacher will urge them to be faithful during the vacation time.

St. Margaret (June 10) was Queen of Scotland. Through her constant prayers she brought her husband back to the practice of his religion. She had eight children, and again by prayer and true Christian training she inspired several of them to enter the religious life.

You can become very powerful through prayers and do what a little boy or girl ordinarily could not do.

> Though many things
> I soon forget,
> This one thing
> Holds its place,
> May I learn it
> As a little child,
> "Hail Mary,
> Full of grace."

INTRODUCTION TO GRADE II

In the second grade there must be considerable repetition of what was studied in the first grade. One reason is the difference of custom as to the time of First Communion; another is that children of this age should learn the fundamentals well rather than be burdened with new matter.

The diction throughout will be simple, using such short words and phrases as will make it unnecessary for the teacher to re-word them for her oral exposition.

The teacher is to remember: the daily recitation covers the matter studied the previous day, whether much or little; the organization reviews a section indicated by Arabic numerals, and is carried out when the class completes a section; the reconstruction covers the whole unit and is carried out when the class completes a unit. The teacher must prompt copiously during these steps, and even then not too much is to be expected owing to the intellectual limitations of these second-graders.

The work of this grade is based principally on the Revised Baltimore First Communion Catechism and this is the text to be used by the pupils where they have no special one. The basic lesson is indicated in parentheses immediately following the title of the unit.

The compilers of the First Communion Catechism, however, advise that additional matter not included in this official text be explained by the teacher. This additional matter with the reference to the Revised Baltimore Catechism No. 2 is given in the footnotes to each lesson in the Revised Baltimore First Communion Catechism. There is no difficulty where the pupils use a special book adapted to these other topics. If only the official First Communion Catechism is used, the teacher must explain the extra topics orally as given in this manual. This procedure is simple because in this part of "I Teach Catechism" only a minimum number of questions from sources other than the Revised Baltimore First Communion Catechism are presented which are well within the range of second-graders. These extra topics are recognized by the fact that no lesson reference in parentheses follows the title of the unit, thus indicating that the matter is not to be found in the First Communion Catechism.

SUMMARY OF TOPICS

(Lessons from the First Communion Catechism indicated in Parentheses)

FIRST SEMESTER OR II B

Unit One: One God (Lessons 1, 2, 3, 7)
    I. Who God Is.
    II. Our Duty to God.

Unit Two: The Ten Commandments of God.
    I. What We Must Do to Be Saved.
    II. God Gave Us the Ten Commandments.
    III. The Particular Judgment As a Motive.

Unit Three: The First Three Commandments—Our Duties to God.
    I. The First Commandment of God.
    II. The Second Commandment of God.
    III. The Third Commandment of God.

Unit Four: The Fourth to the Tenth Commandment—Our Duties to Ourselves and to Others.
    I. The Fourth Commandment of God.
    II. The Fifth Commandment of God.
    III. The Sixth Commandment of God.
    IV. The Seventh Commandment of God.
    V. The Eighth Commandment of God.
    VI. The Ninth Commandment of God.
    VII. The Tenth Commandment of God.

SECOND SEMESTER OR II A

Unit Five: Two Laws of the Church.
    I. The Law About Holy Mass.
    II. The Laws About Meat.

Summary of Topics for Grade Two

Unit Six: Prayer Helps Us to Keep God's Laws.
    I. We Should Pray Sincerely and Earnestly.
    II. We Should Pray With Hope and Perseverance.
    III. Morning, Evening and Table Prayers.
    IV. Prayer for Special Needs.

Unit Seven: Grace (Lesson 8).
    I. Grace Is a Help.
    II. How Grace Comes to Us.
    III. Kinds of Grace.
    IV. Using Grace.

Unit Eight: Grace Through Baptism and Confirmation (Lesson 8).
    I. What a Sacrament Is.
    II. The Sacrament of Baptism.
    III. The Sacrament of Confirmation.

Unit Nine: The Sacrament of Penance Helps Us to Keep God's Laws (Lessons 9, 10).
    I. The Sacrament of Penance.
    II. How to Receive Penance Worthily.

Unit Ten: The Holy Eucharist Helps Us to Keep God's Laws (Lesson 11).
    I. The Sacrament of the Holy Eucharist.
    II. Holy Mass.

Unit Eleven: Our Blessed Mother.
    I. To the Time When the Angel Appeared to Her.
    II. From the Birth of Christ to the End.

UNIT ONE: GOD

(Revised Baltimore First Communion Catechism:

Lessons 1, 2, 3, 7)

I. WHO GOD IS.
   1. GOD IS A SPIRIT.
   2. THE PERFECTIONS OF GOD.

II. OUR DUTY TO GOD.
   1. WE MUST KNOW, LOVE, AND SERVE GOD.
   2. SIN OFFENDS GOD.

What We Shall Learn: We shall begin this year with talking about God. We learned much about God last year but so many new ideas are added now that it is practically a new lesson. We can never learn enough about God, never learn all about Him even though we studied Him every day of our life. First we shall study who God is, how big, how holy, how wise, how powerful He is. Then we shall learn why He made each one of us, what He wants each one to do and not to do in order to get to heaven. We are young and we want to start out right; we want to keep on that one right road that leads to heaven.

I. Who God Is

1. God Is a Spirit

God is our Father.—One time Our Lord called His disciples and the people together in order to teach them how to pray. He began His prayer with the words that you now know so well. "Our Father who art in heaven." Jesus in this instance did not say "My Father" but looking at all the people He said, "Our Father," meaning that God was the Father of every one in that crowd of old men, young men, of women young and old, of children. He meant that God is the Father of every one in this world. God is your Father.

Recall what you learned in the first month of school last year. You love your own father at home, but God is your Father whom

Grade II   I. Who God Is   133

you must love still more. You consider your father a big man, wise and powerful, but you learned that God is the biggest Father of all, big without limit, wise and powerful as can be. As a child of your father you belong to him, must look to him for direction and even help. You belong still more to your Father in heaven who directs you by His commandments and helps you. You may live in a nice home provided by your father who works hard every day to earn enough to bring you this comfort and many others. God your Father has a home called heaven which is more beautiful than any you can imagine; He lives there and He wants to bring you, His child, to that beautiful home. Now let us all recite that prayer composed by Jesus Himself, the "Our Father."

You cannot see God because He is a spirit but nevertheless God is here, there and everywhere. God has no body as you have. You believe in angels, you know that you have a guardian angel, but you have never seen any angels because these also have no bodies. There are many things in this life which you cannot see but they are really here. Sometimes they cannot be seen because your eyes are too weak. When this classroom is dark, nothing can be seen in the air, but when the sunlight streams through the window millions and millions of little particles are seen floating in the air. Some things can never be seen. While I am talking to you, you have a thought of me in your mind; that thought cannot be seen. There are persons in eternity who have no body, yet they are alive. Say, the mother of a boy here has died, her body is in the grave, but the boy believes firmly that his mother is alive in heaven. Once God spoke to Moses from a burning bush. Moses heard God but He could not see Him. We shall see God in heaven because then we will not have to depend on our weak bodily eyes. God is a spirit because He cannot be seen with bodily eyes.

There are three Persons in one God. This is a mystery which all the explaining in the world will not clear up. We believe it on the word of Jesus Christ who even told us the names of the three Persons: the Father, the Son, and the Holy Ghost. We learn the same truth from the holy Bible which in a certain sense was written by God; undoubtedly there is a Bible in your home. *Example:* When your mother goes on a trip to Yellowstone Park she tells you about the geysers she saw there. You never saw those shooting fountains of hot water, but you take your mother's word for it because she would never tell you a lie. So you take the word of Jesus about there being three Persons in God.

Q. 13. How do we know that there are three Persons in one God?
A. We know that there are three Persons in one God because we have God's word for it.

You already know something about the first Person, God the Father, from that prayer, the "Our Father." Perhaps the second Person, God the Son, is better known to you because He came down on earth after which He was called Jesus Christ. The Holy Ghost, the third Person in God is mentioned when the Bishop visits the parish to administer the sacrament of Confirmation; your pastor then explains that the Holy Ghost comes to us in a special way through this sacrament.

Q. 11. How many Persons are there in God?
A. In God there are three Persons—the Father, the Son and the Holy Ghost.

These three Persons are in one God. They are very, very holy, so we called them blessed. They are in on God, so we call them the Trinity which is derived from a Latin word meaning three-in-one.

Q. 12. What do we call the Three Persons in one God?
A. We call the three Persons in one God the Blessed Trinity.

Jesus and the Holy Bible mentioned the three Persons by name. Jesus told the apostles to baptize "in the name of the Father, and of the Son, and of the Holy Ghost." At the baptism of Jesus, God spoke from heaven telling the listeners who Jesus was; He said, "This is My beloved Son." But every time and in every place there is mention of one God only.

Q. 10. Is there only one God?
A. Yes, there is only one God.

Motivation: Now you have reason indeed to say the "Our Father" devoutly, for that is a prayer composed by Jesus Christ and ordered to be said by Him. Moreover today and tomorrow you will practice making the sign of the cross exactly and devoutly. You have seen people making that sign with a gesture that was grand. As one woman said, "I go to hear Father's sermons not so much for what he says but I do like to see him make the sign of the cross." Ah, that is a prayer! Make it slowly, say the words reverently. You are signing yourself with the three Persons of the Blessed Trinity. *A Story:* "Let me see this God of yours" said the Roman emperor. The priest pointed to the sky, "Lift your eyes to the sky," he answered, "God is there." The emperor looked up but the blazing sun made him turn his eyes away. "What?" asked the priest. "You ask to see God and you cannot even look at the sun!"

Organization: What great prayer did Jesus give to the people? Did Jesus here call God "My Father" or "Our Father?" What Father have you besides your father in the home? Where does God live? Since you are His child, where does God want to bring you? Why did God make you?

Why can you not see God? Name one thing in this life which you cannot see but it is there nevertheless. Tell the story of God talking to Moses from the burning bush. Why could Moses not see God then? When will you see God?

How many Persons are there in God? Name them. Explain whether you can fully understand this? How do you know that there are three Persons in God? In what sacrament does the Holy Ghost come to you? What do you call the three Persons in one God? What did Jesus always say about the number of Gods? Is there only one God? In what holy sign do you mention every one of the three Persons in God? How do you make this sign?

2. The Perfections of God

Though you cannot see Him with your bodily eyes God is nevertheless here, there and everywhere.

God was in all those places. During World War II a mother wrote to her soldier son in Africa, "Every night, pray to God." Another mother wrote to her son in Australia, "I am sure that God is with you." A father wrote to his soldier-son in England, "May God care for you wherever you are." Another father wrote to his son in Iceland, "Here in my bedroom I pray for you to God every night." And each son replied, "Wherever I am, I know that God is with me."

True, God is in heaven and He is in your church, but He is everywhere else. Perhaps you never thought that He is also in your home, even in your garage. But what is most important to know is that He is everywhere, no matter where you may be, in this classroom, or in the street on your way home this afternoon. He even watches the boys and girls playing because He is also on the playground. Perhaps you and a companion have tried to count the stars on a clear night. Do you realize that God is on every star and through every star? You cannot hide from God even though you go into the darkest closet.

Q. 5. Where is God?
A. God is everywhere.

Motivation: Love God wherever you may be, for He is present everywhere. Fear God wherever you may be, and never offend Him, for He is in that place. When you retire tonight remember that God is in your bedroom. Kneel down and say your night prayers devoutly.

God knows all things.—In your arithmetic lessons you have studied addition and subtraction. God knows all the answers. You are going to school now in order to become a wise man or woman. You will study much in the years to come, but God always knows the answers. There are people in this world who amaze you with their knowledge, but God knows more. God knows more than is to be found in all the books that have ever been written or will be found in the books still to be written. God knows all things.

God knows everything that ever happened. He knows about Abraham Lincoln and George Washington and every man and woman who ever lived in the United States, and for that matter who ever lived in any part of this world. Adam and Eve lived so long, long ago, but God could tell you exactly how they were created, and what happened in the Garden of Paradise. God knows every single thing you ever did since you were born.

God knows everything that is happening now. He knows what people at this moment are kind and what people are bad. Every prayer being said now as well as every curse uttered now, is known to Him. God knows what you are doing just now, whether you are paying attention or wasting your time.

God knows everything that will ever happen. The future life and death of every one is before Him as in a book. All the people who will yet live and die are known to Him and He knows what every one will do in every future moment. God knows what you will do tomorrow and on every day until you die.

I. Who God Is

Q. 6. Does God know all things?
A. Yes, God knows all things.

Motivation: God knows your most secret thoughts; then try to make them good thoughts. God knows every word you speak; then see that your conversation remains clean. God knows your every action; then make all your actions good. Very soon you are going to confession. Tell God everything because He knows it any way; you cannot deceive God.

God can do all things. He made you and everything in this wide, wide world. In order to make this explanation interesting we will recall the story of the Creation. It will serve as a pleasant review of matter studied last year.

How God makes a Thing.—You have seen men building a big house or a big store. For months and months trucks hauled sand, gravel, lumber and bricks. Then many men labored and sweated for a long time building the foundation, the walls, the roof. You thought that they would never finish the building. God does not do it in that way. He uses nothing; it takes Him no time to make anything. God just says so and there it is!

God made the angels. Before any man was on earth God made the angels, who are spirits, wise, powerful, and holy. Remember, He did not need anything from which to make them but He wished them to be, and they were there at once, millions and millions of them, so many that you could not count them in a lifetime. They, too, were spirits without a body and therefore cannot be seen with our bodily eyes. (The story of their temptation will be told later in this unit, so now we discuss only the angels who remained faithful to God).

Angels are wise; their knowledge is indeed surpassed by that of God, but without having had to learn and study they know everything there is in this physical world. Angels are powerful; one time the Israelites were threatened by the Assyrians and an angel of God descended upon the enemy and in one night slew 185,000 men. Angels are holy; they spend their eternity in the holiest work, adoring the Lord God.

Motivation: We are happy to know that each one of us has a guardian angel who protects, guides, and helps us; he is the messenger who carries our prayers to God. Do you know the prayer to your guardian angel? Do you ask his help when you are tempted?

God made the world. God made everything just by wishing it to be. When it is said that God made the world in six days, it means that God began to make certain things on each of six separate or different days. What He wished on each day, was done in an instant.

On the first day God made the earth. And God said, "Let there be light," and light was made.

On the second day, God said "Let there be a firmament made" and there it was. This is the sky which you can see if you gaze out of the window now or which you behold at night. Do not think that the sky is just nothing; it includes the air which you must breathe in order to live.

On the third day God separated the land and the water, and He made the plants. Thus were made the oceans, the seas, the lakes and the rivers. (Perhaps the pupils will name some). There was warmth on the earth, so God placed into the ground the trees, the grains, the herbs, the vegetables, the flowers, and the grass.

On the fourth day God made the sun, the moon, and the stars. You get an idea of the great power of God when you realize the great size and weight of many of these planets. Looking at them from afar, they seem very small, even the sun does, but actually they are so large that if you could ascend to some of them and walk and walk for a million years, you could not circle them. You think that the earth is large because you have seen so little of it but the sun is many, many times larger than the earth. Think what power it took to make the earth, then think what power God manifested when He made the sun. God can do all things.

On the fifth day God made the fishes and the birds and these have multiplied to the present day. Most boys like fishing. Well, on this day the first fishes were made and from them came those fishes you caught in the stream. Adults go deep-sea fishing and they make catches that are big and strange. All boys and girls, like the birds for their songs and beautiful feathers. Those hundreds of strange looking birds of which you have seen pictures (perhaps the pupils will tell about some strange birds or fish, or describe those they have seen) come from this day.

On the sixth day God made the animals of the earth and last of all He made man. You see, God began with material things, then went to living things in a steady climb, until He came to His choicest creation on earth, man, of whom He said, "Let us make man to our image and likeness." Of no other creations had God said this, for He gave to man alone a soul that was made "to His own image." Only the soul is a spirit as God is and will never die; only to our soul did He give understanding and free will as He Himself has.

Q. 7. Can God do all things?
A. Yes, God can do all things.

Motivation: God is good. He made this earth for man; the heat of the sun to give man warmth and make things grow for the benefit and pleasure of man; the grains, the fish that man might have food; the animals that they might give food for man and help man in his work.

God always was. He never was born for He had no beginning. He lives now, even as you do. If you count a million years ahead, God will still be.

Q. 8. Did God have a beginning?
A. No, God had no beginning; He always was.

Q. 9. Will God always be?
A. Yes, God will always be.

Motivation: God is here all during your life to watch over you and help you. He wants to save your soul. Will you be with God a thousand years from now?

Organization: What did those parents write about God to their soldier-sons in different parts of the world? Name some places where God is in a special way. Is God in other places? Name five other places where God is. Where is God? Since God is in your bedroom, what will you say before you go to sleep?

What do you study in school? What does God know about your studies? What does God know about the past? What, about the present? What, about things that will still happen? Does God know all things? Then why should your talk always be clean, and your actions always be good?

God's Power. How do men build a house? How does God make all things? How did God make the angels? Explain how an angel is wise. What work do angels do in heaven which shows that they are very holy? How did the one angel show his power over the enemy that wanted to destroy God's people? What is the guardian angel? What prayer to your guardian angel do you know?—Who made the world? God worked on six different days. Can you tell what He made on each day? On what day did God make Adam and Eve? What did God breathe into the bodies of Adam and Eve? Explain how many things that God made, were for the good of man. Describe some things made by God which show that He is very powerful. Did God have a beginning? How long will God live?

II. Our Duty to God

1. We Must Know, Love and Serve God.

Why your Parents sent you to a Catholic School.—They sent you there because in a Catholic school you are taught about God. They themselves had taught you as much as they could while you were a little child, but realizing that that was not enough they sent you to the Catholic school that you might learn still better why God made you.

A little while back we learned why God had made all things on earth. He had done it to help man and we said that God is good. You will still learn a great deal to show how good God is to man in other ways but God's good intentions go much further than this present life. God has heaven in mind when He thinks of man, that beautiful place where man will be happy with God for all eternity. God made you for Himself. How honored you are to be made for God!

Q. 3. Why did God make you?
A. God made me to show His goodness and to make me happy with Him in heaven.

In order to get to heaven you must know about God. You have tried to know Him in the last few days as you learned Who God is. You have learned that He is everywhere, knows all things, can do all things, and that He always was and always will be. You have learned too that He is a spirit, that there is only one God, and that there are three Persons in God. Actually from other studies you know much more than that about God, and in the coming months you will learn still more. Your father wants you to know him because he has done much for you. God wants you to know Him because He has done everything for you.

In order to get to heaven you must love God. Certainly God will not want you in heaven if you hate Him. Your parents want you to love them; God wants you to love Him. It is easy to love

Grade iI II. Our Duty to God 141

God when you reflect that He first loved you and that He has done and is doing so much for you. All the chapters in the catechism give you the picture of how God loves you through the Father and the Son and the Holy Ghost, through the Redemption, through the sacraments, through the Catholic Church. Forgetting for a moment how many favors God has showered upon you, God is lovable in Himself; He is all-good, all-holy.

It is not enough to know your father—to say that you love him. You must prove your love by doing the things he wants you to do; in other words, you must serve him. It is that way with God; you must serve Him by doing what He commands and avoiding what He forbids.

Q. 4. What must you do to be happy with God in heaven?
A. To be happy with God in heaven I must know Him, love Him, and serve Him in this world.

Summary by Example: Our Lord told a story of a father who had two sons. The one remained at home to help the father wherever he could. The other got restless, and contrary to his father's wish, went into a far country, forgot his father, and lived a very bad life. Who, do you say, loved his father? Yes, the child who serves God really loves Him but the child who refuses to serve, does not. The good boy will be happy with God in heaven.

Motivation: Now you know why God made you, what God will do if you know, love, and serve Him. You are eager to learn how you can serve God. That you will be told in the next lesson.

Organization: Why do your parents send you to a Catholic school? For whom did God make you? Into what place does God want to bring you? Tell some things which you already know about God? What else must you do besides knowing God? Give one or two reasons why you should love God. What does Mother expect you to do when you say that you love her? What does God want you to do besides knowing and loving Him? Then, what three things must you do to be happy with God in heaven? Tell the story of those two sons and explain which one really loved his father.

2. Sin Offends God

Many Angels loved God: some Angels hated God.—Go backed to the creation of the angels for a moment. Before God admitted them into heaven He gave them a test to prove their love of Him. The angels indeed knew God and loved Him but they still had to serve God. The greater part were faithful and they served. Strange to say, however, many angels said, "I will not serve." That was a big, big sin, to refuse to serve the God who had made them. Those bad angels are now called devils and they try to lead you into sin so that you will never get to heaven.

Q. 23. Who committed the first sin?
A. The bad angels committed the first sin.

You show your love for God when you serve Him in the way He has commanded. You sin when you disobey His commandments.

Q. 22. What is sin?
A. Sin is disobedience to God's laws.

We will return to Adam and Eve, our First Parents, to get another example of sin. When God made them He placed them into a beautiful Garden called Paradise where all they had to do was enjoy themselves. Only one command was given to them to test their love—not to eat of the fruit of a certain tree. If they observed that command, not only would they be happy for time and eternity, but we, their children, would have the same good fortune without any further effort on our part. Certainly God held forth the greatest reward He possibly could for obedience to that one little command. The devil knew of that command and he was determined to spoil their chance and ours to get to heaven. Going into that tree one day when Eve was standing beneath, he told her a big lie, that God's command was nonsense, and that Eve would become very wise if she ate the fruit. Would Eve prove her love for God now by serving Him? Eve believed the devil, ate the fruit, and shortly afterwards gave Adam a piece of it. That was a big, big sin.

Q. 24. Who committed the first sin on earth?
A. Our first parents, Adam and Eve, committed the first sin on earth.

The devil had made Adam and Eve commit a big sin and thereby had spoiled their chance for heaven. What affects us more though, is that he also spoiled our chance, for we are the children of Adam and Eve; each one of us is now born with their original sin on his soul. Adam and Eve were cast out of Paradise, were stripped of most of the great favors God had given them, and made to enter a world where there would be hard work, sickness and death. As we, their children, are born with their sin, so do we suffer the punishments which were given to Adam and Eve.

Q. 25. Is this sin passed on to us from Adam?
A. Yes, this sin is passed on to us from Adam.

Q. 26. What is this sin called in us?
A. The sin in us is called original sin.

Only one person, the Blessed Virgin, was free from original sin.

Q. 27. Was any one ever free from original sin?
A. The Blessed Virgin Mary was free from original sin.

It is hardly right though to blame everything on Adam and Eve, for we too sometimes refuse to serve God. We too commit sins sometimes, doing it by our own free will, by our own act.

Q. 28. Is original sin the only kind of sin?
A. No, there is another kind of sin, called actual sin.

We call this an actual sin for one reason that the act is our own. This time it is not the act of our First Parents or of any one else but our own. The boy who smashes a window cannot say that it was Adam and Eve or his uncle who did the act. He himself did it.

Q. 29. What is actual sin?
A. Actual sin is any sin which we ourselves commit.

Q. 30. How many kinds of actual sin are there?
A. There are two kinds of actual sin: mortal sin and **venial** sin.

Mortal sin is so called because it does so much injury to the soul, it is in fact called deadly. When the American soldier was hit by a bullet, he received a terrible wound. The doctor called it a mortal wound, meaning that the soldier would die from it; he could also have called it a deadly wound. Death strikes us as something fearful; mortal sin is fearful too. In some forms death is horrible as, for instance, when a man is burned; mortal sin is horrible. Now you realize that this sin is a big offense against God. *Examples:* To miss Mass on a Sunday or holyday is such because you refuse God the biggest worship you can give Him on earth; to kill another or to injure him seriously is such because you take away or harm his life which is his choicest earthly possession; to tell a very bad story about another is such because you hurt him in his good name which all men prize highly; to eat meat on Friday is such because you show disrespect to Jesus Christ who died for you on Good Friday.

Q. 31. What is mortal sin?
A. Mortal sin is a deadly sin.

Mortal sin kills the friendship which God has for us. He will not, cannot tolerate this sin in any one. The sinner does the one thing which is really evil in the sight of God, the one thing which God hates. Would you stand for a friend doing the one thing you hate most?—Mortal sin robs the soul of grace. When a soul is good God gives it grace that makes it holy and good. That grace is like a brilliant light that goes through and through the soul like it would through glass. Now the soul is dark, it is bad, it is ugly.

Q. 32. What does mortal sin do to us?
A. Mortal sin makes us enemies of God and robs our souls of His grace.

God hates a bad soul and He will have nothing to do with it. He just does not want it, even in eternity. Such a bad soul will forever be locked out of heaven and will be for all eternity with the other bad souls, the fallen angels who said "I will not serve."

Q. 33. What happens to those who die in mortal sin?
A. Those who die in mortal sin are punished forever in the fire of hell.

Summary by Example: Try to picture a soul in the state of mortal sin. It is dead. There is an ugly stain on it. There is a stench from it that is worse than any stench you can imagine. Heaven is closed to it; hell is open for it; God hates it. What a terrible thing is mortal sin.

Motivation: Think what happened to the angels who said, "I will not serve." From beautiful beings they were instantly changed to ugly devils. Whereas they might have enjoyed heaven for all eternity, they were suddenly plunged into hell where they will endure pain forever.—Think of what happened to our First Parents and to all of us because of their mortal sin. From that day on they had to work hard, to study for what they wanted to learn. Troubles without end came upon them. They had to endure sickness and in the end they had to die. All the troubles you see in this world today and all the troubles you will ever undergo, came as a result of that sin. You must work, must worry; you can suffer accidents and you will often get sick. You are tempted now and may lose your soul, whereas you might have been free and gone straight to heaven. In the end you will become sick and die. God hates mortal sin and He punishes it severely.

In explaining venial sin the fact is ever to be kept before the pupils that it is really a sin even though not so serious as mortal sin. Pupils must not get the impression that it is of little importance just because it is called "lesser."

Lesser sins are also displeasing to God.—Say there is a boy named Albert in this class. He is not really a bad boy; he does not break windows, smash desks, or spill the ink on the floor. For other reasons, though, Albert is a great annoyance to his teacher for he is a great fidget. He plays with his books, rustles his papers, scrapes his feet, moves around jerkily, whispers, giggles. Sister loves Albert indeed because he is not the worst kind of a boy, but she loves him less because he troubles her constantly. The actions of Albert are like venial sin which also displeases God.

A venial sin is not as serious as mortal sin but it is a sin nevertheless. No, it is not like the sin of missing Mass on a Sunday or a holyday, not like killing, nor like ruining a person's good name. Does Mother say that you may injure her in little ways as long as you do not kill her? No, Mother wants you to behave well in every respect. God forbids every kind of sin, like, for example, using His name carelessly, misbehaving in church, disobeying parents or teachers, quarreling, stealing little things, telling lies.

Q. 34. What is venial sin?
A. Venial sin is a lesser sin.

Venial sin does not wholly kill your friendship with God or make you an enemy of God but it lessens the friendship, makes you less loved by Him. *Example:* Joan does not hate Marie because Marie has never committed a serious offense against her; but she does not love her fervently because Marie is constantly doing little things that annoy her. Instead, Joan has chosen Florence as her best friend because this girl is careful never to offend in any way.— Venial sin does not rob the soul of God's grace but it makes it less beautiful and holy. *Example:* Dorothy has a nice white dress but it does not attract the admiration of friends because a few light stains impair its whiteness.

Q. 35. Does venial sin make us enemies of God or rob our souls of His grace?
A. No, venial sin does not make us enemies of God or rob our souls of His grace.

God is displeased with venial sins because He has forbidden them and because they show a lack of love for Him. Do not think that Christ on the cross suffered for mortal sins only; He had to make atonement too for many venial sins, even for the slightest venial sin ever committed. God the Father hates venial sins too because they caused His divine Son great sufferings on the cross.

Q. 36. Does venial sin displease God?
A. Yes, venial sin does displease God.

Summary by Example: When William went out to play ball instead of going to the store as his mother had ordered, he committed a venial sin of disobedience. No, the family did not starve because Mother finally sent Alice for the groceries—it was not a mortal sin. But it was a sin nevertheless because God commands children to obey their parents. God did not cast the boy out of the circle of His friends but He marked down the fact that William was an inconstant friend who occasionally forgot his duty to God. God now saw a little stain on William's soul that made it just a little less holy and beautiful. God had expected greater friendship from William; God was displeased with the boy's conduct.

Motivation: Try, never, never, to commit a venial sin. The sin is not punished with hell fire as the sin of the angels was, or with a long life of punishment as that of our First Parents was. Venial sin is punished in this life and in the next. Here God often visits the sinner with aches and pains and troubles and disappointments. In the next life God has prepared purgatory where the sinner must suffer until the stain of the last venial sin is erased.

Organization: When God made the angels, did He take them into heaven right away? How did God first test them? Tell what happened in this test. What kind of a sin had the bad angels committed?—Where had God placed Adam and Eve? Describe that garden. What was the one command which God gave them?

Tell the story of the temptation. What kind of a sin had Adam and Eve committed?

Is this sin of Adam passed on to us? What is it now called? What one person was free from this sin? Is original sin the only kind of sin? Do men themselves commit sin now? What is such a sin called? How many kinds of actual sin are there?

Mortal Sin. Give two examples of mortal sins. Could you perhaps explain why your examples are big, big sins?—What does mortal sin kill? What happens to the grace in the sinner's soul? Then, what does mortal sin do to us? What happens to those who die in mortal sin? What other persons are in that bad place?

How did God punish the angels who said, "I will not serve?" How did God punish our First Parents for eating the forbidden fruit? Did their punishment pass on to you? Explain some of the troubles you have now because of their sin.

Venial sin. Describe how Albert annoyed his teacher all day. Was he a real bad boy? How did teacher feel towards Albert? Give an example of some venial sins. Are these examples lesser than mortal sins? What is venial sin?—What does venial sin do in regard to friendship with God? What does venial sin do in regard to grace? Joan did not hate Marie but why did she not consider her the best friend? Why did Joan choose Florence as her best friend?—Give a reason why venial sin displeases God.—How does God punish venial sins?

UNIT TWO: THE TEN COMMANDMENTS OF GOD

I. WHAT WE MUST DO TO BE SAVED.
II. GOD GAVE US THE TEN COMMANDMENTS.
III. THE PARTICULAR JUDGMENT AS A MOTIVE.

What We Shall Learn: We know of God's command that we know Him, love Him and obey Him. There is before us the terrifying example of the fallen angels who did not fulfill their duties to God. Our question is: What must we do to please God and to avoid the fate of the bad angels?

First of all we must know and believe certain truths; as the boy would say, "We must know where we are at." We must believe in God or we could not believe that He ever told us anything. Then we must really believe that He said, "Do this; do not do that." We must start out right by believing certain facts.

Next comes the question, What did God tell us to do? The answer is contained principally in the ten commandments which God gave us. To move ourselves to do what God ordered, we shall reflect on the Judgment. God at that time will ask us whether we did what He ordered. Our eternity of reward or of punishment will depend on how we can then answer God's question.—This unit must be taught orally.

I. What We Must Do to Be Saved

He does not know where to go and he is too lazy to go anywhere. Picture a typical hobo sitting beneath a road sign that points to a town going south and another going north. The tramp is fast asleep. This tramp is like many a man who does not know the road to heaven and, even if he does know, is too lazy to go there.

First, we must know and believe. We Catholics are told what to believe. God told us many truths through His holy leaders in the Old Testament. When Christ came on earth He told us many more truths. Today the Catholic Church explains what the prophets of old and Jesus Christ told us. Thus Catholics can be absolutely sure that there are three Persons in God, no more, no less, because the Church says so. Similarly, when the Church

Grade II   **1. What We Must Do to be Saved**   **149**

tells them that Jesus came down to save us, they can be sure that it is a fact. These and many other truths they must believe.

Here is opportunity to review the chief truths the children have thus far been taught to believe. They believe in God and His heaven; that is, why they want to get there. They believe that Jesus Christ opened heaven; that is why they know that it is possible to get there. They believe in the sacraments; that is why they believe that God Himself will help them to get there. An act of faith by the class is in place here.

Summary by Example: To believe is like getting the right start. If a boy wants to learn, he must first believe that there is a school where he can learn, must know the way to the school, must believe what the teacher tells him.

Believing sets us on the right road to heaven but good deeds moves us along the road. *Examples:* It does a man no good to own a farm, if he does not cultivate it; if he does not work hard, he reaps no crops and he will starve to death. It does a man no good to own a store, if he does not work hard to sell his goods; if he does not get busy, he will have to close the business. It does us no good to go to school, if we do not study; if we are lazy, we will remain ignorant our whole life long. So, it does us no good to be in the Catholic Church, if we do not live the correct life of a Catholic. It does us no good to believe what God has taught unless we do what God has taught, that is, obey the commandments of God and of the Church.

A sensible man learns what to do, then he does it. Catholics are taught what to do by their teachers who get the truth from the Church itself. The class gives examples of what the Church through her teachers has taught them thus far. It is not enough for the pupil to know that he ought to obey his parents; he must actually obey. It is not enough for him to know about the Mass; he must go to Mass. The resolution of the pupils is then, first to study the catechism, so that they will learn what to do, and next to do what the catechism tells them.

Summary by Example: On a tombstone in St. Paul's Church, London, is a strange writing which describes the life of the man buried beneath it. It reads: "I didn't know what to believe; I didn't know what to do; I don't know where I'm going." What a puzzled life that man must have led! Evidently he did not know much about God or about the commandments which would have told him what to do. He did not know much about heaven so he did not strive to attain it. He did not know whether he would ever get to heaven because he did not believe enough and did not do enough. He had the wrong start. Believe and do what the Church tells you and you have the right start.

Organization: Describe the picture of the tramp on the roadside. Did he know where he was going? Or, did he care to get there? When is a Catholic like that tramp? What holy men long ago told us what to believe? What Person later on, whom you love very much, also told us what we must know and believe? Tell two things which you know and believe about God. Tell three things which you know and believe about Jesus Christ. Tell one thing which you know and believe about your Catholic Church. What must a boy believe about his school and his teacher if he wants to learn addition?—Believing is not enough. What will happen to the girl who knows that she should study but does not study? What must you do besides knowing that you ought to obey? What, besides knowing about the Mass?

II. God Gave Us Ten Commandments

Read the Bible Story, God Gives the Ten Commandments. The teacher will paint the scene on Mount Sinai in the strongest colors. Her description, vivid and graphic, must convey an impressive idea of the greatness of God, and the almost terrifying importance of the commandments which He then and there gave to Moses for all the Jews. Just to hear them, the Israelites had to make solemn preparation. The manifestations of nature proved that God had the right to say to men: "Thou shalt not" or "Remember"!

God gave the commandments on two tables of stone. There might have been significance in the stone, namely, that He wanted them to be preserved as long as men lived. On one stone He placed the first three commandments because these concern Him more directly: they tell us how to live and serve the Lord our God. The seven commandments on the other stone explain how we can love ourselves truly and love our neighbor as ourself.

Here then we have the answer to, What must we do? God Himself gave us the answer—obey the commandments. *A Story:* An Indian had begged a bag of tobacco from a white man and later found some money mixed with the tobacco. When the Indian returned the money next morning, the white man asked why he had not kept it. The Indian laid his hand on his heart. "In my heart I have a bad voice and a good voice. The good voice said that the money did not belong to me; give it back to the white man. The bad voice said it belongs to me because the white man gave it. The good voice answered that the man gave the tobacco but not the money. All night the two voices fought. I could not get rest until I returned it to you." Either directly or indirectly God had enunciated the seventh commandment to that Indian—Thou shalt not steal.

We are now making progress in the knowledge of our duty to God—to know and to do. First, we will learn the ten commandments—that is knowing. Next we will do what the commandments say—that is doing. Q. Which are the commandments of God? A. The commandments of God are these ten:

1. I am the Lord thy God; thou shalt not have strange gods before Me.
2. Thou shalt not take the name of the Lord thy God in vain.
3. Remember thou keep holy the Lord's day.
4. Honor thy father and thy mother.
5. Thou shalt not kill.
6. Thou shalt not commit adultery.
7. Thou shalt not steal.
8. Thou shalt not bear false witness against thy neighbor.
9. Thou shalt not covet thy neighbor's wife.
10. Thou shalt not covet thy neighbor's goods. (Revised Baltimore Catechism No. 2. Q. 195).

Summary by Example: Albert looked at the leaves covering the front lawn. He recalled his father's order to rake them together. Albert knew about the fourth commandment ordering children to obey their father. That was knowing. Then Albert obeyed the commandment and cleared the yard. That was doing.

Organization: Tell the story about God giving the ten commandments. How many tables of commandments were there? Of what were the tables made? What commandments were on the first table? What, on the second table? By these commandments,

152 Unit 2: The Ten Commandments of God   Grade II

God tells us what to do. Tell the story of the Indian who found some money in the pack of tobacco given him. Name some of the commandments? What did Albert know about the leaves and what did Albert do?

III. The Particular Judgment As a Motive

This section takes the place of the Motivation which is generally added at the end of each unit.

It is left to us to decide whether we wish to obey the commandments or not but God will punish or reward us according to how we have obeyed or disobeyed them. The very first question which God will ask us when we come to be judged will be, "How have you obeyed My commandments?" Then God will go over every single commandment telling us where we have failed or obeyed. He will frown when He comes to a sin and smile when He comes to a good deed. He will ask: Did you take My name in vain? Did you go to Mass? Did you obey your parents? Did you steal? Did you lie? These questions He will level at us at the particular judgment which takes place immediately after our death.

No moment in life can be compared to this one in importance, for on it hinges an eternity of joy or of sorrow. If God finds only venial sins we will be fortunate, for He will sentence us to stay in purgatory until they are wiped out. But purgatory is very painful and to escape it we must now avoid even venial sins. When the last stain of sin is erased, God will take us into heaven where we will be happy with Him forever. But consider the case of the man who has sinned grievously against the commandments and did not repent before he died. To him God will say, "Depart from Me into everlasting fire." Never shall he see God: always will he be in torment.

A Story of Two Heroic Children.—Jacob and Magdalen were two Japanese children who were condemned to death because of their Faith. Jacob was a tender boy, only eleven years old, who fell several times on the rocky road to the place of death. When sympathizing men offered to carry him on their shoulders, he refused saying, "I am following Jesus who walked to Calvary carrying His cross." When the boy saw the fire prepared for him, he said, "Do not weep but be happy because I am happy." Little Magdalen saw how the fire consumed her brother and her parents. She took some live coals and arranged them like a crown in her hair, then she sank down beside the dead bodies of her dear ones and gave her life to God. What do you think the great Judge said when these two souls came to be judged?

Organization: When will the particular judgment take place? Who will judge you then? What questions will the great judge ask? Where will you go if He finds no sins? Where, if He finds venial sins? Where, if He finds big, big sins? What should you resolve to do now? Tell the story of the two Japanese children, Jacob and Magdalen. What do you think the Judge said to them when they came to be judged?

Reconstruction of Unit Two: To do this easily, the teacher need only return to the questions given for the organization of each of the three sections. She will take them in the order given, thus uniting the sections into a unit. This direction will not be repeated as it holds for the reconstruction at the end of every unit.

UNIT THREE: THE FIRST THREE COMMANDMENTS—OUR DUTIES TO GOD

I. THE FIRST COMMANDMENT OF GOD.
   1. WE MUST WORSHIP GOD.
   2. WE MUST HONOR GOD THROUGH HIS SAINTS AND HOLY THINGS.

II. THE SECOND COMMANDMENT OF GOD.
   1. GOD'S NAME MUST BE HONORED.
   2. BAD LANGUAGE IS SINFUL.

III. THE THIRD COMMANDMENT OF GOD.
   1. THE LORD'S DAY IS HOLY.
   2. WE MUST AVOID UNNECESSARY WORK.

What We Shall Learn: When God gave the first commandment He began with the words, "I am the Lord thy God." He placed Himself first because He is first. He comes before ourselves and before our neighbor. The first duty of every human creature is to know, to love and to serve God.

In this unit we shall learn what our duties to God are. We have three principal duties to God and each of these is covered by a special commandment. It is our first duty to worship Him. "Worship" is a new word but it just means that we must in various ways tell and show God that He is our Creator, our Preserver, our Redeemer and our eternal reward. We must act in a holy way towards holy persons, first to the All-holy One who is God and next to His saints who are His holy friends.—In the second commandment we shall learn that His name is holy because it stands for Him and that we owe it great respect.—In the third commandment we shall learn just what actions we must perform in order to worship God.

To the Teacher: The commandments are not given in the First Communion Catechism, so this unit will be taught orally by the teacher. It is necessary to cover them because some of these pupils, perhaps all, will soon have to make this first confession. The few questions taken from the Revised Baltimore Catechism No. 1 are just for the teacher's guidance.

I. The First Commandment of God

1. We Must Worship God

Q. What is the first commandment of God?
A. The first commandment of God is: I am the Lord thy God; thou shalt not have strange gods before Me.

All must worship God, and Him alone. "Worship" means to tell God by word and act that He is our God. We tell Him by word and act that He is our Creator, that He is all-truthful, almighty, all-good. We may not say that any other thing or person is as powerful, as good, as lovable as the real God; doing this we would make gods of other things and persons, and God said, "Thou shalt not have strange (false) gods before Me."

The Great Captain. Neil was talking to his baseball team. "Boys, I am your captain and I want you to respect me as your captain. I want you to believe me when I tell you something. I want you to do what I tell you. I want you to trust me to run the team right."—God is the great Captain of our souls. To believe what God says, to rely on Him, to do what He says, is respecting God for what He is; the other word is "worship."

Wrong Worship. Read the Bible Story, the Golden Calf. Here we have an example of the most serious sin against the first commandment. The people had grown weary of waiting for Moses to come down from the mountain, some even doubting that He would ever return. They brought their gold ornaments to Aaron who made a golden calf for them. They sang and danced around this calf and called it a god; they worshiped the calf as a god. Then God spoke to Moses for He was angry that the people had adored a calf as their god and said He would destroy them. Moses was so angry at the sight that he hurled the two tables of the law to the ground and broke them. He pulled down the golden calf and had it beaten into powder. But Moses prayed for His people and God forgave them.

We dwell for a moment on the awful introduction of this first commandment. Do we not hear the roll of a mighty voice in the words: "I am the Lord thy God"? As if He said: "Remember all the days of your life that I am your God, your Creator; I am the infinite God who made you out of nothing. Never forget it. I will not tolerate anything else or anyone else being made your god. I am the Lord your God."

We must offer to God alone the very great worship that is due to Him; we must by word and act tell God that He is above every creature. We can do this by telling it in plain words. "God, you are my God!" We can also tell it by our daily deeds; when we do what God commands, it is the same as saying, "O God, You are my God. You are so great and so holy that I will do whatever you order."

Faith: With heart and lips we must often tell God that we believe He is our great God, our great Creator, and that we believe whatever He has said, just because God said it. A boy believes in his father; he is proud to point him out to all the other boys. He goes still further; he believes everything his father tells him without question. We too go further and we tell God that we believe whatever He has said. In the Apostles' Creed we say, "I believe in God the Father almighty." In the Act of Faith we say, "O my God, I firmly believe in Thee." In the lessons since the first day of school we learned that there are three Persons in God, that Jesus Christ came down and died for our sins, that the Catholic Church teaches us all things necessary for our salvation. We believe these truths because God Who has given them to us cannot deceive.—The class will learn the Act of Faith from the First Communion Catechism.

Hope: By word and deed we tell God that He is almighty and that we therefore place all our hope in His almighty power. We firmly rely on Him giving us all the help we need to get to heaven. In other words, we tell Him that He is our almighty God. A boy thinks his father so big and powerful that he places all his hope in his help. Does he not tell the other boys, "I'll bet my father is a thousand times stronger than your father?" Only a God can give us all the graces we need to live a good life; when we hope to get them all, we really say, "You are almighty: You are God." Only God can take us to heaven; when we hope to get there, we really say, "You are God; You will do what You promised." Only God can forgive sin; when we hope for forgiveness, we really say, "You are all-merciful; You are God."

Love: We must love God in a way that only God deserves. Our great love then says, "You are God; You are infinitely lovable." We love Him more than anything created because He, our

Grade II   I. The First Commandment   157

God, is above everything created. We love Him as a Being who is all-good, all-holy. We love the all-holy One so much that we will never offend Him by any sin. We go further and love what He loves. Because God loves our neighbor, we love our neighbor; we will try to help him to save his soul. These are works of love that prove our love for God.

Prayer: When we pray to God, we believe that there is a God—that is faith. We expect Him to help us—that is hope. We like to pray to such a beautiful God—that is love.

Children are not to be taught that missing one or several prayers is a sin. Missing prayers becomes a sin only when extended over a considerable period of time, because no one may go for long without telling God that he believes in Him, hopes in Him, and loves Him. Nevertheless, children are to be counseled to confess missing prayers, not necessarily because it is sinful, but because it will give the confessor a probable index to the cause of their sins and will enable him to give them salutary advice for the future.

Though it is not a sin to miss one's morning or evening prayer, it is nevertheless very unwise. Through these prayers we get God's help for the day, and we need His help very much. Just like breakfast—it is no sin to miss a breakfast but it would be unwise, because we cannot do our day's work so well. But it would be a sin to miss all our meals for a considerable time, because we would die. If we miss our prayers for a long time our soul will become so weak that the dread sickness of mortal sin may kill its spiritual life.

Holy Mass is greater even than prayer. In the Mass Jesus is present and worships His heavenly Father for us. No one knows better than our Saviour how to do this. He tells the Father for us, "You are God" and we join our prayers with His. He tells the Father for us, "You have been a good God to give the people all blessings" and we say likewise. Jesus tells the Father, "The people have sinned against You, their holy God, and I ask for their forgiveness" and we ask pardon too. Our Saviour tells His Father, "These boys and girls want more graces so that they can always be true to You" and we bow our heads and pray for more blessings. The Mass is the greatest action by which we can worship God, tell Him that He is our God. We worship God by Acts of Faith, Hope, and Charity and by adoring Him and praying to Him.

Summary by Example: During the reign of Diocletian, a universal decree went forth that all Christians were to be killed. Sixteen boys, recent converts to the Faith, presented themselves before the judge. The judge explained to the youngest of them how he could gain the emperor's favor by worshiping seventy false gods. The boy exclaimed, "There is but one God, the Father of Our Lord Jesus Christ. Your seventy gods shall burn in this fire." The tyrant commanded that the boy be roasted in the fire and shortly afterwards his companions too offered up their youthful lives for the truth that there is but one God. Here was a glorious exhibition of faith and hope in God, of love for God. Their feast is celebrated on September 24.

Organization: What is the first commandment of God? What do you tell God when you worship Him? What did Neil tell the boys on his baseball team? Tell the story of the Golden Calf. How did the people sin here? How can you tell God in a few words that He is above and greater than any one?—You worship God by telling Him that you believe everything He has said; you call it faith in God. Recite the Act of Faith. Name three things which you believe of God. You worship God by hoping in Him. Is God almighty? Name two things which you hope God will give you. —You worship God by loving Him. How must you love God? How can you show your love for God?—Suppose you pray for better health, how do you thereby show hope in God? What morning and night prayers do you say? Why is it very unwise to miss all your breakfasts? Then why is it very unwise to miss all your prayers? What is the biggest prayer of all? Tell the story of the sixteen boys and especially what the youngest one said to the bad ruler.

2. We Must Honor God Through His Saints and Holy Things

God loves the Saints. St. Agatha was the child of rich and noble parents. From her earliest infancy she was consecrated to God; and for the few years of life which God gave her, she served Him faithfully. The wicked ruler of her country, who had heard of her great wealth and beauty, called her before him hoping to lead her from the path of virtue. Agatha saw through his plans and she cried, "O Jesus Christ, I am Thine: save me from this wicked man!" For a whole month she was kept in prison but she answered every new temptation with the words, "Christ alone is my life and my salvation!" At the end of that time the ruler had her murdered and the young soul went to God.

God loved Agatha. While she was in prison He even sent her a consoling vision of the apostle, St. Peter. We cannot help but love this saintly maiden. Because God loved her, He certainly wants us to love her.

Catholics honor God by honoring God's saints. They do not adore or worship them; that would be as much as to say that they are gods. When they honor them they admire them for their virtue; they respect them because they are friends of God. We honor great people here on earth for similar reasons. We honor Abraham Lincoln because he liberated the slaves; we revere our mother because she is a good mother. When we admire God's works, we admire the God who made them. When we honor the saints, it is just as if we said: "Oh God, you must be wonderful to be able to make such wonderful saints."

God is pleased when the saints, His best children, are honored. A Father is pleased when his son is honored. When we honor Abraham Lincoln, we are proud that he lived in the United States, and we love our United States more. So does the honor given to saints turn our thoughts to God from whom they came.

As regards prayer, we beg the saints to ask favors of God for us. They themselves have nothing to give, as God has entire control of heaven's treasury but they go to God, and ask Him to open His treasury for us. We go to the favorites of God, we use the intercession of men and women who are more influential than we, and who are closer to God than we.

This is the time to make the class really practical. Probably the teacher can find a little time to look up the patron saints of some of the pupils. The saints are first of all to be imitated; what is there in the life of a particular patron saint which can be imitated? They were no different from us because children have become saints; St. Agatha is an example of a child-saint and there are many others. Next, they are to be chosen as intercessors before God. The greatest saint is the Blessed Virgin Mary. When we pray to the saints we ask them to offer their prayers to God for us.

We honor pictures and statues of the saints and of Christ. The same reasons why we erect monuments to great men in our parks hold for honoring of images of the saints. We gaze admiringly upon these statues and are inspired to model our lives after men they represent. We treasure a photograph of a dead friend, because we wish never to forget him; that is why, too, we treasure the images and pictures of the saints and of Christ.

Do we sometimes take the photograph of a dear friend into our hands and talk to him? Why? The picture cannot hear, but when we have the photograph before us we can picture him more distinctly. We seem to see him standing before us, and it makes it so much easier for us to talk to him. Seeing a picture or statue of a saint makes it easier for us to pray fervently to that saint. The same line of thought holds with crucifixes. We know that a clay figure has no life and cannot hear but the figure recalls the real Christ who can and does hear. We pray to the real Christ. We do not pray to the crucifix or to the images of Christ and of the saints, but to the persons of whom they remind us.

The teacher might take the pupils into the church and make them acquainted with all the saints whose pictures and images are there, or have them tell what pictures and images they have in the home. Perhaps they can even tell why this or that saint was preferred in the selection. What holy pictures have they?

Summary by Example: When Blessed Mary Hóss was three years old she had a vision of a beautiful boy dressed in rich robes. Being about to partake of her meal, she invited the little stranger to join her but he answered, "My Father has much better fruits in His garden than you have here."

"Where is your father?" asked Mary. "Where do you live? What is your name?"

The boy replied sweetly, "My Father is God the Father: My home is heaven. My name is Jesus and My Mother is the Blessed Virgin Mary." See how sweetly Jesus talked of His greatest saint, the Virgin Mary. See how He loved this saintly child, Blessed Mary Hóss. The child later became a Sister and her model of virtue was the Blessed Virgin from whom she had taken her name. She loved pictures of the saints because they reminded her of them. She often prayed before an image or crucifix of Christ because it helped her to picture Him in her imagination.

Motivation: The saints are very much interested in our welfare. We do not walk the path of life alone, for the saints are ever near us and listen to our call for help. One of the greatest joys in life is to possess friends, and every Catholic boy and girl has friends by the millions, the saints of God. They are our teachers. Every one of them gives us a heartening message: the sixteen boy martyrs tell us to be brave; St. Agatha tells us to be clean; St. Aloysius tells us to visit the Blessed Sacrament often; Blessed Imelda tells us how to receive Holy Communion. The saints are busy friends for they never sleep. If we wake in the night to call on the Little Flower, she listens at once and right away she carries our request to God. When we are truly happy, they are happy with us; when we are sick they sympathize with us. And surely God loves this great big happy family. Today especially we will try to make our patron saint happy by doing something noble which he used to do.

Organization: Briefly, tell the story of St. Agatha. Why did God love Agatha? Does your mother want you to love her friends? Why does God want you to love the saints? Name one great American whom we all honor. Why is this right? Why is it right to honor the great men and women in heaven? Is Mother pleased when her children are honored? Why is God pleased when His children, the saints, are honored? What do the saints do when you pray to them?—Of whom does a saint's picture or statue remind you? How does it help you to pray to that saint? Of whom does the crucifix remind you? Do the saints want to help you? What holy pictures are in your bedroom?

Reconstruction of Division I. Combine organizations 1 and 2 in order.

II. The Second Commandment of God

1. God's Name Must Be Honored

Q. What is the second commandment of God?
A. The second commandment of God is: Thou shalt not take the name of the Lord thy God in vain.

In studying the first commandment, we learn how to honor God's person, or in other words how to honor Him directly. Now we shall learn how to honor something very dear to Him, namely, His holy name. His name really stands for Him because every time we think of God we think of His name and vice versa; we cannot separate the two. The name may be Father or Son or Holy Ghost; it may be Jesus or Saviour or Redeemer, but each one stands for the all-holy God. God cannot be honored without thinking of His name and His name cannot be honored without thinking of God. God Himself is honored by using His name respectfully.

> Philip was roller skating with his chums. Without a moment's warning a heavy truck struck him, killing him instantly. The story is not unusually gruesome as city children are the objects of perennial campaigns, "Look before you cross."
>
> There was a comforting feature about the boy's death; he was a member of the Junior Holy Name Society and had an abiding respect for the name of God. Death called him suddenly but we can presume that he was prepared. William, his companion, heard him say, just as the truck struck him, "My Jesus, mercy!"

God Himself gave the motive for devout use of His name when He enunciated the very first commandment; "I am the Lord thy God." The holy name belongs to the One who created us and we should worshipfully give it our respect. It belongs to the Lord upon whom we depend and we should wisely respect it. "Jesus" is the name of Our Saviour and we should lovingly give it respect. As to the Mother of God and the saints, they are God's friends whom He wants revered; as our best friends, we should talk of them as a friend talks of a friend. Holy things were given by God to aid us in our salvation and we should talk reverently about them as objects dear to God.

Respect for holy names means talking respectfully and even thinking respectfully of any name which stands for a holy person. A name does stand for a person. If that person is noble, his name is noble; if he is a saint, his name is saintly; if the person is divine, His name in a way is divine. "Father" and "Mother" are lovable names because of the love in a father's and a mother's heart and because of the children's love for them. Revering the name, we revere the person, be it God or His saints.

Holy Names are: God, the Creator, our Saviour, our Lord, our Redeemer, Jesus Christ, the Holy Ghost, the Blessed Virgin Mary; the names of the saints, the names of the sacraments and the sacramentals.

Respect can be shown for God's name in various ways. The most common way is to bow the head at the mention of the holy name of Jesus. There is the custom of using little prayers or ejaculations containing the name of God, especially when passing a church; but such phrases must be used with very great devotion, otherwise the habit becomes so familiar as to be futile. Every prayer has the name of God or of His saints. It is well to give to the holy names just a little more attention than to the rest of the prayer. By the second commandment we are commanded always to speak with reverence of God, of the saints, and of holy things.

Summary by Example: A certain soldier had the bad habit of beginning every sentence with the words, "My God!" He was hit by a cannot ball and fatally wounded. When they brought him to the base hospital, the doctor informed him that he could not live. Then the soldier realized what God and eternity meant. He clasped his hands in prayer, looked up to heaven and for perhaps the first time in his life used the words as they should be used. With all the fervor of his heart now he said, "My God!"—For another example the pupils might ask themselves, "How did the Blessed Virgin use the name of Jesus when she stood at the foot of the cross?"

Organization: What is the second commandment of God? Of whom are you reminded when you say "Jesus"? Tell the story of Philip. Mention some holy names. How can you show respect when you hear the name, "Jesus"?

2. Bad Language Is Sinful

It is wiser if the teacher in this grade explains the truth in the proper place. There will be no unfortunate results because seven-year-old children are shocked almost as much by a venial sin as by a mortal sin.

Let the pupils repeat the second commandment. God says, "Thou shalt not." Who is God who thus forbids bad language? He is more than our father and certainly a boy would be careful to obey if Father said, "Thou shalt not." This is the God who owns us more than our own father does and He lays down a strict law here.

How terrible then when a boy stubbornly says, "But I will! I do not care if You do own me! I have no respect for You or Your name! You mean nothing to me! I'll say what I like!"

Nobody likes it. After lunch today Robert came crying to Sister. "The boys made fun of my name, Sister." They made nicknames of it. I don't like them to do that because it is a nice name." God does not like a misuse of His name either.

It is sinful to misuse holy names because it shows disrespect to the person who bears the name. How can anyone call himself a friend of the saints if he uses their names in a careless manner? Any boy will fight if another insults his mother. A Catholic boy should not insult the name of the Blessed Mother. The seriousness of the sin grows when the misuse concerns the name of God. A good Catholic feels like screaming in protest when he hears a curse with the holy name of Jesus.

Two sins are explained under the second commandment. To use God's name without the addition of "damn" is called using His name in vain. To add the word "damn" makes it the sin of cursing. People curse to emphasize a statement or because they are surprised or indignant. Children should be taught the necessity of self-control. Control of surprise and indignation not only prevents sin but it constitutes a good work. Would the one who misuses God's name, be ready like Philip if a truck suddenly ran over him? He is a manly boy who hits his thumb with a hammer and still retains control of his speech. Much can be expected of such a boy.

Summary by Example: In summation of the doctrine contained in this division, the teacher might tell another imaginary example, this time of a bad man who was hit by a truck. Suppose at the instant he saw death threatening him, that he had used the holy name of Jesus irreverently. The next moment he was whisked into eternity. How did that man meet His Eternal Judge?

Motivation: Catholics must be more careful in their speech, when talking about holy persons or things, than any one else. They know so much more about God and His saints that their references to them should be more respectful. How well the saints understood this language! They drew men to the faith by their devout speech. The martyrs during their long sufferings called incessantly upon the holy name of Jesus; they died with the holy name on their lips.

Nothing outside of the sacraments so comforts a Christian in life as the name of Jesus. It is a sweet name, sweet as honey for it seems to melt upon the lips. To say it prayerfully, seems to cool our tempted soul, to revive the sick. O let all pray that they may have the great grace to die with that holy name upon their lips.

Organization: Why do you dislike boys and girls making fun of your name? Tell the story of Robert. Why does God not like

it when you make little of His name? On whose name did the martyrs call when they were dying? What is the last name you want to mention before you die?
Reconstruction of Division II.

III. The Third Commandment of God

1. The Lord's Day Is Holy

Q. What is the third commandment of God?
A. The third commandment of God is: Remember thou keep holy the Lord's Day.

We have learned that we must honor God's person and even His name. Here we shall learn just when we must give God special honor or worship.

God did not want us to forget Him, so He Himself made a law, when we must give Him special worship. If it were left to ourselves, we might easily forget. So He gives us a commandment which He starts with the word, "Remember" and He tells us that we must give Him special worship on Sunday. Of course He wants us to worship Him oftener than on one day but He makes a commandment of the worship that must be given to Him on this particular day. We shall learn moreover how we are to worship Him on Sunday.

> Sunday marks a reunion of God's children. John and Mary longed to see their children once more, for it was a long time since they had left the old homestead to make their homes far away. With shaking hand Mary wrote to the three daughters and the two sons. The answers were that they would be glad to come and that Mother was to let them furnish the meal. And what a joy there was on that day! The children brought great joy to their aged parents and they themselves were consoled and strengthened by the reunion. God too wants to meet His children, yes, He insists on meeting them at regular times.

This third commandment is one of solemn warning, as contained in the word "Remember." We recall how serious and threatening our father speaks when he gives us a warning with the word "remember." He is giving us a very serious order, and if we do not obey Him, we will offend Him severely. Just that word and sharp look makes us think. We are hushed, for Father means what he says. We can imagine that God was very serious when He gave this commandment, as if He said sternly: "I do not ask much of you, but I do demand that you keep holy one day a week to Me, and if you do not, you must beware of My wrath,—remember."

Right from the beginning God insisted on a worship, called sacrifice. Such were the sacrifices of Abel and Cain. When Noe was saved from the deluge, he offered a sacrifice. Abraham was called upon to offer the greatest worship of all—the sacrifice of his own son. When Solomon dedicated the new Temple, the worship continued for several days. God commanded that the people offer Him worship when He gave the law to Moses.

God is the Father of all, who wants His children to gather about Him on certain days to show their respect and love for Him. God has commanded that they worship Him every seventh day in a particular manner, namely on Sunday. Sunday is called the Lord's Day for He wants them to give their principal thought to Him on this one day of the week. He lets them think principally of themselves on the other six days. On Sundays they must gather round Him to worship Him, to thank Him, to ask His pardon for their sins, and to ask His blessing. The Lord's Day should be a day of good works from morning until night, when the faithful add grace to their souls and make themselves more pleasing to Him. They should thank Him that He has insisted on a day when they can pay more attention to their soul's welfare. Millions will be saved because of the good works they do on the Lord's Day. By the third commandment we are commanded to worship God in a special manner on Sunday, the Lord's Day.

Summary by Example: Children often gather about their father to give him special respect and love. One child can play the piano; another can sing. Perhaps teacher has taught one child a little poem for Father. These occasions are most proper; they are pleasant for parents. It is necessary to have such special days in the Church that the faithful remember the duty they owe to their Father in heaven.

The Mass is the principal worship on Sunday. Of all the good works which can be offered to God on Sunday, attendance at Mass is the greatest. It is the prayer of prayers, the work that stands out amongst others like a mighty mountain amid lesser hills. The

Grade II III. The Third Commandment of God

Mass is the great work established by Christ Himself. The Our Father is the greatest prayer because Christ made it, but the Mass is worth more than a thousand Our Fathers. It is a continuation of that work which, of all that Christ did on earth, pleased His Father the most, namely, the sacrifice of the cross. The Mass prayers thank God, ask pardon of God, request His blessing. The Mass is so great a work that it is no wonder God has set aside a special day for us to attend in a public manner. We offer that Mass with the angels who are present in the sanctuary: with Christ Himself who tenders His work and our good work to His heavenly Father. It is one good work offered by Christ and ourselves. **To hear Mass is obligatory on Sundays.**

To miss Mass through one's fault is a mortal sin. The following are unlawful excuses for missing Mass: a journey to the old swimming hole instead of to church; lingering in the pleasant waters when the church bell rings; starting on an excursion before the earliest Mass; journeying to a town where there is no Catholic church, etc. Recreation is not sinful and can even be sanctified by a good intention, but how bounteously would God bless a soul which really would make the entire day the Lord's Day.

Other good works are optional but advisable. The ideal way to spend the Sunday is really to make it the Lord's day by sanctifying every minute, either by prayer or by pious intention. Very often other services besides the Mass are held, and the faithful should endeavor to assist with great fervor; such are Benediction of the Blessed Sacrament and other evening devotions.

Pupils are not to be forced to attend daily Mass, but rather are to be piously urged to attend once or twice during the week, because of the blessings connected therewith. Training children to do a little more than is necessary, insures them at least always doing what is strictly necessary. The Church commands us to worship God on Sunday by assisting at the Holy Sacrifice of the Mass.

Summary by Example: She was a Catholic school-teacher in a little western village where there was no Catholic church. In one town twenty miles to the north and in another thirty miles to the south there were Masses on alternate Sundays. Would you have gotten to Mass? This teacher never missed a Sunday. In one direction she would take a twenty-mile bus ride and in the other a thirty-mile train ride.

Organization: What is the third commandment of God? Tell

the story of the old couple who gathered their children around them for a reunion. When does God want His children to gather round Him? What does He want all Catholic boys and girls to do on Sunday? What kind of sin is it to miss Sunday Mass without a good reason? Why is going on a picnic not enough reason to miss Mass?

2. We Must Avoid Unnecessary Work

Catholics act becomingly on the Lord's Day. *Example:* In many homes there is a celebration in honor of Father on Father's day. Friends are invited; the house is prettily decorated; the children put on their best clothes. All actions that would be unbecoming on this day are avoided. Father is the center of attention as all gather around to pay him their respects and to make the day a memorable one for him.

For the same reason God has made Sunday a day of rest. On this one day He wants the undivided attention of His people. He wants them to worship Him on Sunday with their whole heart, their whole soul, their whole strength. He has commanded it; they owe it to Him.

It is not enough to sanctify the Sunday with the half-hour or hour at Mass but the whole day must be made holy. Catholics may not therefore engage in occupations which are unbecoming on God's day. Hard work under most conditions is prohibited because it takes the mind away from God and makes us too tired to worship Him fittingly.

Unnecessary hard work is forbidden. *Examples:* Washing or greasing an automobile; repairing a house; doing garden or field work; sewing or patching; baking bread; cleaning house; washing or scrubbing floors.

Necessary work is allowed. *Examples:* Cooking the meals on Sundays or holydays; sweeping the kitchen and dining room after meals; dressing and washing and preparing children for church; making the beds; keeping the fires going during the winter; feeding the cattle, milking the cows. The milkman may make his deliveries on Sunday because milk is an important item of food, especially for children.

The following occupations are not considered hard work and are not therefore sinful: studying our lessons; practicing the piano; fishing and boating; driving an automobile for recreation;

III. The Third Commandment of God

any form of recreation as long as it is not too noisy and held too near a church. By the third commandment of God all unnecessary servile work on Sunday is forbidden.

The practical conclusions for the lesson can be the questions: Did I miss Mass through my own fault? Did I come in after the Offertory? Did I attend Mass devoutly? Did I do forbidden work?

A Story: The man was a very avaricious miller. In order to increase his gains he repaired his machinery on Sunday and even continued making flour. Four blocks away lived his competitor, a God-fearing Catholic, who would not let a wheel turn on Sunday even for very great profit, and who always took the time to go to the High Mass on Sundays. You would think the greedy miller would get rich long before his Catholic competitor. Not so: God sees. The greedy man did not prosper with seven days of toil: the man who went to Mass became very wealthy. It often happens that way; God blesses those who go to Mass on Sunday.

Motivation: The consideration of death. We must all be careful about this greatest commandment lest we be suddenly called to account with a mortal sin on the soul. We know not whether we will die young or old. Many a man who had the bad habit of missing Mass, expected to die when he was old, but he died when young and unprepared. It may be tomorrow; it may be today. We may be conscious in our last hours, so that we can make our peace with God. But we may also be unconscious or in such pain that we cannot elicit an Act of Contrition. Now suppose we had done forbidden work on the previous Sunday or even missed Mass. Will death come when we are in bed, surrounded by friends, and the priest at our side? Or will it occur far from home and friends, and far from a Catholic priest? But no matter what happens, if we say, "Oh Lord, I have always sanctified the Lord's Day," we will approach this moment with great confidence.

Organization: Why do you think it would be wrong for you to work all day around the automobile while your father is celebrating his birthday? Why may you do no hard work on the Lord's day? May you mow the lawn on Sunday? May you study your lessons on Sunday? May Mother prepare Sunday dinner? Tell the story of the two millers.—Do you know when or where or how you will die? Then what should you resolve about attending Mass on Sunday?

Reconstruction of Division III.

UNIT FOUR: THE FOURTH TO THE TENTH COMMANDMENT—OUR DUTIES TO OURSELVES AND TO OTHERS

I. THE FOURTH COMMANDMENT OF GOD.
   1. CHILDREN MUST HONOR THEIR PARENTS.
   2. CHILDREN MUST LOVE AND HELP PARENTS.
   3. CHILDREN MUST OBEY THEIR PARENTS.
   4. ALL MUST RESPECT AND OBEY THEIR SUPERIORS.

II. THE FIFTH COMMANDMENT OF GOD.
   1. PROPER CARE OF BODY AND SOUL.
   2. INJURY TO BODY OR SOUL IS FORBIDDEN.

III. THE SIXTH COMMANDMENT OF GOD.
   1. THE DUTY TO BE PURE AND CLEAN.
   2. EXAMPLES OF PURITY.

IV. THE SEVENTH COMMANDMENT OF GOD.
   1. WE MUST BE FAIR.
   2. STEALING IS FORBIDDEN.
   3. WRONGS MUST BE RIGHTED.

V. THE EIGHTH COMMANDMENT OF GOD.
   1. THE DUTY TO SPEAK THE TRUTH.
   2. WHAT THE COMMANDMENT FORBIDS.

VI. THE NINTH COMMANDMENT OF GOD.
   1. ST. STANISLAUS, PURE AS A PURE WHITE LILY.

VII. THE TENTH COMMANDMENT OF GOD.
   1. WE MUST BE SATISFIED, NOT COMPLAIN.
   2. WE MAY TRY TO BETTER OURSELVES.

What We Shall Learn: During the last few weeks we have been studying our duties to God because naturally we must think first of God, our Creator. But God made persons and things; He made us, our neighbor, all the animals, the birds, the trees, the flowers, everything. He made these, owns these and wants us to regard them as His property to be handled accordingly.

We and our neighbor belong to God and so God has given us

seven commandments where He explains our duties to ourselves and to our neighbor. We and the neighbor are like two houses on the same street, owned by the same man. One has as much right to be on that street as the other. So God has made us, has made our neighbor and He has placed us in the same world.—This unit must be taught orally.

I. The Fourth Commandment of God

1. Children Must Honor Their Parents

Q. What is the fourth commandment of God?
A. The fourth commandment of God is: Honor thy father and thy mother.

When God talks of your neighbor, He includes all men, Chinese, Indians, Negroes, white men. Some of these are closer to you because they are related to you or have conferred favors upon you for which you owe them respect and gratitude. Naturally then your closest neighbors are your own parents to whom you owe honor more than to any other human being.

> The Lazy Robin.—A young robin was very lazy and every morning he slept longer than the rest of the robins. Finally came the time for the birds to fly south where it was warmer. The lazy robin wanted to wake up in time to go with the rest because he did not know the way. But again he overslept. Not a robin was in sight and now the lazy little fellow feared that left alone, he would freeze to death. After a time he heard a chirp and there was his mother who had come back after him. She directed his course to the warmer country. If a bird could be grateful, that little robin certainly should have been obedient to its mother as long as it was under her care.

Children must honor their parents. To honor parents means first of all to respect them. A child's parents have a nobler relation to him than the mother-robin had to the lazy little robin. Children owe their parents respect because of the noble place parents have in God's holy plan. God places them over the children. Parents may be poor or sick or not very learned but they are honorable because appointed by God. Suppose the President of this country would appoint the father of a boy in this class to a high office, would not that boy be proud and tell all the other boys about it? God who is greater than the President, has appointed parents to their high office, has given them charge of the children and the home.

Parents deserve respect because they are noble beings who do noble things for children. They spend many hours deliberating how they can help their children for later life, make them useful to God and men. Parents are real heroes because they work and suffer for their children. Many a father and mother has given up his or her life for children. National heroes are respected because they have done great deeds for their country. Parents are doing noble deeds for their children all the time.

Children can show respect to parents by being polite and courteous to them. A cheerful "Good morning" means that they wish them well for the whole day. A loving "Good night" means that they are mindful of the favors which parents showed them during the day. A "Thank you" frequently repeated proves that children know from whom the favors come. When Father or Mother talks, children do not interrupt but listen courteously and attentively. Good children are proud to be seen in the company of their parents.

Not to respect parents is to disrespect them. This means refusing parents that honor which is due to them, making little of them, being ashamed of them.

Summary by Example: The teacher may tell the pupils the story, Joseph is sold into Egypt. Joseph respected his father more than the other brothers did, so Jacob loved him more. To reward Joseph for his respect, the father gave him a coat of many colors. When Jacob ordered the boy to visit his brothers, Joseph listened respectfully and carried out his father's wish at once. No wonder that Jacob grieved deeply when such a respectful son had disappeared.—Then, How can I be polite to my parents today?

Organization: Recite the fourth commandment of God. All people are your neighbors, but who is your closest neighbor? Tell the story of the Lazy Robin. How should that little robin have behaved after it was saved by its mother?—*Respect:* Who gave your parents charge over you? Tell two noble things which your parents do for you when they teach you, when you are sick. How can you show respect to your parents in the morning, at night, during the day? Explain how Joseph respected his father, Jacob.

2. Children Must Love and Help Parents

A Son who loved his Mother.—She was an old mother bent

with the years and crippled with a life of heavy work. Her only joy now was to attend daily, the Mass which her priest-son celebrated at the neighboring parish church. But it was such a long distance to walk. Every single morning, that priest-son drove his car to the old home and lifted his mother tenderly into her seat. People used to watch them when they arrived at the church. How tenderly he grasped her arm and assisted her up one stone step after the other nor did he leave her until she was comfortably placed in her regular seat beside the pillar.

The second duty of children under the word "honor" is to love their parents. They must love all men, but especially their parents. If all men are their neighbors, parents are doubly so. Are they not the greatest benefactors they have? Every stitch of clothing, every bit of food, shelter, education, are all contributed by parents through many long years. Is it not strange how children will run home excitedly and tell Mother that some man gave them a nickel; parents give clothes and food worth ten thousand times more than that nickel. Do children realize that by the time they are twenty-one their parents have spent a large sum on their support, and if the sons or daughters have been benefited by having been given a higher education, how much more their parents show love for them in going to such a burden of expense. The children have not contributed one cent! Do they ever realize how tenderly parents care for them in infancy and in sickness?

True love is not satisfied with sentiment but translates itself into loving words and actions. It is indeed very proper for children to tell their parents often how much they love them. There are many children who kiss their parents before they retire for the night. But loving actions are still better than kisses. Little Jane and Albert can run happily towards Father when he returns from work. Both can assist parents in many ways. They can make good use of their school time because parents wish it. They can take good care of the books and clothes which their parents give them. Jane can help around the kitchen and Albert around the lawn.

Not to love parents may mean to be unkind to them, impolite, ungrateful, to slight them, to hurt them by cutting arguments and remarks.

The practical question is, How can I show love to my parents today?

Summary by Example: Grace told Mother the story of the Lazy Robin. That little robin, she explained, had caused its mother a lot of worry but when the little fellow was in danger of being frozen, the mother returned to save him. Mother Robin reminded Jane of her own mother. Mothers are not trying to make children do hard things just to annoy them. They want only to help their children, to make them good and holy. To show her own love Grace picked a bouquet of beautiful flowers and presented it to her mother.

Organization: Tell the story of the priest who helped his mother.—*Love:* Tell three things which your parents do for you as to clothes, food and a home. How can you act lovingly towards your parents by helping them, by taking good care of the things given you?

3. Children Must Obey Their Parents

Parents try to direct their children wisely. The traffic policeman stands in the center of the intersection directing autos and people to stop or to go. It is not his intention to punish any one but to help all.

"The traffic policeman makes me think of you and mother," Paul said to his father. "You tell me to go ahead and do something. Then you tell me to stop and not do something."

"Yes, that policeman has received his job from the mayor and the people must obey him. Your mother and I have received our job from God and God Himself says that you must obey us."

Parents have received authority from God to rule and to command their children. It should become very pleasant to obey when children realize that the command really comes from God and that by obeying their parents, they obey God. Parents enjoy the same authority in the home as a king in his kingdom. Obedience is necessary to make a home orderly and happy. Parents have the duty from God to make a peaceful home; children have the duty from God to help by being obedient.

Parents have the wisdom that comes from experience and therefore it is reasonable to obey them, "in all that is not sinful";—God is first and no one may command another to offend Him. There used to be a song, "Always take Mother's advice" and the same goes for Father. When Father says, "Do not go to that show," he knows why. Many a time he has heard how little boys end up badly who went to every show. When Mother says, "Jane, help me with the work," she knows why. Many times Jane was told what happens to little girls who are lazy. God Himself rewards children who are obedient. A long, long time ago He said that He would bless those who are respectful, loving and obedient to their parents.

To obey is a duty; to disobey is a sin. It is not for the child to ask whether it likes to do something; the fourth commandment orders it to obey without any "ifs" and "ands." Commands of parents are of two kinds, either to do something or not to do it. Mother may call up the stairs, "James get up!" or she may say, "Dorothy, do not walk over that newly varnished floor!" For either to disobey is a sin, although in the case of children the sin will hardly be more than venial.

No to obey, is to disobey. The sin can arise from a refusal to do something or to avoid something. If Jane refuses to sweep the kitchen floor, she sins; so does Harry who goes skating when Mother told him not to go on that treacherous ice. By the fourth commandment we are commanded to respect and love our parents, to obey them in all that is not sinful, and to help them when they are in need.

Summary by Example: Paul was still talking about the traffic policeman. "You compare me with that policeman," explained Father. "Notice how the officer really helps. If he did not direct traffic, there would be one smash-up after the other and many people would be killed. Mother and I direct you only to help you. We do not want you to go with a bad companion, so we direct you to the opposite route. We do not want you to run a knife into your hand, so we say 'Stop'! We do not want you to follow sin, so we say 'Stop'! We want you to go on the road of a good life so we say, 'Go'! Do you notice, Paul, how kind those policemen are, how they help little children across the street? Mother and I are your kind guides who want to do our best by you because we have been appointed by God to care for you."

The practical question is, Have I disobeyed by parents? And the resolve, I will obey my parents always.

Organization: Describe what the traffic policeman does. How does he help the people as they cross the street? Do your parents want to help you when they say, "Stop doing that," or "Go and do that"? Who gave your parents the right to order you about? Why do your parents know more than you do and why do they mean everything for your good? Tell three things which your parents might order you to do. What did Paul tell his father about the traffic policeman?

4. All Must Respect and Obey Their Superiors

Read the Bible Story, Joseph is made Governor of Egypt. God also gives us other superiors. Joseph was now in new surroundings. Instead of a parent, he now had superiors. As he had respected and obeyed his father, so did he now respect and obey these superiors. He obeyed Putiphar first of all. He did not murmur against the ruler of the land when he was wrongly imprisoned. So signal was his respect for the king that later on he was deemed worthy to be made the Governor of Egypt. Joseph looked upon his lawful superiors as representatives of God.

Our superiors are the bishop, the pastor, the sister in the classroom. If an older person is appointed temporarily to take charge of the home, that person for the time being is our superior. (Only the superiors are mentioned with whom the child comes into contact.)

Scripture is full of exhortations to respect and obey those in authority. Catholics are glad when the President is honored by the large crowds that wish to see him; they think it right when the Army or the Navy maneuver to do him honor. And thus it goes too, with those who hold lesser positions over them.

Great honor is given our bishop when he visits the parish. A procession is arranged for him, in which the children take part. At the altar he is surrounded with much more ceremony than a celebrating priest. It is the bishop's due, because God approves his high place over the people.

Whenever we meet the priest we greet him respectfully. A boy raises his hat. We address him with the beautiful title of "Father" because he is like a father to us and because the fourth commandment bids us to do honor to all in authority.

The teacher in school is given respect because she was appointed by our pastor, and given authority by the parents who send their children to her grade.

Summary by Example: When Joseph became a superior over

others he dealt justly with all the people. He made fair laws for rich and poor and he treated all alike. Joseph realized that his authority came from God and that people owed him obedience only because he was now the representative of God.

Motivation: Jesus gave the great example of obedience. He knew more than any boy or girl in this classroom, knew more than Joseph or Mary because He was God, yet He most willingly obeyed them. When He was a little boy He did just what little children are asked to do today. He went, when He was told to do some shopping for His mother; He obeyed at once, when He was sent on an errand to a neighbor or elsewhere. Often too He helped His mother to dry the dishes. In the afternoon He helped Joseph in the carpenter's shop, and when the day's work was done, He swept up the shavings. And who was Jesus? He was God. If a God could do these simple tasks, we can do them too. Did Jesus our God, perform these tasks of obedience when He was a little boy only? No, He did them for thirty years. If this grown-up God-man could help Mary and help Joseph, then surely little children can help parents and obey them. How shall they prove their respect, love and obedience to their parents today? What did Jesus do and what will they do? They want to become like Jesus.

Organization: How did Joseph act towards his superiors in the new land? Name two of your superiors. How is the bishop honored when he visits your parish? How do you greet your priest? How do you show respect to your teacher? Describe the life of Jesus of Nazareth. Whom did he help? For how long did He help them?

Reconstruction of Division I.

II. The Fifth Commandment of God

1. Proper Care of Body and Soul

Q. What is the fifth commandment of God?
A. The fifth commandment of God is: Thou shalt not kill.

All men are our neighbors, including even ourselves, for God commanded us to love ourselves with a true love, such as will bring us to life eternal. In studying this commandment we shall learn about a terrible sin, namely killing. Now, little children do not kill themselves or anybody else, but the commandment takes in many other sins such as hurting ourselves or others. Killing is a big hurt but there can be also little hurts; we may not hurt ourselves or our neighbor in any way. The commandment goes even further and commands love of neighbor. God has said, "Love your neighbor as yourself." As you want people to do kind deeds for you, so should you do kind deeds for them.

Read the Bible Story, Joseph and His Brethren. The story is an example of how all must take care of their own life and that of their neighbor. Acting on the prophecy of Joseph, the Egyptians expected seven fat years and seven lean years. During the good years they stored their grain to prepare for the lean years. The king and his officers wanted to have enough food to live on when the crops would fail and they saw to it that their people would also have enough food then. The famine that followed was widespread and even Jacob and his family suffered. The Patriarch knew that it was his duty to care for himself and those entrusted to him, so he sent his sons to Egypt to buy food. Joseph could have refused them because of their uncharity to him, but being a man of God he knew that he must care even for his enemies and so he gave them food.

Men are given the years of life in order to serve their God and save their souls. Health promotes long life so that God can be served better and for a longer time. Life and health therefore are precious possessions. They are gifts of God which men must handle as carefully as any other gift. Body and soul, our own and our neighbor's, are gifts from God that must be properly cared for.

Children must take care of their health. They should observe cleanliness of body; bathing and cleaning the teeth are part of this routine. They should be happy when the school nurse examines their eyes, their teeth, their ears. If they get sick, they should willingly do what doctor and parents tell them. Parents provide food in order to preserve their health. If Mother orders the frequent drinking of milk, children should know that it is for their own good to obey. *Example:* When Dad wants to take a long trip he looks over the car carefully, oils it well, puts in good gasoline. He depends on his car to take him over the long distance. The body must carry the soul over the long journey of life; the soul is the valuable passenger. Proper care must be given this vehicle (the body) that it carry the soul through life as long as God wills it.

Grade II II. The Fifth Commandment of God

Children must have a care for the well-being of their neighbor. They must live at peace with their playmates, be pleasant with them, must talk kindly with them and of them. They visit them, play with them in order to make them happy. They try to make them good by giving good example. They try to help their neighbor not only on the road of life but also on the road to heaven. *Example:* Perhaps the little boy next door has a big job of mowing his lawn. Perhaps the little girl in the next seat has difficulty in doing her problems. A little push, a little word is really a very kind work which will please Almighty God.

It falls under this commandment to be kind to animals and not to torment them; they also are gifts of God created by Him for our use and enjoyment. The story of St. Francis and the birds is a good example. By the fifth commandment we are commanded to take proper care of our own spiritual and bodily well-being and that of our neighbor.

Summary by Example: Little Margaret had been badly crippled in an accident and could walk only with the aid of a crutch. The boys and girls loved Margaret because she had always been very kind. Even now she found time to cut out pictures for William and to cover Lucy's books. William, next door, had a new wagon which he called, "Red Flash." Every day he would send Lucy and Stella to get Margaret and place her carefully in the wagon. The fresh air brought color to the cripple's cheeks. Her mother said, "You children are helping my girl very much and I think she will soon be well now."

They loved especially to drive on that street covered by the elm trees. There was a little slope and Lucy suggested that they go faster. "No," said Stella, "we might turn Margaret over and hurt her so badly that she would never get well."

At the end of the street was a little church. The three of them had a way of lifting the wagon over the two outside steps so that they could pull "Red Flash" right up the center aisle. Margaret would bow her head and the other three kneel in the pew to say sweet prayers to Jesus in the tabernacle.

The practical conclusion is, How can I help my playmates today?

Organization: Recite the fifth commandment of God. God forbids big hurts. Does He also forbid little hurts to your own body and to that of your neighbor? How did Jacob try to care for himself and his sons when the famine came? For what purpose does God give you life and health? Then why should you take care of your health, as to teeth, as to baths. What should you do when the school nurse tells you to go to a doctor? Should you eat only sweet things? What about drinking milk? How should you act towards your playmates? How can you help them? How should you treat a pet animal or bird? Tell the story of little Margaret who was crippled.

2. Injury to Body and Soul Is Forbidden

The brothers of Joseph had first resolved to kill him but later compromised by throwing him into a pit.—King Herod killed many little children hoping to kill Jesus amongst them.

Killing another is a very great sin because the murderer takes away life, which is that person's greatest possession. God alone has the right to say when life shall end for any one because God owns every life; a murderer takes to himself a right which belongs to God alone. Killing oneself is also a very great sin because no one has the right to end his own life as it likewise belongs to God.

The fifth commandment forbids any kind of injury to ourselves and others whether very big, less big or little. Whatever human action actually inflicts injury or can inflict it, is sinful when deliberately done. A man injures his neighbor in his own mind when he hates him or desires revenge on him; in this state he pictures himself as hurting him, abusing him. When a boy is angry he fights his playmate in his mind and pictures himself as saying hurtful things to him. In a quarrel two people actually do say mean things that hurt and injure. In a fight they try to do bodily injury to one another. Cruelty is uncharity and we may not be uncharitable in deed or in thought.

To defend oneself against unjust attack is not sinful. Likewise to be angry that God has been offended is no sin. Thus parents and teachers may be justly angry with the lawbreakers in their charge, as long as they do not lose control of themselves. *Example:* Moses was justly angry when he found the Israelites adoring the golden calf.

Dangers. Children should not undertake unnecessary hazards which endanger life. They should not unnecessarily expose themselves to catching colds or any other sickness. When they get sick they should take the medicine the doctor orders. When boys are old enough to drive an auto, they should proceed at a safe speed. Children skating in winter, should stay on safe ice. They should

Grade II — II. The Fifth Commandment of God

cross the streets carefully; they should help younger children across.

Summary by Example: Rob had joyfully rolled the snow together and built a snow-man. He wanted to surprise his sister, Bessie, so he went into the house to call her. Tom, a mischievous boy next door, had watched the operation and now ran across the yard and kicked the snow-man to pieces. When Rob and Bessie appeared they saw only the ruins of the figure. Rob saw his tormentor and picking up a stick he was about to strike him. Then he remembered what his father had once told him, "You are master of the stick while it is in your hand; let it fly and you cease to be its master." In an instant Rob realized now seriously he could injure his enemy. He checked his anger and quietly he and Bessie made a snow-man in another part of the yard. Tom was really ashamed of himself when he saw how nobly Rob had acted. The next day at school he begged Rob's pardon.

A little word may lead to a big quarrel, and a big quarrel to a serious injury. The practical question is, Did I fight or quarrel? Was I angry?

Motivation: Jesus loves our little neighbors and so should we. One time He gathered a lot of little children about Him and blessed them. They were children of the neighborhood, probably of the same age as the pupils in this classroom. He did not ask them a lot of questions first, "What's your name? Who is your Father? Have you nice clothes?" It was enough that they were little friends of God and were therefore His friends.

We must not make any difference between the children that we know. If Jesus loves them, we can love them. Jesus wants to help all of them and we should try to help all. Jesus did just as much for them as He did for us.

Two flowers were having an argument. "I'm nicer than you because I am red." said the first. To which the other replied, "I'm nicer because I am white."

Then the man who owned the flower beds came out and spoke to them. "You are both nice as I like both red and white flowers. I planted you both, so I am satisfied with both of you."

God likes us all and He put us all here. He likes all kinds of children, white ones, red ones, Chinese children and Negro children.

Organization: Tell the story of the bad King Herod. Who gave you life? Who gave your neighbor life? Who alone has the right to end your life or that of your neighbor? Why must you avoid danger to your body. How can you avoid danger like catching colds, when the doctor orders you to take medicine, when you go skating, when you cross a busy street? Is it sinful to quarrel, to fight, to get angry? May a boy defend himself when another hits him? Tell the story of the snow-man. Tell the story of the argument between the white and the red flower. Since God loves all children what should you do?

Reconstruction of Division II.

III. The Sixth Commandment of God

1. The Duty to Be Pure and Clean

Q. What is the sixth commandment of God?
A. The sixth commandment of God is: Thou shalt not commit adultery.

The sixth commandment will be covered very briefly, with more space given to the positive than to the negative presentation. For many reasons, physical and otherwise, children of this age can hardly sin grievously in this regard. Though Sister may catch one or the other doing "something terrible" she may generally judge that the sin was a material one and not a formal one.

At this time we shall learn how we can become the most beloved friends of Jesus. Purity of mind and body is that precious gift which can make us angels on earth and the beloved friends of God. We call the Blessed Virgin "Mother most pure" and we love her for it. Mary is our mother and we her children will learn how we can become more and more like her by being pure.

Consider the example of Mary most pure. The Church places her before us as the model of purity, calls her a virgin, a virgin most chaste, a mother most pure. The pastor calls upon the children to march in the May procession and sing hymns like "Mother purest, Mother fairest." The teacher might tell the story of the Annunciation.

"Modesty in looks." It is not necessary nor wise to see everything. Because unclean thoughts often enter through the eyes, we must keep a good guard on those gates of the soul. Notice how Sisters observe modesty of eyes as they pass through the street.

"Modesty in behaviour." We should wear modest clothes. Our posture must always be modest, especially in play when we are

Grade II   III. The Sixth Commandment of God   183

indulging in violent exercise. By the sixth commandment we are commanded to be pure and modest in our outward behaviour.

Seven-year-olds should be cautioned only about unnecessary impure touches. Probably they are not morally responsible for anything further. The intention to derive pleasure therefrom need not be explained, just that they are unnecessary. Necessary or accidental touches in the bathroom are not sinful.

It will be wise to caution the children against consorting with bad companions, and to advise them of the necessity of prayer to the Blessed Virgin for the gift of purity. As yet they cannot realize the full import of this advice but with the years, perhaps even months, their sex knowledge will grow and they will recall the warning.

Organization: Recite the sixth commandment of God. How pure was the Blessed Virgin? What kind of thoughts must you always have in your mind? How shall you dress? What unnecessary things must you avoid?

2. Examples of Purity

The story offered here is briefly told. It may be well for the teacher to consult a larger work so that she can tell it in greater detail. The aim is to explain how children can preserve purity.

Pure As Snow.—The life of the Little Flower of Jesus affords many inspiring examples of chastity; besides, St. Therese always appeals to children. Quite a story can be made of the miracle of the snow. The little Saint had prayed for snow on the day of her reception. All weather indications were to the contrary that morning but as the people gazed out of the window after the services they saw snow on the ground. After Therese's death, her spiritual adviser told the world how pure this little Saint had been. She did those things which preserve purity. She had a tender devotion to the Blessed Virgin; she loved work; she received Holy Communion daily. She was pure as snow.

Purity is a priceless jewel. As the man who owns a costly gem will take every precaution to safeguard it, we must also use every means to preserve purity. The teacher can make quite a story of an imaginary person who has a valuable jewel in his house.

Prayer is a very powerful help for the preservation of purity. By it we call upon God directly to keep us pure. By prayer too we give our mind the cleanest possible occupation. Prayer cleanses the mind: a clean mind has clean thoughts; clean thoughts make chastity.

Mary has been placed before us as a model of chastity. Being so chaste herself she is interested in keeping us chaste. Daily we should practice some devotion to her in order to get the special benefit of her intercession. Prayer is good but the greatest devotion to Mary is to imitate her. To imitate Mary we must begin with chastity.

Holy Communion increases grace, increases fervor and preserves us from mortal sin. We should receive Holy Communion frequently. The more grace we have, the better we will practice purity. The more fervor we have, the more easily we will practice it.

Summary by Example: To conclude the section the teacher will tell the story of St. Bernadette of Lourdes. It is not necessary to recount it at length here. Every detail proves that a pure child was talking with the "Virgin most pure." The Blessed Virgin revealed herself by a title which indicates the height of chastity, "I am the Immaculate Conception."

The repetition is a story-hour that will impress seven-year-olds far better than explanations. It is necessary only to use the terms, "clean," "pure," "pure as snow" as often as possible.

A POEM

Dear Mother Mary
  As we kneel,
To thy goodness
  We appeal.

Guard us, dear Mother
  Through the day
In all our work
  And all our play.

When darkness comes
  The day to hide,
May we still feel thee
  Close beside.

Mother Mary, keep my soul
  Pure from every sin,
So my little soul will smile
  When He enters in.

—*Adelaide Proctor.*

Organization: Tell the story of the Little Flower and the Snow.

What can you do morning and night to help you remain pure? What sacrament helps you to remain pure? Whom will you imitate for purity? Tell the story of St. Bernadette of Lourdes.

IV. The Seventh Commandment of God

1. We Must Be Fair

Q. What is the seventh commandment of God?
A. The seventh commandment of God is: Thou shalt not steal.

We want others to respect what is ours. Children have toys with which they while away their time and certainly they want to keep these toys. Some children live far away from school and so must bring their lunch for the noon-hour; they expect to find the lunch where they stored it when it is time to eat. They must have books by which to study their lessons; when it is time to study spelling, they rightly expect to reach into the desk and find their Speller. God made a commandment bidding all to respect the things owned by others.

John Linden owned a beautiful bicycle which he called "Speed King." "What a beautiful wheel!" exclaimed Robert. "Where did you get it?" "My father gave it to me for a birthday present."

"I'll give you six mibs," proposed Robert, "if you let me ride Speed King around the next two blocks." "It's a bargain," replied John, "but be sure to take good care of it; it's my bike and I have the right to use it as long as I own it."

"I'll be back in five minutes," and away went Robert. At the far corner two boys ran after Speed King, begging for a ride. "No," answered Robert, "the bike is not mine and I promised to be back in five minutes."

Robert respected the property of his friend. He lived up to his agreement to return in five minutes. When he dismounted he paid his debt of six mibs. By so doing he carried out the rules of the seventh commandment.

God who gave us the right to own things, wants our ownership to be respected by all. God even lets us own many things to give us joy, recreation, happiness and health, like the bicycle, the football and many other playthings. We may own food because it helps us to preserve our body which is a gift of God. Father may own a house or a store because the house gives him and his children protection against the weather and the store helps him to earn money to support his family.

Children can practice the virtue of honesty. They can respect each other's property on the playground, in the classroom and in the home. If they want another's toy, they must ask permission. They should take the best care of borrowed property and see that it is returned in as good condition as they got it. They even practice this virtue in the way they use their own property, their books, their clothes, their toys. They have a responsibility here to their own parents who gave them everything. They must take ordinary care of these because in reality the parents are the owners. Neatness with work, books and clothes is a help because it preserves property. By the seventh commandment we are commanded to respect what belongs to others.

Summary by Example: Recall the story of Joseph and his brothers. They recoiled from the accusation of thievery when the silver cup was found in Benjamin's sack. They were willing to undergo any hardship to erase this stigma. They had been well instructed on the nobility of honesty by their father, Jacob, who himself insisted that they pay in full for the grain they received. To be fair is a great virtue.

Organization: Recite the seventh commandment of God. How must you act towards the pupils who bring their lunch? How must you act about other pupils' books? How was Robert fair when he borrowed John Linden's bicycle? Why may you and your parents own things? What do you own now? How do you want the other boys and girls to handle what you own? How can you be fair when you want a ride on another boy's bicycle? How can you be fair towards your parents by the way you handle your books and clothes?

2. Stealing Is Forbidden

There is no harm in explaining big thefts committed by adult sinners. The teacher will follow, of course, with an explanation of little thefts of which children are sometimes guilty, doing this in a manner that will make stealing appear contemptible.

Dishonest Boys.—Two boys, neither of them very honest were playing marbles.

IV. The Seventh Commandment of God

"You're creeping!" crief Adolph. The other boy extended his shooting arm so far that he was almost on top of the marbles.

The other boy, Bernard, had a complaint. "And you pushed a marble closer to your shooter!"

Along came a big boy whom they had not see until now. First, he stepped on Adolph's shooter and kicked it. Then he scooped up all the marbles of both boys and ran away with them.

Adolph and Bernard had been guilty of cheating. The big boy was guilty of stealing; he was also guilty of unjust keeping because he would not return the marbles when the boys met him on the street next day.

God is just and He wants His children to be just; He says, "Thou shalt not steal." God does not want others to take our property nor does He want any one to cheat us out of it. God's eye sees everything and everywhere. He sees the thief who robs the bank and He even notices the boy who cheats by moving a marble a little closer.

Children may not be dishonest. When children can contract little debts; they must pay them. Sometimes a child promises a neighbor boy a candy bar if he will help him mow the lawn; if that boy gives the service, he is entitled to his pay. Children can practice honesty in the home. They can take equal shares of the work about the house. If they earn something outside, they should tell their parents about it. Parents will probably overlook very small sums, but the practice teaches children that their earnings up to a certain age are the property of their parents. Damaging property is akin to stealing, like breaking a pen, marking up another's book. If Mabel deliberately damages Harriet's bicycle so that it must remain in the repair shop four days, it is almost as if she had stolen the bicycle. If the repair work costs Harriet $4.00, it is the same as if Mabel had stolen $4.00 from her. The seventh commandment forbids all dishonesty, such as stealing, cheating, unjust keeping of what belongs to others, and unjust damage to the property of others.

Summary by Example: Ralph was a great cross to his parents. When the lawn was to be mowed, he let his brother do it while he ran to the playground to play ball. Sometimes he set pins at the bowling alley but he never told his mother about the money he earned. He would borrow a bat from a boy, then take it home with him. His mother spoke to him: "You'll not last long in business if you keep that up. No man will trust you, and besides these acts are sinful."

Organization: What was wrong when those boys played marbles? What must you do when you owe Ellen a dime? What must you tell your parents when you earn money? What warning did Mother give her son, Ralph?

3. Wrongs Must Be Righted

The teacher should not go into too much detail with this section. It is enough to conclude that stolen goods must be returned.

Righting a Wrong. When St. Paschal Baylon was a boy he had a ram with big horns. That ram was wild and one day it broke through the fence and ran into the neighbor's field. In a minute the rest of the sheep followed, ate a lot of grain and trampled down a lot more. Now Paschal was a saint and he grieved because his sheep had damaged his neighbor's grain. He was a thoroughly honest shepherd and he remembered that he must make good any damage that is done. Next morning he brought the farmer enough grain to pay for the damage his sheep had caused.

A thief hurts his neighbor when he steals from him; he hurts him too every minute that he deprives the owner of his property. If a bad boy steals a bicycle he deprives the owner of the joy of riding that bicycle every day that he keeps it. Stolen property can never become the property of the thief; it must be returned to the rightful owner.

To destroy is worse than stealing. It is scarcely ever possible to restore it in a way to give the same satisfaction to the owner as the original property gave him.

Summary by Example: If a boy has a pet dog he would not sell it for $200 because that puppy has an especial appeal to him. If a mean man poisons the dog, the boy is inconsolable. No other dog can take Towser's place. It is difficult to right certain wrongs. Better not to do the wrong in the first place.

For the present the practical questions are, Did I steal? Did I restore the value of what I stole or damaged?

Motivation: A great President, Abraham Lincoln, loved to use the quotation, "Honesty is the best policy." Dishonesty will not take us far in this world, for in the long run cheaters and thieves are always caught. There is no real joy in keeping stolen property, for the thief is always bothered with the thought that he is an enemy of God as long as he keeps what does not belong to him. When people once find out that a man is a cheat or a thief, they will not trust him, will not be friends with him. Certainly, dishonesty will get us nowhere in the next life because God cannot be deceived.

To be honest is to be noble. An honest boy or girl can look anyone in the face. People like to have them for friends. When they have a job they are happy to know that they are not being watched because their boss trusts them. God loves honest souls.

Organization: Tell the story of St. Paschal's big ram. How did the Saint right the wrong? May a thief keep what he stole? What must a boy do who breaks a window in school? Do people trust a thief? Then what must you do?

Reconstruction of Division IV.

V. The Eighth Commandment of God

1. The Duty to Speak the Truth

Q. What is the eighth commandment of God?
A. The eighth commandment of God is: Thou shalt not bear false witness against thy neighbor.

Speak truthfully to your neighbor and of your neighbor. God has commanded every one to love his neighbor in thought, word and deed. The eighth commandment deals principally with love of neighbor as manifested in word; it regards men's speech with one another and of one another. It deals with truth and untruth.

On November 22, the Church celebrates the Feast of the noble and brave St. Cecilia. Perhaps the pupils have seen a picture of this beautiful saint who is generally represented as playing an organ while flowers from heaven fall over the keys. She was brought before the wicked ruler who asked her what she believed. The Saint could have secured her release by telling a lie, but bravely she answered, "I am a Christian." She was subjected to terrible tortures but remained steadfast in telling the truth. Freedom and happiness were offered her but her only answer was, "I am a Christian." God so loved this truthful maiden that He did not let steam and boiling water hurt her. Next a soldier gashed her neck three times with an axe. The Saint lived for two full days even after that and her great joy was that God still gave her strength to say, "I am a Christian."

To "bear false witness" means telling false or untrue stories about our neighbor.

Speech was given to man to enable him to communicate his thoughts truthfully to his neighbor; his tongue and speech are gifts of God which must be used as God intended. All the world admires a man who tells the truth. Men have become heroes for speaking the truth under stress. From their earliest years, children should be taught to speak truthfully no matter how difficult this may be. Even though they later become the most learned people in the world, they will never be truly esteemed unless they are truthful. *Example:* Mother asks who took the cookies from the jar and while it is difficult to admit it, the truthful girl says, "I did it." The boy slides into second base safely; he tells the story later without any exaggerations that would make the feat more heroic than it truly was.

We should train ourselves to say kind things of our little neighbors. Every time we say a kind word about them, our guardian angel puts a good mark in his book for us and when we come to be judged he will show all those marks to God. If children grow up with this good habit they will be loved by everyone because people like to hear kind words spoken. They will be loved by God who wants them to be kind to their little neighbors. By the eighth commandment we are commanded to speak the truth in all things.

Summary by Example: Father had given Jack a beautiful tool-box for his birthday. One day while Jack was downtown, the younger brother Tommy played with the tools. The saw slipped and he made a cut in a beautiful chair. Tommy looked at the gash regretfully, thinking, "What will Mother say?"

Mother had heard the noise of the falling tool-box and she entered the dining room. Right away she saw the damage that had been done. "Did you do that, Tommy?"

The boy was only in the second grade but he had heard Sister tell the story about the truthful St. Cecilia. He hesitated just a moment, then he said, "Yes, Mother, I did it."

Organization: Recite the eighth commandment of God. Tell the story of St. Cecilia. Could she have saved her life by telling a lie? Why did God give your your tongue? May you tell little lies of excuse? How would Harry tell an untruth when he explains how he slid into second base? Tell what a good boy Jack was when questioned about the beautiful chair.

2. What the Commandment Forbids

God said in the commandment that we may not bear false witness, meaning that we may not tell false stories, namely, lies. A lie is saying something which we know is not true for the purpose of deceiving another. Thus fairy stories or bedtime stories are not lies because there is no real intention to deceive.

The fault of lying is not uncommon even among children of this age. Too often it is a way out of everything. Little failings can easily grow into the vice of lying. The girl will exaggerate about the good time she had the evening before. The boy will add a few points to his story about the ball-game if it makes him appear more heroic. When Father searches for the rake, the boy does not admit that he used it yesterday and does not know where he left it.

Recall what trouble the brothers of Joseph brought upon all by their lie that a wild beast had devoured the boy. That lie covered up their attempted murder of Joseph and their selling him to the traders. The lie did not comfort Jacob because he grieved for years over the loss of his boy. How ashamed they must have felt when Joseph years afterwards revealed himself to them! God had severely punished their lie. Lies killed Jesus. When He was brought before the rulers, the Jews told lies about Him. The Father in heaven hates lying because it caused His divine Son so much pain.

Lying brings lots of trouble. If a friend hears that he has been lied about, he will no longer be afraid of the liar. Lying has ruined people. If Lydia lies about Catherine, perhaps the other girls will not like Catherine any more. If Edward lies about James, perhaps the other boys will not let James into their games. If children lie in the home, perhaps an innocent one will be punished.

Boys and girls know that they must respect each others' books and playthings, but each child has something which is worth more than a hundred playthings. His best property is his good name.

It is pleasant to hear someone say, "He is a good boy" or "She is a good girl." We would be shocked if someone pointed to a certain child and said "That little girl is a liar" or "That little boy is a thief."

Raymond was a good honest boy, going to the second grade. School was just closing when one of the girls noticed that her pencil was missing. Right away a boy pointed at Raymond, "You stole it, Raymond Sears; you are a thief."

"I didn't, I didn't," cried out Raymond. "I wouldn't steal a pencil from anybody."

Sister did not believe the accuser but Raymond was brokenhearted. He ran home crying. "Mother!" he said, "A boy called me a thief before the whole class. I don't want to go to school any more. I cannot face the class again."

But Raymond, at the bidding of his mother, went to school. As soon as the prayers were said, Sister spoke to the class, "Raymond Sears is an honest boy who would not steal anything. The boy who accused him wants to beg his pardon because he admits he made a mistake and should not have used such a rude word." The apology restored Raymond's good name but it did not take away his great grief of the day before.

It is forbidden to talk unkindly of others. All people have faults, even the little boys and girls in this classroom, but it is sinful to bring these faults into our conversation. It is wrong to say, "She is mean" or "He is unfair" when there is intent to injure that girl or boy. Sometimes a little girl gets jealous when another has more friends, so she says nasty things about the girl. Sometimes a boy is jealous because he cannot play ball as well as another, so he says that the other boy is unfair.

God certainly blessed Sister when she defended Raymond the next morning in school. Sister herself felt good all day because she had said a kind word for the little boy. The boy who had accused Raymond did right when he acknowledged his fault and begged Raymond's pardon. The eighth commandment forbids lies and harming the name of another.

Summary by Example: Nat had so thoroughly enjoyed his April Fool jokes that he resolved to keep them up. Soon the boys gave him the nasty name, "April Fool" and they did not believe anything he said. It happened that there was a ball-game one day and a boy knocked a fly from the far end of the field. Nat saw that the ball was going straight for Richard Straus. He cried, "Duck, Richard, or you'll get hit." Now Richard never believed any story of Nat's and did not believe in this warning. But this was one time that Nat had spoken the truth. The ball hit Richard on the jaw and injured him severely—A liar is not believed even when he speaks the truth.

Motivation: The liar has a hard time to get back. John, caught in a trick one day, got out of it by lying. He thought that was smart, so he tried it another time and again he escaped punishment. It was not long before lying was a habit with the boy. Then one day an older boy called him a liar and proved him a liar. John had never realized how terrible that word "Liar" sounds, and how it robs one of friends. He grieved over the situation and resolved never again to lie. It took the boy a long time to convince his chums that he had changed, until he stood up in class one day and bravely admitted having done something of which another boy was accused.

Organization: What lie did the sons tell their father Jacob, about Joseph's disappearance? What trouble did this lie bring upon the aged father? How do you think the brothers felt when Joseph told them who he was? Who lied about Jesus during His passion? How can lying about James make trouble for him on the baseball team? Tell the story of Raymond who was accused of stealing a pencil. You may not talk unkindly of others. What might be an unkind thing to say of a boy in this classroom?

Reconstruction of Division V.

VI. The Ninth Commandment of God

1. St. Stanislaus—Pure As a Pure White Lily

Q. What is the ninth commandment of God?

A. The ninth commandment of God is: Thou shalt not covet thy neighbor's wife.

St. Stanislaus Kostka came from a noble Polish family. As a child he showed such purity of soul that he was looked upon as an angel on earth. When unclean talk came up, he would turn pale and if it continued any length of time he would faint. The boy was so pure of heart that it is said he never was disturbed even for an instant by a contrary thought.

Unit 4: Fourth to Tenth Commandments   Grade II

This ninth commandment calls for the exercise of a high grade of purity. In the sixth commandment God tells us that we may not do anything that is not pure. Now in the ninth commandment God tells us that we may not even *think* of something that is not pure, or *want* to do something that is not pure. Our Lord once said that He wanted not only the outside of the cup to be clean but also the inside. We can be clean inside by thinking only of clean things; then we are clean in mind and heart.

The explanation to seven-year-olds must of necessity be brief. No attempt is made to explain "covet" or "neighbor's wife." The teacher just states that the commandment forbids us to entertain impure thoughts; nothing is explained about impure desires. The writer does not even counsel the regular review by the class. The story of St. Stanislaus is the theme for this section.

The Blessed Virgin, our Mother most pure, treated St. Stanislaus as a special object of her love and St. Stanislaus gave love in return, for he always said, "She is my mother." While he attended the college at Vienna he was treated roughly by his brother Paul. The Saint became dangerously ill and feared that he would not be able to receive holy Viaticum before he died. The people with whom he boarded were non-Catholics and besides, Paul refused to get a priest for him. But the pure angels in heaven take care of a pure angel on earth. His patron, St. Barbara, appeared to him in the company of two angels from whose hands he received the body of Our Lord. Our Lady herself cured him and bade him enter the Society of Jesus. A few days later she appeared to him with the divine Infant whom she placed in his arms. How happy was that Infant to nestle against the heart that was as pure as a pure white lily. Once St. Stanislaus ran away from his brother; when Paul tried to pursue him, Paul's horse would not budge. He did enter the Society of Jesus, but God gave him ten months only of that happy life. St. Stanislaus had written a letter to our Blessed Lady asking that he be allowed to spend the Feast of the Assumption with her in heaven. The boy was not very ill but on the morning of the Feast, Mary most pure appeared to him with a host of virgins. She called and the pure saint went to heaven to spend an eternity with the other saints who were pure as pure can be.

We must keep our mind on clean things. We can do this if we talk about clean things and if we seek healthy recreation. The ninth commandment forbids all thoughts and desires contrary to chastity.

Grade II VII. The Tenth Commandment of God 195

Motivation: Stanislaus was a mere boy but he became a saint. Will some little boy or girl here become a saint? The answer is, all can become saints if they remain pure as pure as a pure white lily.

A POEM

Take my body, Jesus,
  Eyes and ears and tongue;
Never let them, Jesus,
  Help to do Thee wrong.

Take my heart and fill it
  Full of love for Thee.
All I have I give Thee:
  Give Thyself to me.—*Anonymous.*

Organization: Recite the ninth commandment of God. What would happen to St. Stanislaus when he heard unclean talk? What, when this talk continued? What kind of thoughts must you have in your mind? What did St. Barbara and two angels do for this Saint when others would not let him receive Holy Communion? What happened to Paul's horse when he tried to catch St. Stanislaus? When did the Saint want to die? When did he die?

VII. The Tenth Commandment of God

1. We Must Be Satisfied, Not Complain

Q. What is the tenth commandment of God?
A. The tenth commandment of God is: Thou shalt not covet thy neighbor's goods.

The tenth commandment calls for a high grade of honesty. In the seventh commandment God forbids actual stealing; in the tenth He tells us that we must not even want to steal, or think of wanting to steal or to be dishonest. In this tenth, God commands us to be honest in mind and heart.

Read the Bible Story, Esau sells his Birthright to Jacob. This is the story of two young men, each of whom desired what the other had and both of whom suffered very much after they obtained what they desired. Esau was very hungry and he desired the mess of pottage which Jacob had. Jacob on the other hand desired to be the leader of the Jewish people, whereas Esau as the oldest son was to have that office. The trade was made; Jacob gave the pottage to Esau; Esau gave his future high office to Jacob. But what troubles followed it! Esau had made a foolish bargain: Jacob had made a tricky bargain. Jacob indeed gained much but he had to run away from home because his brother became very angry when he realized into what an unequal bargain his desires had led him, and during the years that followed he suffered a great deal.

Some in this life receive more, some less. Some are born wealthy, some poor; some healthy while others are sick; some are talented and others are not.

Each must be contented with what he has. If a child can have only poor clothes, it must be satisfied; so also with health or sickness, more talents or less talents. Good children will be happy that a little neighbor has more. If a boy has more, he should share it with others; if he has more playthings, he should let others share his toys. No one in this world has everything; no one is entirely happy; all have their troubles. Health is more than wealth. Goodness is a far more valuable possession than either; it brings more happiness than either.

Heaven is not won by health, good clothes, great talents; it is won only by good works. A poor boy in heaven is infinitely better off than a rich boy in hell. The greater the goodness of any one, the greater will be his happiness in heaven. If a child is not so well clothed, not so gifted, not so healthy, he has a better chance to get to heaven than his more favored companion. Our Saviour loved the poor, the sick, the downtrodden.

Summary by Example: Harold sat on the sofa pouting, for he wanted a new pair of skates. Jane whimpered because she wanted a new dress.

Mother spoke: "If I had the money to buy skates or a new dress, I certainly would do so. Dad has no steady employment and it takes every cent just to make a living."

"Alice has a new dress," mumbled Jane.

"Yes, Alice has but her father is better off than yours. Both of you should go out and play with the toys you have. If you keep on thinking of what others have, you will be very unhappy."

Organization: Recite the tenth commandment of God. Tell the story of Esau and Jacob. How was each greedy? Did their greediness bring them happiness? How can you be contented as to clothes, your health? What might you do if you have more playthings than a little neighbor?

2. We May Try to Better Ourselves

Read the Bible Story, Esau forgives Jacob. Many years passed by while the brothers remained enemies. The enmity which their unholy desires had caused, was making life bitter for them both. Finally, both came to the conclusion that it was not worth while and they met near the River Jordan and forgave each other. They were friends ever afterwards, each seeking his own gain and comfort in his own sphere, and both became great in the land of Israel.

We too are allowed to desire an improvement in our lot as long as we use honest means to attain our objective. A pupil may be ambitious to head the class. A girl may desire to have better clothes. If the boy works honestly to get his marks and the girl resolves to earn a little extra money, there is no fault, no sin. An honest purpose coupled with honest means is all that is required. Such ambition is not sinful; it is even praiseworthy.

We may not be lazy. The boy who is satisfied to wear dirty clothes or to remain at the foot of his class, is just plain lazy. The girl who is not ambitious to make her bedroom tidy, is lazy too. Honest effort to get ahead is commendable. We must not condemn a man who is rich or has a large home; if he gained it by honest effort it is his and we have no right to criticize.

Table of Sins for a Child's Confession

1. Did I say my prayers every day?
   Did I say them well?
2. Did I take God's holy name in vain?
   Did I curse?
3. Did I miss Mass on Sunday or on a holyday?
   Did I misbehave in church?
4. Was I obedient?
5. Did I get angry?
   Did I quarrel?
6. Was I pure in touch and thought?
7. Did I steal anything?
8. Did I tell lies?
   Did I say mean things?
9. Did I eat meat on Friday?

Motivation: A great task is completed. We have learned what we must do and what we may not do under the ten commandments

Unit 4: Fourth to Tenth Commandments — Grade II

of God but mostly we have learned how we can please God and gain heaven. Our Lord said that if we want to prove our love for Him, we must keep the commandments. There will never come a day when we are free from this obligation, and there is no person in the world who is excused. We remember how the commandments began, "I am the Lord thy God." We will obey because of the God who gave them and because the results are so important. When the devil whispers to us to be lazy and not go to Mass, we shall answer, "God said, 'Keep holy the Lord's day.'" When the devil says, "Be unkind," we shall reply, "But God said, 'Thou shalt not'." Now we know exactly what God will ask us at the Judgment, ten questions, Did you keep the ten commandments? We hope to answer, "God, I always remembered Your words, 'I am the Lord thy God' and I kept Your commandments."

To the Teacher: In many schools pupils make their first confession in Advent of their second year. These pupils already received some instruction on the method of confession while they were in the first grade and now they have just completed the study of the ten commandments. It will be easy to recall what they learned about Penance by using first-grade material or even by consulting the later instruction of unit nine of this year.

Organization: Suppose each does it honestly, may Jack try to get to the head of the class, may Rita try to get better clothes? How could each succeed? Is it wrong not to care at all about getting good marks?

Reconstruction of Unit Four.

SECOND SEMESTER OR II A

UNIT FIVE: TWO LAWS OF THE CHURCH

I. THE LAW ABOUT HOLY MASS.
   1. WE MUST OBEY THE LAWS OF THE CHURCH.
   2. THE MASS ON SUNDAYS.
   3. THE MASS ON HOLYDAYS.

II. THE LAW ABOUT MEAT.
   1. HOW THE LAW AFFECTS CHILDREN.

What We Shall Learn: In the first semester we were taken up principally with laws made by God, the ten commandments which God gave us through Moses. But God now has a large organization which takes the place Moses once had; this is His Church. God gives us laws now through His Church as He once gave them through Moses. God no longer speaks to us directly but He speaks through His Church, tells the Church what she should tell us. He guides her so that she makes no mistakes when she tells us. The Church has given us six principal commandments but just now we will study only those two which affect children, the law about Mass and the law about abstinence from meat.—This unit must be taught orally.

I. The Law about Holy Mass

1. We Must Obey the Laws of the Church

The Catholic Church makes laws. A law is a kind of rule, it is a commandment. Thus, Father may tell Alfred, "Rake the leaves." Father has given Alfred a law, a commandment to do something.

God speaks to the faithful through the Catholic Church. When a man goes to a far country for a long visit, he places a man in charge of his business while he is gone to give orders in his place. Christ Himself had established the Catholic Church and when He ascended into heaven He gave this Church charge of the faithful, to teach them and to rule them.

Recall the Bible story, Feed My Lambs, Feed My sheep. Before Christ departed, He gave His Church the same rights and powers that He had. He blessed Peter telling Him that

He would be the head of this Church. Peter was to feed the lambs and the sheep, that is, the faithful, as Christ had fed them during His lifetime. Peter was to feed them with the sacraments and other graces. He was to guide and rule them through counsels and commandments as a shepherd does for his lambs and his sheep.

Peter also was given the right and duty to make rules and laws for the faithful who are the lambs and the sheep. Now a good shepherd does not let his sheep do what they please but makes them go where he directs. He does not let them eat everything or go everywhere. In other words, he makes laws for them. Peter was given the right to make laws for the faithful.

Our Holy Father, the Pope, today takes the place of St. Peter. When St. Peter died, another Pope took his place and so it went on and on, one Pope followed another until the present-day Pope. If Father should die, our home is not broken up and the rules of the home do not stop because Mother now takes Father's place. Every Pope as ruler of the faithful has had the right to make laws and the Pope today has that right.

The Pope makes laws that will help the faithful to lead good lives and guide them to heaven. Every once in a while our pastor reads a letter from the Holy Father in which he asks his lambs and his sheep to do something, to observe some law. The Popes have made six big or principal laws and these still remain the six big commandments of the Church. Men still admire these six because they bring order into the Church and help the faithful to become holy. We will study only two of the six which relate to children of this age.

Summary by Example: St. Stephen, King of Hungary, had a true love for the people committed to his care. During his lifetime he did everything possible by laws, gifts and personal example to spread and increase the faith in his country. He was anxious that provision be made to continue this holy work after he died. He asked the then-reigning Pope to appoint more bishops to care for the spiritual needs of the Hungarian people. The Pope exercising his right to rule the faithful did appoint eleven bishops to care for the flock in that Catholic land.

Organization: The Catholic Church has given us laws. Can you give another word for laws, beginning c-o-m? Through what Church does God give us laws? Tell the story of Jesus saying to

Peter, "Feed My lambs, Feed My sheep." Are you one of the lambs of the Catholic Church? Does a shepherd let his lambs do what they like or does he make them do what he thinks is right and good for them? Who now takes the place of St. Peter in the Catholic Church? May the Pope make laws for you? What big laws has he made?

2. The Mass on Sundays

This division will be treated briefly because it is mostly a review of the third commandment of God which the pupils studied in the preceding semester.

The third commandment of God reads, Remember thou keep holy the Lord's day. That commandment was given through Moses several thousand years ago and the Sabbath day or Saturday was designated as the one to be kept holy.

Christ and the apostles changed the day to the first of the week, namely Sunday. Our Lord Himself had performed His most important miracle on a Sunday when He rose from the dead on Easter Sunday. He had established His Church on a Sunday when He sent the Holy Ghost upon the apostles on Pentecost Sunday. These two Sundays are the biggest and most important Feasts in the Church; therefore the Church commanded the observance of Sunday instead of Saturday.

The Church prescribes how the Sunday is to be kept holy. In the third commandment, God had ordered men to keep the day holy; here the Church tells us of an altogether special way to keep the day holy. When God spoke to Moses there was no Mass. The Mass came with the Church; and since the Church rightly considers the Mass the greatest worship men can give to God, she orders that the faithful make the Sunday holy by going to Mass.

The Mass is such a very great act of worship that it is a very great sin to miss it on Sunday. We are excused from attending Mass only if we have a very good reason as, for example, sickness or long distance from the church. A Catholic who through his own fault misses Mass on a Sunday or holyday of obligation commits a mortal sin.

Summary by Example: A man who had not been to Mass for a long time had a dream one night. He dreamed that he was again going to Mass and an angel behind him was counting his steps. Turning around he asked the angel why he was following and why he was counting his steps. "I have been sent by God to count your steps," replied the angel. "For every step you take in going to Mass, you will be rewarded in eternity." The dream was so impressive to the man that henceforth he made the necessary sacrifices to get to Mass every Sunday.

Organization: On what day of the week did Jesus rise from the dead? On what day of the week did the Holy Ghost come down on the apostles? Then why is Our Lord's day on Sunday? You must keep the Lord's day holy. How does the Church tell you to make it holy, that is, what must you do on Sunday? What kind of sin is it to miss Mass on Sunday if you have no good excuse? Tell the story of the angel who counted the steps of the man going to Mass.

3. The Mass on Holydays

The Church has other days besides the Sundays which she wants the faithful to keep holy and offer to God.

The Church has feast days as all nations and people have them. The United States has its big celebration of Independence Day on July 4, but it has other days like Thanksgiving and Washington's birthday. Parents commemorate a great event when they celebrate the anniversary of their wedding. We ourselves have a birthday and a name day, more properly called a Saint's day, meaning the Feast of the patron saint whose name was given us in Baptism.

The Church gives us other holydays besides the Sunday. On these days something very important happened which she wants us ever to remember; a great mystery is celebrated which has great meaning for our spiritual life. For example, a great event took place on Christmas Day when our Redeemer was born. The Church wants us always to remember Christmas Day because the Christ was born for us, so she makes it a holyday.

The first commandment of the Church is: To assist at Mass on all Sundays and holydays of obligation. The Church has given us six holydays. On these six, we must go to Mass, and the law is just as strict as for the Sunday. When any one of these days falls on a school day, the pupils are excused from school, not that their work is so very hard but that the Church wishes to give them joy when all should be joyful about the feast.

The holydays of obligation in the United States are these six:
  Christmas Day (December 25).
  The Circumcision (January 1) also called New Year's Day.

Grade II — I. The Law about Holy Mass

Ascension Thursday (40 days after Easter)
The Assumption (August 15).
All Saint's Day (November 1).
The Immaculate Conception (December 8).

The Church calls these holydays of obligation. It means that we are obliged to go to Mass on these days unless we are lawfully excused.

The holydays are to be observed in other ways like the Sunday. Thus Catholics are not permitted to do unnecessary servile work on these days. The Church generally makes an exception for the wage-earners in the family for the reason that their wages are necessary for the support of the family and the cessation from labor would mean a considerable loss of necessary income. It would also mean a big disturbance in a factory or an office were the Catholic to stay away on certain days leaving all the work to non-Catholics.

Summary by Example: Clyde, a Catholic, was talking with Robert, a non-Catholic.

"Why didn't you go to school today?" asked Robert.

"Because this is Ascension Thursday. All Catholics must ever remember that Jesus went to heaven to prepare a place for all men. On this day too Catholics have a special Mass which tells them about Christ's Ascension and all go to Mass to recall the day and to thank Jesus.

Robert thought a while. "Really, that's a very fine thing to do, but your father is working in the factory today. Didn't your father remember?"

"O yes, he did," replied Clyde. "He went to a six o'clock Mass. We need Father's wages to support us, and besides, the boss would not let him lay off a day. In my case though it is different. I do not earn wages so I am not permitted to do hard work. For example, I would not be permitted to wash the automobile today."

Organization: Do you go to school on Thanksgiving day? Has the Church got other feast days beside Sundays? Name one such big day, and give one reason why the Church wants the people to keep it holy. How many such big extra days are there in all? What must you do on these six days? May Simon, aged 13, wash the automobile on a holyday?—Then, what may you not do on a holyday?

Reconstruction of Division I.

II. The Law about Meat

1. How the Law Affects Children

Picture the Crucifixion. That great event took place on a Friday. The Church never wants its members to forget that great day. Our life in the Church is not all holydays and feast days, no more than our life at home is. Like Father at home, the Church tells us to do certain things and also not to do certain things. To show our gratitude to Jesus Christ for the Crucifixion and to make us remember always this great event, the Church asks us to abstain from meat on Friday.

Control of our eating habits is good for us. Mother often says, "Now you have had enough salad" or "You better not eat pie today because you are not feeling well" or "Better drink more milk and less coffee if you want to get strong."

In the case of abstinence from meat on a Friday, the reason is far more important. Christ suffered for our sins on Good Friday and we in turn offer this little sacrifice for our sins and show our love for Christ by suffering a little with Him. A day of abstinence is a day on which we are not allowed the use of meat. The second commandment of the Church is: To fast and abstain on the days appointed.

All Catholics over seven years of age are forbidden by the Church to eat meat on Friday. When Friday comes around we say, "Jesus died on Good Friday and we in turn offer this little sacrifice for our sins." To show our love for Him we do not eat meat on other days during Lent, on the Wednesdays all day and on Holy Saturday till noon. It is quite a sacrifice for American children to abstain from meat so often because they are accustomed to having it at most meals. The good Catholic child will say, "Jesus suffered so much for me, so I can deny myself a little bit for Him." Jesus said that He wants us to follow Him on the way of the cross because that way alone leads to heaven. Wasn't He thirsty and wasn't He hungry then on the way of the cross? Truly then our little acts are the steps to heaven. All baptized persons seven years of age or over are obliged to observe the abstinence days of the Church.

Sometimes children are excused from abstaining from meat on the Wednesdays of Lent. When Dad works hard, he needs meat to keep up his strength, so the Church permits him to eat it once

Grade II — II. The Law about Meat

a day on all Wednesdays. Now Mother has lots of work and she has not the time to cook one kind of a meal for Dad and another kind for the children. The Church is very kind so she says that in this case all the members of the family may eat meat once a day. Indeed, children under twenty-one may eat meat several times a day when it is otherwise permitted.

Motivation: A priest was once asked, "What are the outstanding marks of a Catholic who will die a Catholic? How can you tell whether a Catholic will remain such? What are the signs of a faith that will never fall away?"

He was asked about avoiding this sin and that sin, "Will that save a Catholic in the end?" To all such questions he replied, "It helps very much but it is not the sign of lasting faith. No one can tell you how to make salvation sure. The only advice is that you should do all that God commands."

"But can't you tell us of some practices which would lead you to think that the doer will remain a Catholic to the end?"

"If you will let me judge only from my own experience, I would say that there are two practices, never missing Mass and never eating meat on Friday. These are commandments of the Church and perhaps God wants us to be humble enough to obey the Church He has appointed to speak for Him. Perhaps the reason is that the Son of God is so closely connected with the two: He becomes present on the altar during the Mass; He died for us on Good Friday."

Perhaps these two practices are not the infallible marks but they are at least indications of an enduring faith.

The practical conclusion is that every child in this classroom will resolve never to miss Mass, never to eat meat on Friday. Now when they are young is the time to make such a resolution.

Organization: On what day was Jesus Christ crucified? How can you show your love to Jesus who died on a Friday? What law did the Church make for you for the Friday? What can you say to Jesus when you do not eat meat on Friday? Of whom do you think during Lent? Are there more days during Lent when you may not eat meat? If your dad is working hard during Lent may he eat meat on Wednesdays? Why?

UNIT SIX: PRAYER HELPS US TO KEEP GOD'S LAWS

I. We Should Pray Sincerely and Earnestly.
II. We Should Pray With Hope and Perseverance.
III. Morning, Evening and Table Prayers.
IV. Prayer for Special Needs.

What We Shall Learn: In the last unit we learned that grace is necessary for salvation, that only through grace can we avoid evil and do good, that only by grace can our soul be made fit to enter heaven. Since grace is so important, the question rises in every child's mind, How can I get more and more grace? In a preceding unit we learned that we can get grace through prayer. We shall learn therefore how we should pray so that God really listens to what we say. God does not listen to a carelessly said prayer but He wants to be asked in the right way; we shall learn how to ask Him in the right way. Next we shall learn just when we should pray. While we always need grace, there are troublous times when we need a great deal of grace. We shall learn when these times are. —This unit must be taught orally.

I. We Should Pray Sincerely and Earnestly

The lesson is indeed a repetition in part of the matter which was studied in the first grade. This time the Presentation is different and only two phases are selected, They have a very practical bearing for the seven-year old child. It is far better to cover simple fundamentals thoroughly than to go on with too difficult details.

Our Lord gave men the Example of Prayer.—He was about to choose His first apostles, a very important work indeed, because His future Church would be ruled by these men. The Scripture says that He spent the whole previous night in prayer. He wanted to get grace for the apostles, so He prayed most earnestly to His heavenly Father. At another time, He even told us how to pray, so important is this work; He said, "Thus shall you pray" and He gave us the Our Father. When Jesus entered upon His agony in the Garden, He prayed three times. If the God-Man prayed, then we should pray. The question only is, How shall we pray?

Grade II I. We Should Pray Sincerely and Earnestly

We must mean what we say when we pray.—*A Story:* Raymond Beck asked Father Murray why God does not hear all our prayers. Father had the answer, "I was in your classroom this morning and asked you to read for me. When you had finished, I asked you what you had read and you couldn't tell me. Next I asked you to read a little poem and to put some feeling into it. Instead, you read it in one tone and it sounded like the addition table. You were not interested in your own words, and you did not interest the other pupils either, in fact, one of them fell asleep."

"That's true, Father, I was just a sleepy head."

Father continued, "That's the way some people pray to God. Why should God be interested if they themselves show no interest? By the way, Raymond, have you heard Jack's parrot? Jack has trained it to say several sentences from the Hail Mary."

"Yes, I have, Father, but God doesn't listen to the parrot because the parrot doesn't know what it is saying; a bird can't mean what it says."

"Well, some people pray like that parrot. God doesn't listen to their parrot-prayers either."

Our prayers must come from the heart. A boy who, instead of kneeling upright, slouches at the side of the bed when he says his night prayers, does not know what he is saying. What he does say comes from the lips and not from the heart. Our Lord told a story about the Pharisee who went into the Temple to pray. The man said his prayer loudly and distinctly but the prayer was not heard. He pretended to be pious but in his heart he was not a pious man; his prayer was not holy; it did not come from a good heart. We cannot mean what we say when our heart is not right.

We must really want what we ask for.—*A Story:* "Why didn't you give my son a job?" Mr. Simpson asked the boss. "Because he didn't want a job. When your son asked me, he slumped in his chair and he seemed more worried about the way his cigaret burned than in a job. He showed no eagerness in his voice and when I talked to him, he was generally looking out of the window. He was in a great hurry to end the interview because he wanted to play ball down on the corner lot. No, he didn't really want a job and he asked for one only because you forced him."—That is the way many people pray to God; they do not put their mind into what they say, do not lift their mind to God.

We must pray earnestly and eagerly. We do make a serious mat ter of it when we ask for a cure from sickness but we become indifferent and careless when we ask for virtue or for grace or for favors for others. We are interested in what we can see or in what helps towards present comfort or joy, but we are not eager enough to do something for our soul. Does a pupil here wish to be kind, obedient, industrious? How earnestly will he pray for these virtues. He must put his heart into the prayer, must keep his mind on what he says. Prayer is the lifting up of our minds and hearts to God.

Summary by Example: A banker had some very important work to do, so he locked himself up in his office and forbade any one even to rap on the door. A clerk who had not heard the order, did rap several times but the banker paid no attention. To pray is a very important work and we must close the doors of our eyes and our ears. If the devil raps, trying to distract us, we pay no attention to him and go on with our prayers. We are bankers who must buy heaven with golden prayers. Do we mean what we say when we pray? Do we really want what we ask for? We must really lift our minds and hearts to God.

Organization: You need grace all through life and sometimes a great deal of it. How can you get more grace? What did Our Lord do the night before He chose His apostles? What did Jesus do during His agony in the Garden? How did that boy, Raymond Beck, read? Did any one in the class pay attention to his reading? Using this example, how do some people pray to God? Does God then pay attention to poor prayers? Fill in the missing word: Our prayers must come from the ...... —Recall the story of the boy who asked Mr. Simpson for a job in the factory. How did the boy act while he was asking for the job? Did the boy really want the job? Why did Mr. Simpson not give him the job? Why must we earnestly want what we pray for? Supply the missing word: Our prayers must come from the .... Tell the story of the banker who locked the doors, not wishing to be disturbed. Against what must we lock our mind and heart when we pray?

II. We Should Pray with Hope and Perseverance

David placed His hope in God and Won the Battle.—The youth, David, was to battle the giant, Goliath. The giant armed with sword and spear felt sure he would destroy David. The boy told Goliath that he placed his hope not in weapons nor in his own strength but in God, saying, "I come to thee

Grade II II. We Should Pray with Hope and Perseverance

in the name of the Lord." God was so pleased with the boy's trust that He helped him and the onlooking armies beheld the unbelievable sight of David overcoming and slaying Goliath.

We must fight against another Goliath, the devil. Temptations like giants are ready to conquer us. Worries and misfortunes, seeming unconquerable, threaten to beat us to the ground. Like David we will hope, saying, "I come in the name of the Lord." As God helped David, so will He help us to conquer these giants in our path.

God wants us to pray with confidence or hope. When we pray with hope we tell God that He is able to help us. By our prayers we tell God that He is almighty and can help us in everything. Now God is almighty and He is pleased when we tell Him so. He helps those who trust that He can help them but He rejects those who say that He cannot help.

Suppose a little boy here prays that God will help him to learn his lessons better. Can God help? Sure He can, because He is almighty.

We should never stop asking for help.—It is so easy to say a short prayer but it shows real hope when we keep it up. A boy who wants a new pair of roller skates asks his father not only once but many times and finally the father gives in. We do not always receive the answers to our prayers at once because God wants to test our hope. He knows that we have real hope only if we continue our prayers for days and often for weeks. We learned last year that we worship God by hoping in Him. Our hope is genuine when we never stop asking for help.

Sometimes we do not obtain what we ask for even though we do pray properly. A mother does not give baby a knife even though it says, "Please, Mamma" because the child might injure itself with the knife. Sometimes we ask for things that would hurt us and God like a good father does not give it to us. But Mamma gives the baby a cookie instead of a knife and God always gives us something instead, something better. So we can truthfully say that God always hears us if we pray properly.

Summary by Example: A little girl, Margaret, just came into the rectory. "O Father," she said, "I have such good news. The doctor said I may walk without crutches."

Two years ago Margaret contracted a severe affliction of her hip. She was taken to the Research Hospital where the doctors said she would never be able to walk. After a long treatment she was able to walk with two crutches, but the doctors held out no further hope for her. But Margaret prayed, making one novena after the other, and today she gleefully announced the answer to her long prayers of hope, "O Father, the doctor said I may walk without crutches."

Motivation: Our Lord has promised, "If you ask the Father anything in My name, He will give it to you." Our heavenly Father certainly has everything we need because He is infinite and He shows His love to His divine Son by giving whatever He asks. Jesus will present our prayers to the Father if we ask properly. We have learned that to ask properly we must mean what we say, really want what we ask for, feel sure that God will help, and never stop asking for help. When we do not pray properly Our Lord just disregards our prayers and does not even present them to His Father.

Organization: Hope. Why is God pleased when we show hope in Him during our prayers? Can God help? Is God almighty? Perseverance. Should we be always satisfied with one short prayer? What should we do when we do not get the answer to our prayer right away? Does Mother give the baby a knife when it cries for it? Why does God not answer every prayer? Tell the story of the little cripple, Margaret, who prayed a long time for help.

III. Morning, Evening and Table Prayers

The Flowers tell a Story.—The flowers teach us what we should do for God the first thing in the morning. Caroline and her mother were walking through their garden early one morning. The flowers looked up at the sun smiling a pleasant, "Good morning," and laughing through the veil of dew because another bright morning had dawned. The story the flowers told, made mother and child happy and both breathed deeply of the perfume that rose in the air. Mother spoke: "Wouldn't it be nice if all little children were like the flowers in the morning? Do you notice that morning prayer of the flowers, that sweet perfume they are sending to God? They thank God for having made them, and for having sent them the beautiful, warm sunshine. They never forget their perfumed morning prayer."

Grade II   III. Morning, Evening and Table Prayers   211

We should say morning prayers devoutly. God should be thanked for keeping us safe through the night. Many were led into temptation during the night but God closed our eyes in sleep so that we could not sin. Many died and while some were prepared, others were not and now are lost forever. Many contracted grave illnesses but our eyes are bright and our cheeks show the flush of health. Life is a precious gift and the risen sun tells us that God is giving us another day of it. This day can mean a closer approach to God by good deeds or a departure from Him through sin. A morning prayer will bring fresh graces so that we are of those who will come nearer to Him this day. Prayer can even bring us help for our other duties, to study hard, to help father and mother; it can remove a danger that threatens friendship, health or life.

By saying evening prayers we ask God to be our Guardian for the night. *A Story:* Stephen and his father were passing a store late one night. The boy could see a flashlight moving inside the dark building and he wondered whether a robber were stealing things. "No," replied his father, "that man is a watchman appointed by the owner of the store. He is the guardian of the building all night, seeing that no doors or windows are open, that no fire breaks out and that no thief enters." When God is asked through the evening prayer, He sets Himself up in our bedroom as Watchman over us. He sees to it that the windows of our soul are kept shut so that no evil thought enters. He can give us restful sleep, letting no sickness or accident disturb it.

Our evening prayer should be twofold in character. First, we must make an Act of Contrition for the faults we may have committed during the day. If God calls us then during the night we are prepared to meet Him. Secondly, we should thank Him for all the favors He gave us during the day just closing.

There are special times during the day calling for special prayers. Thus, devout Catholics always say Grace before and after meals. Food is meant to give health and if it cannot be digested properly, it brings sickness. Health is so important because people can work better when they are well and can be more cheerful to all. Before meals therefore all should ask God to bless their food that it really bring them health. Food itself is a gift from God for which thanks is due Him. A good boy thanks his parents even for the smallest favor and all of God's favors are big. Many a poor child has nothing to eat or very little. We thank God for the food by saying Grace after meals.

212 Unit 6: Prayer Helps Us to Keep God's Laws Grade II

Summary by Example: When Margaret the little girl with the crutches told of her cure, Father said, "But now you must thank God every day the rest of your life. God gives new favors to grateful children." Margaret replied, "O, I have already taken care of that, Father; I have promised God to say a rosary every day in thanksgiving."

Organization: Tell the story of Caroline and her mother going through the flower garden. Morning prayers. From what did God save you during the night? What do you need for the day ahead of you? Then why should you say morning prayers? Evening prayers. Tell the story of the night watchman in the store. Who is your Watchman while you sleep? From what can God save you during the night? Then why should you say night prayers? For what do you ask in the Grace before meals? For what do you thank God in the grace after meals? How did the cripple Margaret show her thankfulness to God when she received the answer to her prayers?

IV. Prayers for Special Needs

Andrew's father had been injured in the mill and could get about only with the aid of a cane. He was explaining to Andrew, "I couldn't get very far without this cane; I would soon fall. This cane, Andrew, makes me think of prayer. You cannot get very far in life without prayer. For soon you fall into sin when you forsake that cane."

We should pray for ourselves. God is almighty who can help in all our needs. We need success in our work, protection from danger, health, strength against sin, fervor to do good. Faith is necessary because it helps us to see; hope encourages us to persevere; love makes duty easy. Prayer gives us this necessary faith, hope and love. Are we not asking for things at home all day long? For our soul we need to ask just as many times because God wants us to sanctify every hour and every minute. Just now God asks each one here to pay close attention so that this hour will count for heaven. No wonder the Scripture says, "We ought always to pray."

When danger threatens, or when needs press, there is special reason for prayer. The man who is attacked by a wild beast calls on his friend to aid him; the man who is starving begs for bread. The devil is like a roaring lion who wants to devour us. His roar is a

Grade II — IV. Prayers for Special Needs

temptation to sin and when we hear it we must call upon God, our best Friend, to aid us. The soul gets so weak sometimes that it feels unable to do good deeds. Then it goes to God and prays for the bread of grace. Sickness can cause pain, trouble and loss of time, but prayer can comfort and even cure. There is a shrine in St. Anne de Beaupré in Canada to which people come who have afflictions declared incurable by the doctors, yet after a few days of prayer many go home relieved, and some cured.

We should pray for others. Our friends are often in need too and they need the assistance of our prayers. Parents should be remembered daily for many reasons, but chiefly because their cares and needs generally relate to the children. Father is out of work and he worries that he may not be able to provide for his family. Mother is sick and she worries about getting the meals for the children. God commanded us to love our neighbor as ourselves. To love him as God commanded it, we must come to his assistance when he is in need. Another close neighbor is the Pope, our Holy Father, who daily begs for the assistance of our prayers that He may be saved from the snares the enemy plots against him and may successfully carry out the great task assigned to him. The Poor Souls are always in great affliction, and prayerful Catholics are continually coming to their aid. We should pray especially for ourselves, for our parents, relatives, friends and enemies, for the souls in purgatory, for the Pope, the bishops, and priests of the Church, and for the officials of our country.

Motivation: Life is often like a rainy day when the streets are slippery. On such a day Dad puts chains on the car so that it will not slide all over the road, fall into holes, and bump into trees or other automobiles. The chains give the car a firm grip on the road. The devil tries to make the road of life slippery for us because he wants us to fall into the holes of sin or bump into grave occasions of sin. We must put the chains of prayer on our soul, for they give us a firm grip on the road to heaven. When we neglect prayer we are on the slippery road and we do not know where we will end. Prayer keeps us in the right lane. If the hole of sin opens before us we can confidently steer our soul around it. If bad companions are recklessly driving on the same road we can grasp our wheel firmly and avoid bumping into them.

Organization: What did Andrew's father, injured in the mill, use to get about? Why is prayer like a cane that supports us?

214   Unit 6: Prayer Helps Us to Keep God's Laws   Grade II

Why must we pray for ourselves? What do we need that we should pray for? Why should you pray for others? Name some particular persons for whom you should pray? What will you ask God to give these persons?

Reconstruction of Unit Six. Combine the material offered in all four organizations.

UNIT SEVEN: GRACE

(First Communion Catechism: Lesson 8)

I. Grace Is a Help.
II. How Grace Comes to Us.
III. Kinds of Grace.
IV. Using Grace.

What We Shall Learn: Shall we be able to keep the commandments of God and of the Church? It is not always easy to do the good deeds there ordered or to avoid the sins there forbidden. The devil is so cunning that, if we are not on our guard, he can make good deeds appear as of little account and bad deeds as very desirable. We are so little, so weak and we fear; often too we are just plain lazy. But really, need we fear? No, God will give us help; we call God's help, grace. God will give us greater strength to do and greater light to see. We shall learn therefore what grace is, how many kinds of grace there are and how we can get grace.

I. Grace Is a Help

The topic of grace was covered briefly in the first grade. It is, however, repeated here because of its importance and because the angle of sanctifying grace is now more fully explained. The term "sanctifying" is not used because it means little to a second-grader.

Life is a journey to eternity during which man needs much help. There are bright days on that journey and dark days: the bright days are those where we go along cheerfully and easily do the will of God; the dark days are those when we are troubled and find ourselves weak in doing God's will. There are voices along that road, some trustworthy, others deceitful: the trustworthy are the words of our guardian angel; the deceitful are the temptations of the devil.

Everyone needs a great deal of help to go through life safely, and get to heaven. He must be pleasing to God while he makes the journey and particularly pleasing at the end. He must overcome many temptations and must do many good deeds and this at times can be very difficult. Left to himself, he would be lost on the way and never arrive in heaven. To enable us to do what is right, God gives us help; this help is called grace. Grace is therefore something which God gives all men to help them save their souls.

Grace is a gift. A gift is something we get without having earned it. When Arthur gets a pair of roller skates for Christmas, he receives a gift because he did not have to buy them. Man had no right to grace in the first place. When Adam, our Father, sinned, heaven was shut against him; all then lost the right to heaven and whatever could have helped them to get to heaven. Many, many years later Jesus Christ redeemed mankind with His blood and reopened thereby the gates of heaven; that was the first gift. God in His goodness went still further and supplied men with the necessary help to get to heaven, when He gave them grace; that was the second gift. Men received something to which they had no right; it was a gift. *Example:* Mr. Alard gave his eldest son permission to go to a fair in a far-off country—the first gift. Next he gave him the means to get there and back; he supplied him with money—the second gift.

Grace is a heavenly gift. It comes from heaven; it helps men to do heavenly things; it helps them to get to heaven. God gives men many gifts; in fact, He gives them everything they have, but not all are heavenly gifts, that is, they were not given primarily, and solely to help them get to heaven. *Example:* A boy may have the gift of cleverness; that gift helps him to learn his lessons easily, helps him to grow up into a wise man but not necessarily a man loved by God. It helps him in school but does not necessarily help him to get to heaven because he may use it for a bad purpose and thereby lose his soul in hell. If the pastor should give a boy here ten cents, that would be a gift but not a heavenly gift; it came from the pastor. Grace comes from God and helps men to do good deeds by which they merit heaven and so it is called a heavenly gift. The gift of grace makes them holy; only holy people will get to heaven.

Summary by Example: David wants to make a trip to St. Louis but he has no food, no money. A friend gives him a lot of books and David sets out on his journey. The books are well-bound and interesting but before he has gone fifteen miles, he gets very hungry. The books are a nice gift but they will never help him to reach his destination. A traveler sees the tired boy and after some questioning, says to him, "Here son, is twenty-five dollars to buy food and drink on the way." That money enables David to complete his journey. Grace is the right kind of a gift that will help men journey to heaven; it is the only kind of a gift that will help men get to heaven. Grace is a gift of God that helps us get to heaven.

Organization: What voices can lead you away from the right road to God? To whose voice should you listen? Fill in the missing letters: Grace is a .... Who earned the graces for you? Did you have a right to grace or is it a gift? Where does grace help you to go? Now tell in your own words what grace is. You are now set on a journey to heaven. What are the bright and the dark days on this journey? What can spoil your trip to heaven? What does God give you to help on the trip to heaven? Who opened the gates of heaven for you?—Grace is called a heavenly gift. Is being clever a heavenly gift? Does being clever bring you to heaven? Can a clever boy lose his soul? What helps you to do heavenly things, to get to heaven? Tell the story of David making a trip to St. Louis. Will books help you to get to heaven? What will?

II. How Grace Comes to Us

Little Catherine walked into the grade this morning displaying a ten-dollar bill in her hand. Every one knew that Catherine was too young to earn that much money, so they crowded around her to ask, "Where did you get that money from? Who earned it for you? From whom did you get it?" When we know that a boy or girl has grace, we can ask the same questions, Where did you get it? Who earned it for you? From whom did you get it?

We learn first who earned the graces. Jesus Christ came on earth to do many things for us. At the end of His life, He suffered and died for us. (The pupils can explain when He suffered and how He died.) Those sufferings were worth more than all the diamonds and all the gold in the world. Our Saviour offered them to His Father to pay for several things. He offered them to the Father to buy graces for us so that we could get to heaven. He could buy so many graces that people can never use them all, no matter how many people are still to be born. A millionaire has earned more money than his children will ever need for a decent livelihood. So, Jesus Christ earned more than enough graces for all people. We say that Jesus earned the graces for men.

We get the graces from another Person of the Holy Trinity.

All three Persons have a part in the salvation of our souls. The Holy Ghost distributes the graces to us. *Example:* Father earned good wages this week so he goes downtown to buy suits, shirts, ties, dresses and stockings. Mother then divides them amongst the children; she give out the articles as the children need them or do something that deserves them. So Christ earned the graces but the Holy Ghost distributes them and thereby makes us holy. The Holy Ghost sanctifies souls through the gift of grace.

Any one in heaven can get the graces for us from the Holy Ghost. You do not go to your father every time you need a dime. You often get it from your mother who gets it from your father.

Summary by Example: The people of Egypt had worked hard in their fields and God had given them big crops. The grain was stored in big buildings and Joseph, the son of Jacob, was appointed the distributor. In a country far away Jacob with his eleven other sons needed grain. The old man did not himself go to Egypt but sent his sons, and Joseph gave them the grain. So Jesus worked for the graces and the Holy Ghost distributes them. Now people can go to the Holy Ghost or they can send some one else like the Blessed Virgin to get the graces for them.

Motivation: We love each Person of the Trinity because of what Each has done for us. God the Father is so big and yet He loves every boy and girl in this grade. Just think of how much God the Son suffered during His Passion and with every step He thought of us. This boy's name and that girl's name went through His mind. He said, "I am suffering for James and Mary and John and Lucy and all the children. I want to buy them many, many graces so that they will save their souls." And the Holy Ghost loves us; He said, "I am the Spirit of Love and I love these children too. I want to give them the many graces so that they will grow into little saints." Now just to show our thankfulness to the Holy Trinity, we will all devoutly make the sign of the cross, then recite the Glory be to the Father.

Organization: What did the girls ask Catherine when she showed them a ten-dollar bill? What can you ask the boy who has grace? To whom did Jesus Christ offer His sufferings? Were the sufferings worth more than gold? What did Jesus buy with those sufferings? For whom did He buy the graces? Who has charge of all the graces now, that is, from whom do you get them now? Can you still pray to Jesus or to the saints for grace? Who gives them in the end? Can you ask your mother for a dime? Did Jacob himself go to Egypt for grain? Whom did he send?

III. Kinds of Grace

More will be said here about actual grace than about sanctifying grace. To explain the latter with even relative completeness, would only confuse. The terms "actual" and "sanctifying grace" are probably too difficult for the second-graders. To distinguish between the two graces, the teacher may use the phrases—the "grace that helps us" and the "grace that makes us holy."

The Grace That Helps (*actual grace*).—This grace helps us to see and gives us strength. *Example:* Mr. Wilson, a man of about sixty years, is totally blind. On this particular morning he stands at his front door, preparing to go downtown. He needs help to wind in and out amongst the rushing crowds and to cross the dangerous streets. He certainly needs someone to take the place of his eyes, to guide his steps. There is a joyful yelp around the corner and his trained police dog, Prince, dashes up to him. Prince has a harness around his chest and a long strap hangs from it; Prince is a "Seeing-Eye" dog. Mr. Wilson takes hold of the strap and Prince guides him through the streets. The dog is very powerful and when he feels that Mr. Wilson is weakening, he leans forward in his harness and even pulls him along. Prince supplies sight for Mr. Wilson and even strength.

All people need guidance to know what to do, and strength to do what is commanded. Many a time people are like that blind Mr. Wilson; they do not know where to go, what to do. They weaken like Mr. Wilson and they need something to lend them strength. To get through life safely sin must be avoided, good deeds done and that is not always easy.

God does give this help to all and it is called "grace." When a man is tempted, the devil says that the sin is nice, is pleasant. Then God sends grace and the man sees through the trick of the devil; he sees that the sin is mean and that it offends God. Or, a girl is asked by her mother to dry the dishes; that is a good work. But the little girl is a little bit lazy; she thinks there are too many butter plates and she feels like leaving them in the sink. The girl needs strength and patience. God does send her grace; she sees how even this little task is meritorious and she cheerfully goes to her task. In the first place grace helped the man to avoid sin; in the second place, grace gave the little girl patience and courage to do a good deed. Actual grace is a supernatural help of God which enlightens our mind and strengthens our will to do good and to avoid evil.

The Grace That Makes Us Holy (*Sanctifying Grace*).—Jesus Christ earned another kind of grace. This grace changes the soul and gives it new relations. It is like changing a tramp into a gentleman or like giving American citizenship to a foreigner. The grace is poured into the soul, becomes part of it, permeates it through and through like the sunlight filling a church, like the presence of the Blessed Sacrament which makes a church of the lowliest hall.

Naturally this grace makes the soul holy and pleasing to God. But God thinks so much of the person possessing this grace that He adopts him as a child would be adopted by rich parents and become a member of their family. The Holy Ghost loves that holy soul and makes His home there just as a friend stays at your home when he finds a gladsome welcome. The soul is a friend of God now, it is fit for heaven and has a right to heaven.

Q. 39. What does grace do to the soul?
A. Grace makes the soul holy and pleasing to God.

Summary by Example: The Grace That Helps Us.—Dolores has just gone to Holy Communion. The eyes of her soul are bright now and the devil will not easily deceive her. On the way home she goes into a grocery store. She could easily steal a nice red apple but grace tells her it would not be honest. She buys a Baby Ruth candy bar when in walks a poor little friend. Now Dolores would gladly eat the whole bar but grace tells her to give half to her poor friend and she does.—*The Grace that makes us holy.* But Dolores got something else by her Holy Communion; God put some grace right into her soul and before God she is a holy little Catholic lady. That grace made her soul beautiful before God. She belongs to God's family now; she is His child. The Holy Ghost loves her; He has made a regular little church of her soul because He is in her soul. Dolores is marked for heaven because the Holy Trinity wants good little girls like Dolores to be with them in heaven.—A man found a watch in the mud. That watch was like a soul before it has grace. He brought the watch to the jeweler and had it repaired and polished. Then the glistening watch was like a soul that has grace.

Organization: The grace that helps us. Tell the story of Mr. Wilson and his dog, Prince. What will help you when you are tempted? What will help you when you want to do good? Give an example of each.—The grace that makes us holy. Is there another kind of grace? What does this other grace do inside your soul? Is God pleased with the soul then? Into what family does God take this holy soul? What does the Holy Ghost do for this holy soul? Where will the soul go if it dies in this state?

IV. Using Grace

Grace comes to us all through life. We breathe air all day long and we scarcely ever think of it. The Holy Ghost gives us many graces during life that help to save our soul, many for the asking, many even without asking.

> Sometimes on a hot summer day the room is so stuffy that we cannot seem to get enough air. Then we open all the windows and the fresh draft makes us feel better. There are many times in life that our soul is gasping for more grace, meaning that it is tempted and troubled. Then we must open the door of our souls to grace.

In any need or trouble we can be helped by grace, and more and more as we get more grace. The man who is sick, who is sorrowful can use extra grace; so, the boy who is severely tempted, the girl who wants to do many good deeds.

Prayer brings more grace. The morning prayer brings extra graces for the day. A short visit to the Blessed Sacrament will give extra grace to overcome a temptation or to bear some sorrow. Attending Mass will certainly give enough extra graces to do many good deeds on that day. When Cardinal Pacelli visited the United States, he was shown many beautiful Catholic churches. He always went before the Blessed Sacrament and spent from fifteen minutes to a half-hour in prayer, no matter how many engagements were waiting.

If grace is used well, it will bring many helps. The pupil who eats a sufficiently nourishing breakfast will have sparkling eyes and red cheeks, he will be quick to understand what the teacher says, he will be strong to go through the work of the day. Grace well used is like a meal for the soul, making it alert to understand a duty and strong to perform that duty.

God does not force any one to use grace. The boss at the factory will not force a laborer to eat, but if that laborer pushes his lunch aside he will grow weak; he will not have the strength to do his work. A man can push grace aside too but he will get weak and eventually he will catch that terrible sickness which is called sin. Little Mildred always toyed with her food so that finally she got very thin. One day she was careless enough to go into a house where there was a large red sign, "Keep out,—Chicken Pox." Next day Mildred's face was spotted; she had caught the chicken pox because she was so weak. Little children should make good use of all graces so that their soul remains strong. If they do not use grace well, they will catch the sickness of sin. The principal ways of obtaining grace are prayer and the sacraments, especially the Holy Eucharist.

Summary by Example: We want to make the entire day holy. Donald told his mother that he would work for her all day. He had bought some flower seeds and all morning and afternoon he was busy sowing them in her garden. Our soul is a garden too and we should spend the whole day sowing the seeds of good deeds into it. Every morning we should do as that boy did, tell God that whatever we do on that day is done for Him and our entire day will really be holy.

Every hour or so Donald ran into the house to tell his mother what he was doing for her. It always encouraged him to work harder and always gave his mother new joy. So we should often repeat the offering of our good deeds to God. Many children say several times during the day, "All for Thee, sweet Jesus!"

Motivation: We want a little plan for every day of our whole life. Grace is so necessary that we must have it, and lots of it. We are going to be very careful and devout with our morning prayers. We will always ask God and the saints to give us many extra graces during the day. We will ask God to make us wise so that the devil will not be able to fool us with his temptations. We will ask God to make us strong so that we will do what is commanded. By the morning prayer we will offer every thought, word and deed of the whole day to God. Just think, making 365 days in a year holy to our good God.

Organization: Tell three ways by which you can get more grace. Does God force you to use grace? What will happen to you if you do not use grace? Why did Mildred catch chicken pox? What sickness will afflict your soul if you do not use grace? How can you make the whole day holy, so that every thought, word and deed is given to God?

Reconstruction of Unit Seven.

UNIT EIGHT: GRACE THROUGH BAPTISM AND CONFIRMATION

(First Communion Catechism: Lesson 8)

I. WHAT A SACRAMENT IS.
II. THE SACRAMENT OF BAPTISM.
III. THE SACRAMENT OF CONFIRMATION.

What We shall Learn: We have learned about grace, and now we shall learn that Jesus Christ instituted, or made, certain means through which we can receive grace; these are indeed the principal means and they are called sacraments. Next we shall learn about two of these sacraments, one of which the children have already received, namely Baptism, and the other which they will receive in a few years, namely Confirmation.

I. What a Sacrament Is

God could give you this great help of grace in any way He chooses. He could give it directly to you, only He did not choose to do it in that way.

Santa Claus. At Christmas time your parents could hand you the nice doll or the toy automobile but they do not do it in that way. Instead they have Santa Claus bring you those attractive gifts on Christmas morning. Santa has charge of the playthings and he gives them to the good children.

God has given the Catholic Church charge of His great and many gifts of grace. The Holy Ghost has taught the Church what to do with those graces and how to distribute them amongst the people. While He was here on earth, Jesus Christ instituted or made seven principal means through which grace comes. These seven means are the seven sacraments.

Q. 37. How does the Catholic Church help us to gain heaven?

A. The Catholic Church helps us to gain heaven especially through the sacraments.

A sacrament is a certain kind of ceremony. The words and the actions of the one giving the sacrament are the ceremony. In many parishes during May there is a ceremony which is called the

Crowning of the Blessed Virgin. Little children march, sing and pray and at the end one of their number places a crown of flowers on the head of the statue. In the case of a sacrament the ceremony is called a sign; it is called an outward sign because any one who wishes may hear the words and see the actions in a sacrament.

Q. 38. What is a sacrament?
A. A sacrament is an outward sign, instituted by Christ to give grace.

Summary by Example: Suppose Jesus Himself would come into this second grade and speak to you as follows: "I am going to build a beautiful fountain in your playground. Every child who is neatly dressed and drinks the water from that fountain, will have all its sins washed away." Actually Jesus did build seven fountains of grace and He called them sacraments. All who are well disposed and receive these sacraments, receive grace of forgiveness and grace of strength.

Organization: Who brings gifts at Christmas time? Who has been appointed to bring you the gifts of grace? Who has taught the Catholic Church how to give out these graces? What seven means did Jesus Christ institute through which you can receive grace? What do you mean when you say that a sacrament is a sign? What is meant by an outward sign? What is a sacrament?

II. The Sacrament of Baptism

You were scarcely a week old when sponsors carried you to the parish church. Mother and Father had talked about this ceremony several times every day since you were born. You, of course, did not know anything about it but they knew what wonderful things this sacrament of Baptism would do for your soul. When the sponsors brought you back from church, every one was very happy that you were baptized.

Q. 40. What sacrament have you received?
A. I have received the sacrament of Baptism.

The sacrament of Baptism produces wonderful effects in our souls. Every child born into this world has original sin on its soul. In that state the child is not a friend of God nor is it a member of the Catholic Church. Should the child die in that state it can never enter heaven but will spend its eternity in a place called Limbo. Now the priest uses that sign or ceremony which was instituted by

226   Unit 8: Grace Through Baptism and Confirmation   Grade II

Jesus Christ and he baptizes the child; the priest pours water over the child's head and says, "I baptize thee in the name of the Father, and of the Son, and of the Holy Ghost." Instantly the child is freed of original sin and becomes a member of the Catholic Church.

Besides the above effects, the child is made rich in the grace of God. It is now a child of God, and should it die in infancy it will join the other children of God in heaven. If the child grows up it will now receive very many graces to conduct itself as a true member of the Catholic Church.

Q. 41. What did Baptism do for you?
A. Baptism washed away original sin from my soul and made it rich in the grace of God.

Summary by Example: A baby was born next door. It was a rather sickly child, so the parents hurried it to the church to be baptized. They were afraid that the child might die in the state of original sin and thereby be forever shut out from heaven. Actually, the child did die three days after Baptism. Now the mother always says, "I have a little angel in heaven."

Motivation: Do you ever thank God for the great gift of Baptism? You pride yourself on the fact of being a member of the true Catholic Church but that honor came to you through Baptism. Stop a moment right now and thank God for this great grace.

Organization: What sacrament did you receive when you were just a few days old? Where would you have gone had you died in infancy without Baptism? What does the priest do and say when he baptizes? What sin is thereby washed away? To what new family does the child then belong? Where will the child go if it dies after three days?

III. The Sacrament of Confirmation

Life is a long Road. During the many years before us, we are faced with many difficulties and temptations which can lead us off the road. A man started out on a hundred-mile trip to Chicago. He set out in the right direction but he soon got off the road and never completed his trip because friends persuaded him to enjoy himself on the way. Soon his time was up and he had to turn back. The devil tries to make us take up our time with sinful enjoyment; and the first thing we know, life is over and we have not gained heaven.

Jesus Christ understood how we are tempted, how weak we are, and how we can be taken off the road by sinful pleasure. So He gave us other sacraments which can strengthen us against attack and can bring us back to the right road if we have strayed.

Q. 42. Are you preparing to receive other sacraments?
A. I am preparing to receive the sacraments of Confirmation, Penance, and Holy Eucharist.

Not this year but in three or four years these pupils will receive the holy sacrament of Confirmation. This one of the other sacraments is intended to give us strength to live and act like soldiers of Jesus Christ. A soldier fights the enemy: the confirmed one goes bravely into the battle against the devil. A soldier is proud to profess that he is an American; the confirmed one is proud to profess that he is a Catholic. A soldier cheers and strengthens his companions; the confirmed one strengthens the faith of other Catholics by word and example. A soldier goes into other countries and tells the people about his glorious America; the confirmed one tries to spread the Faith amongst non-Catholics.

Q. 43. What will Confirmation do for you?
A. Confirmation, through the coming of the Holy Ghost, will make me a soldier of Jesus Christ.

Summary by Example: On Pentecost Day the apostles were confirmed by the Holy Ghost. A mighty wind shook the house where they were sitting, and tongues of fire appeared over each one of them. In that moment they became soldiers of Jesus Christ; from that day on they were changed men. We remember how they had run away in fear when our Saviour took up His sacred Passion, but they ran away no more because now they were fearless. They went into far-away countries to spread the Faith. When wicked rulers threatened them with death, they were even happy to suffer for Jesus. All of them endured terrible tortures and eleven of them died a martyr's death. Confirmation had brought about this change.

Organization: Why did that man not complete his trip to Chicago? What can stop you from completing your trip to heaven? What sacrament did Jesus institute to make you strong? How can you then act like a soldier of Jesus Christ? What will Confirmation do for you? When were the apostles confirmed? How did Confirmation change the apostles?

Reconstruction of Unit Eight.

UNIT NINE: THE SACRAMENT OF PENANCE HELPS US TO KEEP GOD'S LAWS

(First Communion Catechism: Lessons 9 and 10)

I. THE SACRAMENT OF PENANCE.
   1. WHAT THE SACRAMENT OF PENANCE IS.
   2. WHAT THE SACRAMENT DOES.
II. HOW TO RECEIVE PENANCE WORTHILY.
   1. WE FIND OUR SINS.
   2. WE ARE SORRY FOR OUR SINS.
   3. WE MAKE UP OUR MINDS NOT TO SIN AGAIN
   4. WE TELL OUR SINS TO THE PRIEST.
   5. WE ARE WILLING TO DO THE PENANCE THE PRIEST GIVES US.

What We Shall Learn: We have studied the ten commandments of God and two of the six laws of the Church. It is possible, even for children, to sin against those commandments. The questions then arise: Must we then carry those sins on our soul all through life and even into eternity? Is there a way to regain the friendship of God? We fear to face the eternal Judge with sins of any kind on our soul. Happily, we shall learn that there is a means by which sin can be erased from the soul and the friendship of God can be regained. This means is the worthy reception of the sacrament of Penance. We shall learn that the sacrament also gives many other graces. Since Penance does so much we shall learn how to receive it worthily.

I. The Sacrament of Penance

1. What the Sacrament of Penance Is

A brief review of the topic of sin is in place here: the effort is worthwhile since it will make the proper background for what follows. More time should be given to explaining the seriousness of venial sins because these will regularly constitute the matter of childrens' confessions.

By the sacrament of Penance the sins committed after Baptism are forgiven. "Forgiven" means wiped out, erased, cancelled, pulled out by the very roots. It means pardoned, even forgotten completely as if they had never been committed.

Grade II   I. The Sacrament of Penance

Like two pieces of furniture, one perfect, the other with a stain. The stain on the latter is wiped out, varnish is applied, and in the end no one can tell the difference between the two. *Example:* Clare spilled some ink over Father's beautiful table. She was inconsolable because she knew how Father valued that blue and gold table. Big Brother came to her rescue and with sand paper and the addition of a little varnish he made the table as good as new. Sin is a stain on the soul but the priest comes to the rescue and makes the soul as good as before.

Original sin with which every child is born, is washed away by Baptism; in the case of an adult even actual sins are forgiven.

The great purpose of Penance is achieved through the absolution of the priest. "Absolution" means a loosing, a setting free, an erasing of sin.

Christ gave this power to erase sin to the first priests, the apostles, and to their successors, the priests today, when He came through closed doors and said to them, "Whose sins you shall forgive, they are forgiven them." Today therefore the sinner goes to the priest and the priest frees him from his sins with the words, "I absolve you." When the priest says those words He speaks for Christ and it is the same as if Christ said "I absolve you."

Q. 44. What is the sacrament of Penance?
A. The sacrament of Penance is the sacrament by which sins committed after Baptism are forgiven.

Summary by Example: One time ten lepers came to Our Lord to be cleansed of their dread disease. He could have cured them Himself but He choose to impress upon them the importance of the Jewish law of that time which required that the Jewish priest witness or certify to the cleansing. But Our Lord also meant that in future times, men who had sinned would have to present themselves to the priests of the Church so that their sins could be forgiven. He said to them therefore, "Go, show yourselves to the priest" and by going to the priest they were made clean. Today sinners are told to go to the priest when sins afflict their soul and the absolution of the priest makes them clean.

Organization: What sins are forgiven in the sacrament of Penance? What sacrament takes away original sin and any other sins which have been committed before Baptism? What did Big Brother do for Clara who had spilled the ink on the table? Was the table as good as new? Is our soul as good as before when the priest forgives all our sins? What does the priest say when he forgives our sins? Could Our Lord have cured those ten lepers? To whom did He send them? To whom does God send us when our soul is sick with sin? What is the sacrament of Penance?

2. What the Sacrament Does

Not all the effects of Penance are explained here as the pupils can hardly grasp, for example, the concept of temporal punishment or the restoration of merit.

The forgiveness of sin is the first and most important effect of the sacrament.

> One time some people brought a man suffering with the palsy to Our Lord. Did Jesus cure his bodily sickness right away? No, because bodily sickness was not the man's worst affliction. That man had sins on his soul and sins are the biggest evil in the world. Our Lord thought first of that worse disease and first He cured him of it by saying, "Thy sins are forgiven thee." The Saviour made this sacrament of Penance to take away the biggest evil, namely, sin.

Penance gives that grace which makes the soul holy and pleasing to God. *Example:* Charlotte went parading down the street in her new white dress when all of a sudden she slipped and fell into a puddle of mud. Did Mother only clean the three black spots? No, Mother washed the dress, starched it, ironed it and even put pleats into it. God is not satisfied with erasing the guilt of sin from the soul but makes the soul as beautiful as before and sometimes more beautiful by giving it much grace.

Penance takes away punishment and restores the sinner to the friendship of God. One who commits big, big sins is cast out of the family of God and, if he does not repent, will finally be cast into hell. When the sinner commits a mortal sin, he must receive the absolution of the priest. When grace enters his soul, he is taken back into that family and once more is a child of God. The penitent regains the right to heaven; if he dies now, even though he had confessed mortal sins, he will go to heaven. If only venial sins were confessed he will stay in purgatory for a shorter while. But, if he made a perfect confession, he will not have to go to purgatory at all.

Grade II — I. The Sacrament of Penance

The sacrament of Penance also gives us graces that help. In Penance God not only gives the jewel of holiness but He gives graces to protect that jewel. These graces are like military guards; they fight off the devil who wants to steal the rich jewel. God forgives sin, then gives graces to enable us to avoid sin in the future. He asks the penitent to lead a life doing good works; these graces help him to perform good works.

Penance is like a medicine that heals a bad sore of the soul. After the healing, it gives protection against the return of the sore.

Summary by Example: In the Tower of London is an immense glass case into which the English king has placed his jewels. Every year thousands of people come to the tower to see the golden crown, the jeweled scepter and many other precious stones. The king not only placed the jewels there but he made arrangements that they be guarded from theft. Night and day British soldiers with gun on shoulder guard the case. So God after Penance gives the soul the jewels of holiness, then gives other graces that protect that jewel.

Motivation: The forgiveness of sins is one of the greatest blessings which Our Lord and Redeemer left to us. Christ's great mission on earth was to erase sin. During His life on earth His most consoling words always were, "Thy sins are forgiven thee." He thought so much of this mission that He suffered and died to accomplish it. And now He has left us priests who carry on that work by forgiving sins as He did. How thankful should we be that we have this great means to return to God's friendship after we have sinned! How we should love and honor the priests who can erase sins from our souls!

Organization: The people brought a man to Our Lord who was sick and who had sins on his soul. Which trouble did Jesus cure first?—After a confession what does God give the soul that makes it holy and pleasing to Him? What is the punishment for a big big sin? What is the punishment for a venial sin? What happens to the punishment when big and little sins are confessed? Will a big, big sinner who has gone to confession, then dies, go to heaven?—Penance also gives the grace that helps. What does that grace help you to do? In whose name does the priest forgive sin?

Reconstruction of Division I.

II. How to Receive Penance Worthily

1. We Find Our Sins

"What is worth doing, is worth doing well." This is especially true of preparing for a sacrament from which we expect so many graces. We learned in a previous lesson that the sacraments always give grace, if we exert ourselves to receive them well. To receive the sacrament of Penance, five things are necessary. The first step is the examination of conscience; this must be done in an orderly manner.

If a boy has to mow the lawn, he does not run all over with the lawn mower making criss-crosses in every direction. Such a procedure would take him longer and the job could scarcely be well done. Instead, he diligently cuts one row beside the next and thus he gets all the grass. So with the examination of conscience we finish one commandment at a time and then go on to the next.

In the examination of conscience we try to find our sins. Two blind men sat by the roadside begging when they heard that Our Lord was coming that way. Right away they set up the cry, "Lord, help us to see," and when Jesus came up, He did help them to see. Before the examination of conscience, we should pray, "Lord, help me to see: help me to see my sins."

The examination is always to be made in the order of the commandments, because skipping haphazardly from one to the other might be the occasion for omitting some sins. If system is used in this matter, much of the disinclination to confession will have been overcome.

A second important part in the examination is the computation of the number of sins. Therefore as they come to each sin, the pupils ask, "How many times?" Again and again this month they will repeat: "After each sin, I find out how many times?"

And when they have found the sins and number of times for each, they should memorize the list so that they can tell them to the priest without hesitating or stumbling. Such a practice will help to make confession easy for the penitent, as well as for the confessor who will be spared many questions.

Summary by Example: "I just got my glasses today," said Sarah McLean to her chum Ella. "Everything looks quite different now; I see things now which I never saw for a long time."

Spectacles are to the eyes what grace is to the soul. When we examine our conscience we must ask God for spectacles, namely, His grace to find our sins and the number of times.

The examples and stories must emphasize, "I must find my sins: I must find the number of times."

Organization: How should a boy mow the lawn? What order should you follow when you try to find your sins? Why should you first ask for God's help? When you find sins, what else must you find out about them? Tell the story of Sarah's spectacles and make the application to this lesson.

2. We Are Sorry for Our Sins

Sorrow for sin is necessary. Four little boys were rowing a boat along the shore of a creek. Many a time their mothers had warned them, "Don't rock the boat." But, one little mischief started rocking and soon all four with many shouts and laughter, were teetering from side to side. The boat turned over and all four were plunged into the dirty water. Luckily the water was shallow, so no one drowned but they were a sorry sight as they stepped on shore, drenched to the skin and their clothes covered with slime and mud. They were sorry but for different reasons.

One was sorry because his clothes were dirty; another, because he was afraid of getting a cold; a third, because his mother would punish him; a fourth, because he had offended his good mother. The first three were not truly sorry because they thought only of themselves. The fourth, a boy named Charles, was truly sorry because he thought of the one he had offended. The first three would again rock a boat if they would not be caught; the fourth, Charles, resolved right there never to repeat the offense.

Contrition means to regret having committed the sins. We often say, "I am sorry; I made a mistake; I wish I had not done it; I hope the other person will forget my mistake"—that is sorrow or contrition.

We are sorry because sin offends God.—When we do something against the orders of our mother, she is sad and disappointed, is displeased with her child. In short, she is offended. Sin offends God who is so good; it is an insult to God's goodness and holiness.

In true sorrow there is a hatred of sin. We hate that stain on our soul; we are sorry that we made the mistake of committing a sin;

we hate mistakes. Sin is a stain; we hate dirty stains especially the ones that stain the beautiful soul.

It follows as a natural consequence that he who is truly sorry, will resolve not to repeat the offense. This brings in the resolution not to sin again, which will be treated more fully in a subsequent division. Contrition is sincere sorrow for having offended God, and hatred for the sins we have committed, with a firm purpose of sinning no more.

Summary by Example: A boy steals an orange from the grocer's window but scarcely has he finished eating the juicy fruit when he realizes his fault. God said, "Thou shalt not steal" and he is sorry for having offended God. Yes, the juice was sweet and he is still enjoying the taste but he realizes too that there is now a stain of guilt on his soul. He hates that stain more than anything in the world and he resolves never again to be so thoughtless.—Hatred of sin constitutes the only difficulty in the class review as children sometimes think they have to hate, for example, the orange which was stolen. They need not hate the orange, only the stain of sin made by stealing.

Why we are sorry for mortal sins.—Read the Bible Story, The Prodigal Son. Here is ingratitude to a good father, a sinful life. But here too is remorse after sin, true sorrow. The son realized that he had committed a great evil, that he had offended the best of fathers, that he had forsaken a beautiful home, that he was condemned now to work on a farm caring for swine.

Sin is the greatest of evils. It was sin that made Jesus suffer and die. Every other apparent evil like sickness can with a good intention be made meritorious but sin can never be anything but a real evil. Even a venial sin is a greater evil before God than a fire or a flood.

Sin is an offense against God, Our Creator. If it were not for his Creator, the sinner would not even have that tongue that sins, those eyes that sin, that body that sins. The tongue that sins, the eyes that sin are gifts of the Creator. Whether he sins mortally or venially he uses God's very gifts to offend God.

Sin is an offense against our Redeemer. The penitent places himself at the foot of the cross. He sees that pitiable figure of Christ, the crown that presses on His sacred head, the nails that

II. How to Receive Penance Worthily

pierce His hands and feet, the mutilated body stretched and racked on the cross—his sins did that. He contemplates Christ's anguish of soul—his sins did that. No one in all the world, no one in all eternity ever loved him more. Yet no one in all the world, in all eternity, has he offended more. Venial sins too are an offense against our Redeemer.

Sins bring punishment. Sins shut him out of heaven. He considers the beauties and joys of heaven; he has lost them by sin. What a terrible loss! Mortal sin condemns him to hell. He feels the pains and despair of hell. That is what he has gained. What a terrible bargain he made! Venial sins are punished in this life or in purgatory.

Summary by Example: All these are reasons why the sinner hates that stain on his soul, why he grieves to have offended God. He has been like the Prodigal Son. He has offended God, the best Father; he has traded the beautiful home in heaven for hell.

Why we are sorry for venial Sins.—Freddie was an adventuresome little boy of eight years. Mother had taken him and his two younger sisters on a picnic in the woods. Against Mother's orders, Freddie went on a tour of exploration. He enjoyed the wild berries and walking up the creek but every step took him further away from Mother. The berries upset his stomach; he slipped into the water; a big thorn pierced his hand. Now he needed Mother and he called for her. Would he find his good mother? Night was coming on. He had gone far from her side.

Every venial sin takes us further away from the side of God. The venial sins are like the berries which Freddy ate because they upset our soul. They are like thorns that pierce the soul. Then comes the night; that is the temptation to commit a mortal sin. Will the sinner come safely through this bigger temptation? He has wandered from the side of God by venial sins. Will he now wander still further away?

To repeat, venial sin is likewise an evil which the all-holy God can never permit. God is a good Father Who does not deserve even the slightest offense. He is so holy and sin is un-holy. Venial sin is punished sometimes in this life, generally in purgatory. Pains in this life can be severe but those in purgatory are more severe. Venial sin delays the sinner's entrance into heaven.

Many venial sins may lead to the commission of mortal sin.

They make the sinner careless so that he makes little of the occasion to mortal sin. They waste the grace of God and make him less worthy of God's special help.

Summary by Example: Peter was sleigh-riding down at the viaduct and with each ride he was trying to get closer to the side of the hill without going over. But he finally did go too close and over he went, sleigh and all, into the icy creek below. Father was sorry that his son received a gash in his leg but when Peter asked him to fix the sled he became just a little impateient, "I have fixed that sled for you again and again, Peter, but you do not appreciate my help. This time you can fix it yourself." The boy who commits many venial sins is going too near the edge like Peter did and he may go over. He does not appreciate the graces his Father in heaven is giving him.

Organization: Tell the story of the boys who rocked the boat and fell into the muddy water. Which one of them was truly sorry? Supply the missing word: "In my act of sorrow I must be sorry because I have offended ..... Why are we sorry? Which is the biggest evil, a venial sin or a big flood? Who gave the sinner the lips and eyes with which he offends God? What did sin do to Our Saviour on the cross? Where will a man go who dies with a big, big sin on his soul? Supply the missing word in these sentences: Venial sin is a bigger .... than a big fire; venial sin offends ....: venial sin hurt .... on the cross; a person who dies with venial sins must suffer in ....; venial sins lead to big, big ..... Tell the story of Peter sleighriding at the viaduct.

3. We Must Make Up Our Minds Not to Sin Again

The sorrow of the Prodigal Son was sincere because his resolution to do better was sincere. He was willing to go back and to live humbly after this, "Let me be one of your hired servants." The very fact that he undertook the long journey homeward was proof of his amendment.

Before God forgives us He demands not only sorrow but a complete return to Him by the promise to do better in the future. Never again will we be ungrateful, so unloving. Never again will we endanger that eternal reward for the short pleasure of sin. Never again will we be so foolish as to exchange an eternity of pain for a momentary joy here on earth. We will not even run the risk of going to purgatory for a venial sin; we will not even offend God in a slight matter.

To make sure that he will not sin again, the penitent resolves to take no more chances. He resolves to avoid everything that might lead him into temptation. The word "occasions" means nothing to these pupils, so call it rather "danger of sin."

Picture a Waterfall.—Donald puts out from shore in a boat. "Go back, it is dangerous!" cries his father. The boat out too far, gets caught in the swiftly moving current, is swept over the brink of the falls. That current is like the danger of sin that can sweep the soul away.

Examples of persons, places and things that may be dangers:

Persons: A boy who is always cursing is a danger for any one as it may get others into the bad habit. Such a boy should be shunned.

Places: To him who is addicted to drunkenness, a tavern is an occasion.

Things: A bad book can put unholy pictures into the mind. Resolve never to linger around any dangers to sin lest you yourself fall into sin. The moth that flies too often near the flame will get burned. "He that loves danger, shall perish in it," Ecclus, III:27.

Q. 45. What must you do to receive the sacrament of Penance?

A. To receive the sacrament of Penance I must:

1. Find out my sins.
2. Be sorry for my sins.
3. Make up my mind not to sin again.
4. Tell my sins to the priest.
5. Do the penance the priest gives me.

Summary by Example: Do you know something about Mary Magdalen who stood at the foot of the cross? Was it not brave of her to have pushed through the hostile crowd and stand there with her Saviour? Had not Magdalen once been a big sinner? Yes, indeed, but she washed her Saviour's feet with her tears of sorrow and the Saviour forgave her. Was that enough? No indeed, but Magdalen so perfectly amended her life that she became a saint and as a heroic saint she followed Jesus to the cross. The sincerity of our amendment proves the sincerity of our sorrow.

Organization: What did the Prodigal Son promise to do when he was sorry? Is a boy who has broken a window, really sorry if he intends to break another? Supply the missing word: I must make up my mind ..... to sin again. We must also avoid the dangers of sin. Mention just two dangers, for example, to a man addicted to drunkenness, to a boy inclined to talk unkindly. What five things must you do to receive the sacrament of Penance?

4. We Tell Our Sins to the Priest

She Told Her Sins.—Read the Bible Story, Mary Magdalen is Forgiven. The teacher is to say a few words about the sinfulness of this woman. Now Magdalen was sincerely determined to make her peace with God. Regardless of the sneers of onlookers she went forward bravely, yet humbly. The grace she expected was so great that she would do everything that was required. She would brave the sneers of the onlookers, cast herself at the feet of Jesus and confess her sins.

If we wish to obtain forgiveness we must go to confession, that is, tell our sins to the priest. Christ says also to our pastor, "Whose sins you shall forgive, they are forgiven them; and whose sins you shall retain, they are retained."

There is no occasion for nervousness. The priest will not interrupt; he will give us plenty of time. He will speak only if the hesitation of the penitent indicates that he is confused for the moment.

From a human viewpoint confession is not a very pleasant task. The little mental discomfort can be offered up as an act of penance. Entering the confessional, we kneel, and making the sign of the cross we say to the priest: "Bless me, Father, for I have sinned"; and then we tell how long it has been since our last confession. If this is our first confession, we say, "This is my first confession."

The confession of mortal sins. The obligation to confess all mortal sins must be explained as something apart from the life of the child, something which adults do at times. We do not wish to make them familiar even with the thought of mortal sin. *Example:* The ten locked doors: A man was searching for a treasure in a certain castle but there were ten locked doors between him and the treasure. Every door had to be broken down before he got his prize. Every mortal sin is a locked door between the big sinner and God. Mortal sin is the big obstacle that must first be removed. Every mortal sin is like a door that bars the way to God. If there are ten mortal sins, there are ten obstacles and every one of them must be removed.

The confession of venial sins. These sins are like cobwebs in the door that leads to God. Mary Magdalen was not satisfied to be just another friend of Christ but wanted to be His very dear friend. She was not satisfied to be partly clean of soul. She acknowledged by her actions all the petty venial sins which had gradually led her to more serious sins. Her reformation was complete.

There is indeed no obligation to confess slight sins but a loving friend is not satisfied to do only the things which are of obligation but will do everything to please his friend. The devout penitent will confess also his venial sins because he knows that it pleases God.

We must tell the number of times we committed each sin. If a boy be truly sorry he will tell his mother the whole truth about breaking windows and not conceal the fact that he broke quite a number.

The rule of telling the number of times pertains only to mortal sin. Nevertheless, it is advisable that even the number of venial sins be confessed. It will be a healthful little shock to the boy and girl, thus to learn how frequently they have been faithless. If we cannot remember the exact number of our sins, we should tell the number as nearly as possible. using the phrase "about so many times."

Summary by Example: Recall the case of Mary Magdalen. She went to confession; we must go to confession. She knelt at the feet of Jesus; we kneel before the priest who takes the place of Jesus. She confessed all her sins; we must confess all big sins and advisedly also little sins. She was forgiven; we will be forgiven.

Organization: To whom did Mary Magdalen tell her sins? To whom must you tell your sins? Supply the missing word: Whose sins you shall ...., they are forgiven them. Who said these words? To whom did He say them? How do you start your confession? Tell the story of the ten locked doors. What sins must be confessed? Why does a pious girl tell her venial sins?

5. We Are Willing to Do the Penance That the Priest Gives Us

The Penitent is like a sick Person.—Nora had a sore throat so she went to the doctor. She listened closely to the advice the doctor gave her about treating the throat ache and about taking precautions so that it would not recur. Willingly too she took the medicine that he gave her.

After his confession the child listens to the salutary advice of the confessor. The priest advises the child kindly. He tells him how to avoid committing those sins in the future, urges him to pray and to do good deeds. He tells him to be faithful both in the Big Test of mortal sin and the Little Test of venial sin. Sometimes, indeed, his instruction is very brief; but whether it is brief or long, we should listen intently. It is always impressive.

Just as Nora took the medicine which the doctor gave her, so must the penitent accept the penance which the priest gives him. It generally consists of some prayers which we must say. This penance is a little punishment which he undergoes for his sins. *Example:* Elmer disobeyed. Later the boy acknowledges the fault to his father. The father says to him: "I had intended to punish you quite severely but even with your admission I cannot overlook your fault entirely. As punishment, you will have to remain in the house for two evenings." Without confession our punishment might be very severe; after confession it is much less, namely, the penance the priest gives us.

The priest absolves us. Read the Bible Story, Jesus Quiets the Storm at Sea. Christ uttered only a few words and the storm stopped and the sea became calm. In the sacrament of Penance, He utters only a few words through the priest and peace and calm enters our soul. The words are "I absolve you from your sins, in the name of the Father and of the Son and of the Holy Ghost. Amen." Let us cooperate with the good God. When the priest is giving us absolution, we should say from our heart the Act of Contrition in a tone to be heard by him.

Q. 46. How do you make your confession?
A. I make my confession in this way:

1. I go into the confessional and kneel.
2. I make the sign of the cross and say: "Bless me, Father, for I have sinned."

3. I say: "This is my first confession" (or, "it has been one week, or one month, since my last confession").
4. I confess my sins.
5. I listen to what the priest tells me.
6. I say the Act of Contrition loud enough for the priest to hear me.

It is better to perform the penance right away because putting it off might cause us to forget it. We should remain in church a while and say other prayers begging God for still greater grace that we may never again commit those same sins or any other.

Summary by Example: Let us follow the case of Nora who had a sore throat. She dutifully took the medicine which the doctor gave her. She followed his advice later to wear rubbers when the streets are wet. She got instant relief and was completely cured in a few days. She had resolved to follow all directions of the doctor and it was a long time before she was similarly afflicted. We must show ourselves willing to do everything that is necessary to have our sins forgiven. We perform the penance and try to follow the advice given by the confessor so that we shall never sin again. We pray to Jesus, to the Blessed Virgin, to all the saints to help us.

Q. 47. What do you do after leaving the confessional?

A. After leaving the confessional, I say the penance the priest has given me and thank God for forgiving my sins.

Motivations: Father Barry of Notre Dame University wrote a story, The Purple Stole. A rich man was dying and as he tossed feverishly from right to left, he called upon his nurse to get him help. She called in the banker who could offer thousands of dollars to buy help. "No, not that," cried the anguished man. She called in influential friends but they could not offer him any consolation. Then his guardian angel appeared to him but the angel had not what the man wanted. Even the Blessed Virgin had not what he wanted. Then in the doorway appeared a humble priest in a purple stole. The sick man's eyes lighted up, he raised himself in his bed, he cried, "That's the man I want; only he can forgive me the many sins I committed."

How we should respect the priest who alone has a power that not even the guardian angel or the Blessed Virgin has! The priest in the confessional is the best friend any one can have. He is true because he will never reveal anything that is told him. He is a helper who will assist us to lead a better life. He is like Christ in the storm for by his absolution he says to our soul, "Be still" and the waves of sin subside and peace comes to our soul. The time for confession should be a happy one; we are going to our best friend.

Organization: What did Nora do when she visited the doctor in regard to her sore throat? What does the priest advise the penitent? What little punishment does the priest then give him? Supply the missing words in the sentence by which the priest forgives your sins: I absolve you from your sins in the name of the ......, and of the ..., and of the Holy Ghost. What prayer should you say while he absolves you? Tell the story of the storm at sea. How does the priest calm your soul in confession? When should you say your penance?

Reconstruction of Unit Nine.

UNIT TEN: THE HOLY EUCHARIST HELPS US TO KEEP GOD'S LAWS

(First Communion Catechism: Lesson 11)

I. THE SACRAMENT OF THE HOLY EUCHARIST.
   1. WHEN AND HOW IT WAS INSTITUTED.
   2. WHAT THE HOLY EUCHARIST IS.
   3. WHAT HOLY COMMUNION DOES FOR US.
   4. HOW TO PREPARE BODY AND SOUL.
   5. HOW TO RECEIVE HOLY COMMUNION.

II. HOLY MASS.
   1. OUR LORD'S MASS.
   2. THE PRIEST'S MASS.

What We Shall Learn: Step by step we have been learning of ever greater graces which Our Lord gives us to avoid evil and to do good. Penance takes from our heart the evil that we have done and gives us the grace to avoid doing it again. Now comes a sacrament whose main purpose is to help us to do good. In this sacrament we again meet our own priest but we meet principally Him who earned the graces and who is called the great High Priest. This time we receive Grace itself, that is, Christ Himself. Because of this the Holy Eucharist is the greatest sacrament of them all. We will devoutly study how we got this great sacrament. Then, filled with a desire to receive it, we shall study how we are to prepare in body and soul for receiving it. We wish to receive it in the right way because the Holy Eucharist confers wonderful benefits on the individual and on the whole human society.

I. The Sacrament of the Holy Eucharist

1. When and How It Was Instituted

It would be no egregious blunder for the teacher to refer to this sacrament just as communion. Children of this age do not distinguish between the sacrament and the reception; the word "Eucharist" with the best of explanations will still mean little to them. Correct terminology might be attempted but the pupil is not to be reprimanded for replying with the term that is simplest for him.

Greatest Love.—Read the Bible Story, Jesus Institutes the Holy Eucharist. On this night when the great sufferings He was to endure, were causing Him sorrow, Our Lord was thinking first of us. At the hour when our sins were about to hurt Him, He could provide us with this lasting sign of love. Just when wicked men were laying plans to crucify His body, He could give us that body for the food of our souls.

How holy, how sublime, how divine His act, as He took the bread into His holy and venerable hands and raised His eyes to heaven! What did He think of as He raised those eyes to heaven! Of us, of how He would love us more in this sacrament. He thought of these children, how on their Communion Day He would say, "Take you and eat; this is My body." Oh, we must thank Him a thousand times that He loved us so. Christ instituted the Holy Eucharist at the Last Supper, the night before He died.

When Our Lord that night said, "This is My body." it was His body. When He said, "This is My blood," it was His blood. When He said to the apostles, "Take you and eat," He gave them His own body to eat. When He said, "Take you and drink," He gave them His own blood to drink. The apostles received Him; they received Holy Communion from His own hands. This was the first communion in the world. How wonderful! How fortunate were these apostles!

Our Lord loved not only the apostles but us too. What He gave them, precious as It was, He would also give us. How would He do it?

Remember God is all-wise and all-powerful. Right there at the Last Supper He gave a great power, one which only God had. He gave those priests, the apostles, about Him (for they were priests), the very same power that He had just used. He gave the great power to all the priests who would yet live. Henceforth all priests could take bread and wine and by pronouncing those same words that He had used, change them into His body and blood; they pronounce the words during the Sacrifice of the Mass. That great power would never cease as long as there was a priest left on earth. And that is the story of how we received the sacrament of the Holy Eucharist. What a power! How wonderful are priests! What a gift!

Grade II   I. The Sacrament of the Holy Eucharist   245

Q. 49. When does Jesus Christ become present in the Holy Eucharist?
A. Jesus Christ becomes present in the Holy Eucharist during the Sacrifice of the Mass.

Summary by Example: Many, many years ago, long before Jesus came on earth, there lived children just like you. They belonged to a people called the chosen people because God loved them very much. These people were wandering from Egypt to a new land, through a desert where little grew, and soon all the people and especially the children became very hungry. God loved these children and He did not want them to starve, so He sent some very sweet bread down from heaven. It came down very much as rain does and it fell every morning except Sunday. The mothers went out with baskets and collected enough for themselves and their children. God showed His love for the children of long ago by sending them bread from heaven. But, He loves the children of today even more because He sends His own Son from heaven to be their food and they can get this food every morning, even on Sundays.

Organization: Tell the story of the Last Supper when Jesus gave us the Holy Eucharist. Supply the missing words: Take you and eat: this is My ...... Take you and drink: this is My ...... Who said these words? To whom did He say them? What then did the apostles receive? Did Jesus give the same power to change bread and wine into His body and blood also to the apostles? Did He give this same power to our priests today? When does the priest change the bread and wine? Tell the story of the food that God sent from heaven when the Israelites were hungry. What food for your soul does God send daily from heaven?

2. What the Holy Eucharist Is

The Holy Eucharist contains Our Saviour Jesus Christ.— You have pictures of Jesus and looking at them you say that He is beautiful and lovable—this Jesus is in the Holy Eucharist. You recall the stories of His kindness to the afflicted, for example, to the two blind men—this Jesus is in the holy Eucharist. You remember that story when He used His almighty power to raise Lazarus from the dead—this Jesus is in the Holy Eucharist. He made a saint of Mary Magdalen— this Jesus is in the Holy Eucharist.

Unit 10: Holy Eucharist Helps Us to Keep God's Laws Grade II

We take another presentation. *The body*—this is the body which Mary clasped to her breast, the immaculate body, the most beautiful body which ever walked the face of the earth. Here are the eyes that wept over the children of men; the feet which walked wearily up and down Galilee, searching for lost sheep; the hands which blessed and healed the sick; the voice which spoke sweet words of forgiveness to penitent Magdalen.

"And blood"—This is the blood which flowed from His head crowned with thorns; which fell in red drops from His mangled hands; which ran from His pierced and Sacred Heart.

The soul—This is the soul which conceived such beautiful thoughts as "Let the children come unto Me"; the soul that felt sorry for Mary and Magdalen when their brother Lazarus died; that said, "Come to Me all you who are burdened"; that willed to forgive Magdalen; that willed to help the five thousand and multiply the loaves for them.

God, Divinity.—This is the God who raised Lazarus from the dead, the almighty God who restored sight to the blind men, who in the end raised Himself from the dead and thereby proved that He is God.

Q. 48. What is the sacrament of the Holy Eucharist?
A. The Holy Eucharist is the sacrament of the body and blood of Our Lord Jesus Christ.

But we do not see His face, we do not feel the clasp of His arms, do not hear His gentle voice, when we receive the Host. Jesus is so bright that we could not look into His face. He is so mighty that we could not stand before Him.

Jesus is so bright. One time Our Lord was transfigured before Peter, James and John. His face shone like the sun. The apostles could not look at Him and they fell to the ground as if dead. In the Host Jesus is bright too but He hides His brightness under a covering that looks like bread and tastes like bread. Holy Communion looks like bread but It is Jesus.

Jesus is so mighty. As God He is so big that He can darken the sun and make the rocks quake. But He does not want to frighten us by dazzling us. He wants to come near us, wants to rest on our little tongues so He hides His mightiness under the shape of a little round piece of bread. Holy Communion has the shape of bread but It is Jesus.

Q. 51. Do you see Jesus Christ in the Holy Eucharist?
A. No, I do not see Jesus Christ in the Holy Eucharist because He is hidden under the appearances of bread and wine.

Q. 50. Do you receive Jesus Christ in the sacrament of the Holy Eucharist?
A. I do receive Jesus Christ in the sacrament of the Holy Eucharist when I receive Holy Communion.

Summary by Example: There was a mighty king who had hundreds of diamonds in his crown and even more jewels in his robes so that human eyes could not gaze steadily at him. His throne was covered with silver and gold. The people spoke in whispers of their ruler and they approached him with fear. But that King loved his subjects and he desired to go amongst them and do good to them. If he appeared in his glittering robes the people would not come near, so he put on an ordinary dress over his robes. Then the people knew him only as a kind prince who loved to associate with them, discuss their needs and help them. Wherever he went large crowds followed him.—So Our Lord in the Eucharist covers himself with an ordinary appearance like a common robe so that He can associate with us, help us. Every morning therefore large numbers of people come confidently to the altar railing to receive Him.

Organization: You receive the body of Jesus in Holy Communion; tell something about that holy body. You receive the blood of Jesus; tell where that holy blood was shed for you. You receive the soul of Jesus; tell how kind that soul was when Lazarus died. You receive Jesus, God; tell what Jesus, God, did for the two blind men.—You do not see Jesus in Holy Communion; with what appearances does Jesus cover Himself? Could you bear to look at Jesus if He came in all His brightness? Tell the story of that rich king who covered himself with a common robe in order to go amongst his people.

3. What Holy Communion Does for Us

We want to know now why Jesus comes to us, how Holy Communion pleases Him, and how it helps us. The king who covered his robes with ordinary clothes, was made happy by the love of his people and the people were helped by the gifts he gave them. The king came closer to his people.

248 Unit 10: Holy Eucharist Helps Us to Keep God's Laws Grade II

Holy Communion brings us closer to our God. Sacred Scripture says that at the Last Supper, St. John reclined on the breast of Jesus. What did the apostle hear in the beats of the Sacred Heart that evening? He was closer to Jesus than the other apostles and he must have been filled with love, for the Scripture refers to him as "the disciple whom Jesus loved." In later years St. John did write more sweetly about His Saviour than any other apostle.

Holy Communion helps us to love Jesus more. When we receive Jesus we are closer to Him even than St. John was and He will teach us to love Him even as He taught the apostle. He makes us feel how good He is to us, and we love Him for it. He tells us how great, how beautiful, how holy He is and we love Him more.

Holy Communion helps us to love others. At the Last Supper Our Lord had a long talk with His apostles and again and again He told them to love one another. No one, He said, could love Him unless he also loved his neighbor; no one could keep the commandments unless he loved his fellow-men. In Holy Communion Jesus talks to us just as He talked to His apostles, telling us to love one another. We see all the other children coming to the communion rail and we realize that we are all of one family, all are adopted children of God. We go from Holy Communion and we speak more kindly to our little friends, do more kind acts for them.

Holy Communion brings grace. The sacrament increases grace in the soul, making it still holier and still more pleasing to God. A gold watch is beautiful to look at but with the aid of a chamois cloth the jeweler can make it shine more and more. Every Holy Communion makes the soul shine more brightly before God.

Holy Communion keeps us from sin. Our Lord came into this world to keep us from sin and He comes into our heart for the same purpose. He strengthens us against the one thing, namely sin, which can separate us from Him. *Example:* The school doctor visited the class because so many pupils were suffering from colds. He not only gave them a medicine for the cold but he immunized them against diphtheria because that dread sickness could keep them out of school and could even kill them—as a friend he preserved them from a big evil. So Jesus, our Friend, not only helps us at the moment of Holy Communion but keeps us from sin in the future.

Grade II I. The Sacrament of the Holy Eucharist

Holy Communion helps us to do good. We can do all things in Him "who strengthens us." The boy cannot push the stalled auto but with Father's help he can. We may lack the power to do a certain good deed but with the help of Jesus in the Holy Eucharist we can do it. Does the child find it difficult to work industriously, to be obedient, to be kind, to tell the truth? Then let that child receive Holy Communion and all these things will be much easier to practice. A man was famished, and he found it impossible to do his carpenter job. He ate some bread, and he not only felt strong to continue but he loved his work. So if we feed on Holy Communion we will be strong to do good deeds and we will love to do them.

A man who lives in the doctor's house is not likely to get sick so often because he is constantly under the doctor's observation and can instantly get medical help when necessary. So we must bring the great Doctor, Jesus, often into the house of our heart by frequent and if possible daily Communion and He will tend us every day.

Summary by Example: The teacher will make the comparison with bread. Bread enters the body and becomes a part of it as Jesus enters the soul and becomes united with it.—When our hunger is satisfied with bread, the whole world appears in a more cheerful light and we are more inclined to be kind and indulgent with our friends; the Eucharistic Bread makes us love our neighbor more.—Bread gives strength to the weak and greater strength to the strong. Bread gives strength to fight off colds and so Holy Communion gives us courage to fight off sin.—Bread gives us bodily warmth so that we can enjoy our work and so Holy Communion gives us joy and spiritual desire to do more good.

Motivation: As the people in His lifetime loved to come near to Jesus, so will we love to be near Him and with Him through Holy Communion. When He was born three kings followed a star over a long journey and when they saw Him, were so transported with joy that they adored and offered Him gifts of gold, frankincense and myrrh. Holy Simeon held Him in his arms and said that now he had nothing more to wish for, to live for, now he was ready to die. When the Saviour preached on the seashore the crowds pushed so strongly against Him that He had to preach from a boat. So shall we go to the communion rail because we want to hear Jesus talk to our souls. He preached in the little temple at

250 Unit 10: Holy Eucharist Helps Us to Keep God's Laws Grade II

Capharnaum and the people brought their sick and He healed them. We shall gather in our church because we want Him to heal us of our sins. He sat in the shade of a tree and the little children came and climbed on His lap. We shall go into the soft quietness of the church and tell Him how we love Him.

Organization: What apostle did Jesus love especially? What did Jesus let St. John do at the Last Supper? Whom then will you love most of all in Holy Communion? Does Jesus also help you to love your little friends more? Does Jesus give you that grace that helps? What does this grace help you to do? What did holy Simeon say when he held the infant Jesus in his arms?

4. How to Prepare Body and Soul

In the course of this section the teacher should find time to review the Acts of Faith, Hope and Charity. It is necessary also to repeat the method of confession if this class is about to make its First Communion.

Jesus gave the examples for the preparation of Body and Soul.—The Last Supper is really divided into three parts, each leading to the next. First, Our Lord and the apostles carried out the rules of the Old Law concerning the eating of the paschal lamb. Secondly, Our Lord washed the feet of His apostles. Thirdly, He gave them Holy Communion.

The apostles observed the rule about eating; they were cleansed by the washing of the feet; they received. We follow the example of the apostles when we receive Holy Communion. We must observe the laws of the Church regarding this Sacrament; we must be cleansed by confession; lastly, we receive Holy Communion. This is the procedure or the rule that the Church lays down for us.

The rule of eating or fasting. By command of the Church no food nor drink, except plain water, may be taken from the previous midnight. Jesus must be the first food on Communion Day.

The cleansing or washing of the soul. The preparation of the soul begins with confession. Pious souls will want to have even the slightest stain of venial sin removed. They desire Communion ardently; they wish to do everything necessary to cleanse the soul and to receive worthily.

The child will think often of his Lord the evening before receiving. Recreation should be becoming and conversation carefully guarded so that no wrong word escape the lips. The evening prayers will be more than usually devout and there will be added a short act of desire for Jesus in the Blessed Sacrament. The last word will be, "Jesus keep me holy and pure, guard me in sleep as I want to receive You in a holy heart tomorrow morning."

Q. 52. What must you do to receive Holy Communion?
A. To receive Holy Communion I must:

1. Have my soul free from mortal sin.
2. Not eat or drink anything after midnight.

Summary by Example: A story of Desire: Years ago children were not permitted to receive Communion at so early an age. Blessed Imelda entered the Dominican Order at the age of ten and when this incident occurred she was not yet fourteen. She loved Our Lord in the Blessed Sacrament intensely and above all she longed for the day when she could receive Him in Holy Communion. Imelda had seen the other Sisters receive and now she knelt alone in her pew. Suddenly, a heavenly fragrance filled the air. A radiant Host hung in the air above Imelda. Jesus had miraculously come. The chaplain was called and he held a golden paten beneath the Host. It descended; he took It in his fingers and placed It on the tongue of Imelda. "How is it possible," cried Imelda, "to receive Jesus in one's heart and not die for love!" And Imelda closed her eyes and died in the embrace of her Lord.

Organization: What did Jesus do for the apostles before He gave them Holy Communion? How will you clean your soul before Holy Communion? Jesus and the apostles kept the law. What law about food and drink must you keep? Of whom will you think often the evening before? Will you say your evening prayers well? Tell the story of Blessed Imelda.

5. How to Receive Holy Communion

The Great Day: In our preparation and thanksgiving we should show such a love for the Eucharist as St. Tarcisius had.

There was no priest available to bring the sacred Host to a Christian prisoner, so little Tarcisius begged permission from the Bishop to undertake the dangerous mission. What an honor that he, a little boy, could carry the almighty God to a future martyr! The Bishop agreed, wrapped the Host in a

Unit 10: Holy Eucharist Helps Us to Keep God's Laws Grade II

white cloth and sent the boy on his way. Piously and modestly he carried the precious package next to his breast.

"There goes Tarse;" cried some ruffians, "he is carrying the Christian charm." The boy's arms became like steel as he pressed his Lord to his bosom and the rowdies could not budge them. He would not let go of the package containing the Host although they beat him cruelly. An approaching soldier, Sebastian, frightened them away but Tarcisius lay on the street dead.

The soldier happened to be a Christian and he knew what the little Saint had clasped next to his breast. He unwound the arms, once like steel, but God had worked a miracle—the Host had vanished.—Will we guard closely the gift that we have received from heaven?

A greeting to God should be on the child's lips upon rising. The morning prayers will be more than usually devout. The child will dress modestly, then walk silently to the church or place of assembly. Though the clothes are better than usual, he must think only that they are given to him to show greater respect for the Divine Guest.

Arrived in church, there will be acts of Faith, Hope, Love and Desire. Again and again he will repeat, "O Lord! I am not worthy."

The time of Holy Communion is the precious time, the goal of desire, an opportunity so rare that millions never get it. It may mean the reception of such graces for the children as they never dreamed possible. When that moment has arrived the communicants must forget the church around them, forget the boy or girl beside them, just lose themselves with God. They must use every minute; they cannot lose a second. The minutes are golden; they are worth hours. They must absorb the strength of Communion like a loving saint.

Q. 53. What should you do before Holy Communion?

A. Before Holy Communion I should:

1. Think of Jesus.
2. Say the prayers I have learned.
3. Ask Jesus to come to me.

See the Bible Story, Jesus Blesses the Children. The actual

Grade II   **I. The Sacrament of the Holy Eucharist**   **253**

moment of reception is now here. The child is to be like one of those fortunate children whom Our Lord blessed.

The first prayer on returning to the pew will be one of adoration. Jesus Christ whom they have received, is God the Son, the second Person of the Holy Trinity. They greet Him again and again as God. They tell Him how happy they are that God has at last entered their heart.

The thanksgiving after Communion is a very holy and beneficial act. Not one of those moments may be wasted because the children have the unusual opportunity of talking directly to Christ within their heart. There must be Acts of Faith, Hope and Love according to the set prayers or still better as composed by themselves. There will be sweet offerings of self.

Finally come the prayers of petition. The children ask God to help them in body and soul. They remember their parents, pastor, teacher, all their friends; they pray for the Holy Father. Childrens' prayers are very powerful before God and at this time they have a special efficacy.

On that day of Holy Communion special care should be taken that no sin be committed and no sin should ever again be committed by one who has been favored so wonderfully. The child will resolve to approach the Holy Table often because Communion helps him to love his Lord better, to love others, to get more grace, to keep from sin, to do good—"give us this day our daily bread."

Q. 54. What should you do after Holy Communion?
A. After Holy Communion I should:
    1. Thank Jesus for coming to me.
    2. Tell Him how much I love Him.
    3. Ask Him to help me.
    4. Pray for others.

Motivation: God is determined to save men if there is the least effort to cooperate on their part. He created man in the beginning and offered him heaven. When man spurned the offer, God did not abandon him but promised to send a Redeemer some day to buy back that lost opportunity. The Redeemer came and offered His life to buy heaven for men. He left them the Holy Eucharist where again and again He gives them the grace to save their souls.

Are we persevering too? Are we willing to give our Redeemer that little cooperation He asks for? Are we ready to come to Him often in Holy Communion?

Suppose that a child spends fifteen minutes every week in the company of a very wise man, would it not become wise? Suppose that it spent fifteen minutes every week in the company of a very good man, would it not become good? People would judge the child by the company it keeps and would say it is a wise or a good child. People are judged by the company they keep. How nice when it is said that a boy or girl enjoys the companionship of Jesus! Yet the child can do this every week, every day in fact. If a child spends a quarter-hour every week or several times a week in the company of Jesus through Holy Communion, people would have to say it is a very wise and a very good child because the association with the Saviour would really make it wise and good.

Organization: Tell the story of St. Tarcisius. Tell what you will do immediately on rising on the day of your Holy Communion. Why do you get nice clothes for Holy Communion? How will you behave on the way to church? Tell the story of Jesus blessing the little children. Do you receive God? For what will you thank Him? For whom will you pray? Will you receive Him often?

Reconstruction of Division I. Combine all organizations in order.

II. Holy Mass

1. Our Lord's Mass

To explain the Mass of the Last Supper to children is difficult. Two explanations are presented here, both of which may be tried: the first one, though more difficult, presents the Mass at the Last Supper as a prior offering of the sufferings to come; the second is simple and just draws parallels between Christ's Mass and the Mass today. (This division must be taught orally.)

FIRST EXPLANATION: Our Lord did something else at the Last Supper besides giving us Holy Communion. First, He offered His body to His Father in heaven, then He gave His body to the apostles to eat. First, He offered His blood to His Father, then He gave It to the apostles to drink.

Instead of waiting for tomorrow to offer Himself to His Father on the cross, He offered Himself now. *Example:* A boy knows that he must ungergo a serious operation tomorrow. He cannot keep it out of his mind, so he says, "O God, I offer You all the pains I will suffer tomorrow; I am ready; I am ready," Our Lord longed to offer Himself, He could not wait, so He made the offering at the Last Supper. In a Mass Jesus offers Himself to His Father. This was the Mass of Jesus.

On the cross Jesus would say, "Heavenly Father, I offer You My body; I offer You My blood in payment for all the sins of the world." He did not wait but now He held to heaven the Host that was His Body and He said, "I offer You this body now which will be tortured and crucified." He held towards heaven the chalice that contained His blood and He said, "Heavenly Father, I now offer You My blood which shall be shed on the cross."

Summary by Example: A boy telephones a sick friend, "I am giving you my sweater for keeps; I'll bring it to you tomorrow." That boy no longer owns the sweater although he will not deliver it until tomorrow. So Jesus here gave up His body and blood, although the offering would be completed only on the following day.

SECOND EXPLANATION: Our Lord offered a Mass at the Last Supper. He took bread and wine and He blessed them; at the Offertory our priest likewise takes bread and wine and blesses them. Our Lord changed the bread and wine into His body and blood; our priest at the Consecration likewise changes the bread and wine into Christ's body and blood. Then Our Lord gave His body and blood to the apostles in Holy Communion; at the Communion of the Mass, our priest likewise receives, then gives the people Holy Communion.

In the olden times such an offering was called a sacrifice. The priests of the Old Law used to offer lambs in sacrifice just like this; they would kill the lamb, burn it and offer it on the altar to God. Here Jesus turned his face towards Calvary where He would be killed tomorrow and offered Himself to His Father.

Organization: Did Jesus wait until the day of the Crucifixion to offer Himself to His Father? What then did He do before He gave His body and blood to the apostles?—Our Lord at the Last Supper offered bread and wine. When does the priest offer bread and wine? Our Lord changed them into His body and blood. When does the priest change them? Our Lord gave Holy Communion. When does the priest give Holy Communion? Then the priest's Mass is the same as the Mass of Christ.

2. The Priest's Mass

Jesus pleased His Father infinitely with His offering of Self on this day. In His great love for the Father He had arranged a plan whereby He would continue this pleasing offering every day until the end of the world.

Example: A priest goes into church and makes a quarter-hour's adoration; then realizing how much it pleases God, he resolves to make that adoration every day. Jesus wanted His Mass to be continued every day until the end of the world.

Our Lord continued His Mass through the priests. He gave the apostles power to do what He had just done, namely, offer up a Mass. He wanted all the priests who succeeded them to have the same power to do just what He had done, namely, offer Mass. He turned to the apostles and He said, "Do this." He spoke to all priests when He said, "Do this." Then and there He gave the apostles and all the priests the power to do what He had just done, namely offer Mass to God.

The priest is like Christ. Every morning priests offer Mass, doing just what Christ did and just the way He ordered it to be done. Jesus took bread; the priest takes bread. Jesus said over the bread, "This is My body"; the priest takes bread and says over it, "This is My body." Jesus took wine and said over it, "This is My blood;" the priest takes wine and says over it, "This is My blood." Jesus held the body and blood aloft to His heavenly Father offering them to Him; the priest does the same. In His mind Jesus said, "O Father, I offer You this body and blood in worship, in thanksgiving for all Your Favors to men; I will offer them to You as a payment for the sins of men, as a prayer that You will shower richer blessings upon men." The priest says, "O Father, with this body and blood I worship You, I thank You, I ask pardon, I beg for new blessings."

Summary by Example: *A Story:* A battle fleet one time encountered such a heavy storm that every ship was threatened with destruction. On the admiral's ship there happened to be a little child. The admiral raised the child in his arms and looking up to heaven, cried: "For the sake of this innocent child, O God, have mercy on us!" And the storm abated. If God will have compassion on men when a little child is held up to Him, how much more will He have mercy on sinners when His own Son is held up to

Him during Mass! He will accept our worship as we offer that Son to Him; He will be pleased with our thanks, for we return Him the gift of His divine Son; He will be moved to pardon our sins because we offer the body and blood of His Son in payment; He will listen to our request for new blessings because we speak through His Son.

Motivation: But what shall we do, how shall we assist at Mass? We should do just what we would have done had we been privileged to see the Mass of our Saviour at the Last Supper. We would not have been late and we would not have been in a hurry to leave the table. We would not have played with the dishes on the table or shuffled our feet or gazed about at the furnishings. Our eyes would have remained on our Saviour; we would have followed His actions, His words, even the thoughts in His mind. With Him we would have offered the body and blood to the Father, would have adored, thanked, asked for pardon, prayed for new blessings. So during Mass we must not play, not talk, not shuffle, not look about. We must keep our eyes on the altar and on the Host or chalice whenever they are visible. We must pray as Jesus prayed at the Last Supper, as the priest prays now, telling God that we adore and thank Him, we ask pardon for our sins and beg for new blessings. We shall be especially attentive at the three principal parts of the Mass: the Offertory, the Consecration, the Communion. At the Offertory we shall ask Him to cleanse our soul. At the Consecration we shall adore Him as our God. At the Communion we shall receive Him either in reality or in spirit.

Organization: Supply the missing word: Do .... in remembrance of Me. Who said this? To whom did He say it? What then were the apostles supposed to do? Were the apostles, priests? Did Jesus then say this to all priests? What does the priest do in his daily Mass that is the same as what Jesus did? Tell the story of the storm and the little child whom the captain held up to God. Was the ship saved? Whom does the priest in the Mass hold up to God? Will Jesus help us? How will you attend Mass? What are the three principal parts of the Mass?

Reconstruction of Unit Ten.

UNIT ELEVEN: OUR BLESSED MOTHER

I. To the Time When the Angel Appeared to Her.
II. From the Birth of Christ to the End.

What We Shall Learn: During this year we have learned much about mother-love and father-love. From there we went further to learn how God loves us and how we must love God. During these explanations we also heard much about another mother, the Mother of Jesus Christ. Now to finish the school year we will study the life of this most wonderful of mothers, learning how she loves us and in return resolving how truly we will love her. It will be a pleasant and comforting story to take with us into our vacation.

I. To the Time When the Angel Appeared to Her

The teacher will refer to the Bible History for a more complete story of the following incidents. Each mystery is to be treated as an independent unit, with explanation by the teacher, followed by recitation by the class.

Mary's Birth. The Blessed Virgin was the child of a very pious couple, Joachim and Anna. From the very first instant of her existence, Mary was free from the stain of original sin, being the only human being to whom this privilege was ever accorded. The great mystery is recalled by the Church on December 8, the Feast of the Immaculate Conception of the Blessed Virgin Mary. All Catholics must attend Mass on this day as it is a holyday of obligation. Just what town was Mary's birthplace has never been agreed upon. Some place it in Bethlehem, some in Jerusalem, and very many in Nazareth, a village of Galilee.

The Child in the Temple. At the age of three, her parents brought Mary to the temple. Pious legend tells us that Mary received her education in this great Temple of the Jewish people. Undoubtedly, during this training period, she with other maidens performed light tasks about the vast building, such as sweeping and dusting, and preparing for the great crowds which continually visited there. To a girl of Mary's virtue and high purpose, these tasks must indeed have been pleasant.

Mary and Joseph. When Mary was fourteen years old, the high priests appointed a holy man, named Joseph, to be her protector and provider. The two left Jerusalem, traveled north, and took up their abode in the village of Nazareth. We can picture the humble little home with the flat roof, its living quarters in the front and carpenter shop in the rear. Everything is spotlessly clean and sweet; flowers climb over the walls. Her life at Nazareth was a quiet, ordinary one with meals to prepare, clothes to mend, floors to clean, yet it had a wider scope too through the edifying example of virtue which she gave to the townspeople.

The Annunciation. One day, as Mary was engaged in prayer, an angel named Gabriel suddenly appeared in the room and announced to her that she was to be the Mother of the long-awaited Redeemer. At first, Mary was very much disturbed that so great an honor should come to her, but when the angel explained further, she answered: "Be it done to me according to thy word." The conversation between Mary and the Angel is part of the Angelus, a prayer recited thrice daily by Catholics to commemorate this event.

The Visitation: So overjoyed was Mary at the glad tidings that, like any person with good news, she resolved to visit her cousin Elizabeth and tell her about it. The Scripture says "she hastened" and we can picture her walking with joyful, rapid step towards a village located about four miles from Jerusalem where Elizabeth lived. The journey ordinarily took many hours, but Mary was so full of joy that she did not feel the hardships or even notice the passage of time. When they met, the Holy Ghost inspired Elizabeth to address Mary as the Mother of God, and Mary answered: "My soul doth magnify the Lord." These words are likewise the first lines of a prayer, the Magnificat, which the Church uses daily in the Divine office. Elizabeth also had joyful news to discuss, namely, that she was to give birth to John, afterwards called the Baptist, who would prepare the way for the Redeemer. Mary remained about three months with her cousin after which she once more returned to her little home in the province of Galilee.

Motivation: Mary is our most powerful intercessor in heaven. Christ granted His Mother's prayers on earth, as witness the marriage at Cana, then how much more will He grant them in heaven. Any good son will listen to the petitions of his mother, and Jesus was the best Son of all. If the prayers of the saints, his servants, have such power before God, how much more those of His mother? In heaven she is closer to God than any saint, and therefore her petitions have first place. The saints have achieved great sanctity by devotion to her; we can do the same. Give examples. We pray particularly to her for the grace of final perseverance; the Church teaches that it is practically impossible to persevere unto the end without Mary's help.

Organization: Review the story contained in each paragraph.

II. From the Birth of Christ to the End

The Journey of the Blessed Virgin and St. Joseph to Bethlehem to be Enrolled. We hear of Mary again as, in obedience to the Emperor's command to be enrolled as citizens of the Roman Empire, she and Joseph undertake the long journey to Bethlehem. The order was that each person was to be enrolled in the place where his family originated, and hence the journey to Bethlehem the city of David from whom Mary was descended. Probably this trip took over thirty hours, for as they moved along the road by the Jordan river they were impeded by thousands of other travelers, who were similarly making their way to the cities of their forefathers. Arrived at Bethlehem, no room was found for them in any of the inns, so the pious couple proceed a little beyond the city and prepared to spend the night in a stable or kind of cave.

The Birth of the Saviour. On that night the angel's promise was fulfilled, for the Saviour of the world was born. A little later the same night the shepherds, heeding the voice of an angel, came to adore the new-born Infant. (Full details must be given from the Bible Story.)

The Presentation. The Jewish law demanded that forty days after the birth of a male child, mother and son be presented in the Temple. Most probably Joseph placed Mary and Jesus on a mule's back while he walked alongside. The pious couple were not able to make the customary offering of a lamb on this occasion, so instead they presented the sacrifice of the poor, a pair of turtle doves or two young pigeons. Quite a dramatic event took place during the ceremony, as the aged Simeon took the child in his arms and prophesied the redemption of Israel. The old man was so overjoyed to have lived to see the Redeemer that he exclaimd he had nothing further to live for and was ready to die. A moment afterwards a holy woman, Anna, prophetess, announced to all that this Child was the hope of Israel.

The Three Kings. After the Presentation, the Holy Family either returned to Bethlehem directly, or first went to Nazareth and then moved to Bethlehem. While at the latter village, they received the visit of the Magi or Three Kings. The actions of the Three Kings tell the pupil how he must conduct himself toward Jesus when he receives Him in Holy Communion.

The Flight into Egypt. Soon after the departure of the Three Kings, Joseph received the heavenly message to flee into Egypt with the Child and His Mother on account of the evil designs of Herod. This wicked king on hearing that the King of Israel was born feared that he would be supplanted. By ordering the slaughter of the innocent children in Bethlehem he hoped that Jesus would be amongst the slain and could therefore never take his place. Being thoroughly worldly-minded, Herod could not realize that Jesus was not to be an earthly king, only a King of souls. Egypt was not altogether an inhospitable country, as a large Jewish colony existed there. The journey just to the confines of Egypt would take about ten days and we do not know to what town or village in this strange land they went. Neither do we know positively how long the Holy Family remained.

The Return from Egypt. When Joseph received from the angel the news of Herod's death, he "arose, and took the child and its mother and came again into the land of Israel." Joseph had intended to settle in Bethlehem, but warned by the angel that Archelaus, also a wicked King, ruled in Judea, he went north into Galilee and once more dwelt in Nazareth. In all these trials Mary obediently followed the guidance of Joseph.

The Finding of the Child Jesus. The Gospels make only one reference to Mary during the Hidden Life, that is, when she and Joseph lost the child Jesus when He was twelve years old, and found Him after three days, teaching in the Temple. The story is so well known that it needs no recounting here.

The Hidden Life. For thirty years Jesus lived with His mother in the humble home of Nazareth. The life was ordinary, as that of any family of rather poor circumstances. Undoubtedly, Mary daily received the assistance of Jesus in performance of her household tasks, and we can be certain of the same in regard to Joseph. Altogether, these thirty years were the happiest ones for Mary. (The teacher may spend considerable time here explaining to the pupils a day's routine in the home at Nazareth, a life which even these pupils can imitate in many respects.) During the later part of the hidden life, St. Joseph died, and we picture him as passing away with Jesus on one side and Mary on the other.

The Public Life. Mary's name is mentioned only three times during the public life of Jesus Christ. The first describes the marriage feast at Cana, where at her request Our Lord worked His first miracle; it is our first picture of the powerful intercession of Mary. During the three apostolic years, Mary effaced herself almost completely. Second reference is made when she happened to be on the outskirts of a crowd when Jesus was preaching. When Our Lord was told of the presence of His Mother, He replied that he who did the will of His Father was His brother and mother. When on another occasion a woman called His Mother blessed, He replied that blessed are they who keep the word of God. Jesus did not by these words depreciate the dignity of His Mother, but He wished to emphasize the value of holiness. Most probably Mary often allied herself with those pious women who followed Our Lord and ministered unto Him.

The Passion. Since the Passion of Christ occurred during the Paschal week, we find Mary in Jerusalem. Not the Gospel, but tradition has handed down the story of Mary meeting her Son on the Way of the Cross. The Gospel though, is very plain in stating that she stood at the foot of the Cross when He was expiring. The same source describes the words of Christ in her regard, when He gave her to the world as its Mother, and when He placed her in charge of St. John. We have the second great picture of Mary here, where she is placed over the whole world as the mother of all mankind.

After the Resurrection. St. Ambrose is the authority for the belief that she was the first person to whom Jesus appeared after the Resurrection. Probably she was present when He appeared to a number of His disciples in Galilee and again at the time of the Ascension. On Pentecost day, the Holy Ghost descended upon Mary as He did on all the apostles and disciples gathered in the upper room at Jerusalem.

With St. John. About Mary's life after Pentecost, scholars lean to the opinion that St. John took her with him to Asia Minor. On a hill about nine miles from Ephesus, a house was discovered later in which Mary is supposed to have lived. Some scholars maintain that she remained in Ephesus only a short while, and that she stayed for the greater part of this period about Jerusalem. At the end, more students agree at least that she died of love, her great desire to be united to her Son either dissolving the ties of body and soul, or prevailing on God to dissolve them. There is no certain tradition as the year of Mary's death. One great authority places her death at 48 A.D., that is, about fifteen years after her Son died on the cross.

The Assumption. The whole Catholic Church believes that Mary's body was not corrupted in the grave, but was miraculously assumed into heaven. It was fitting that so holy a body as Mary's never be subjected to the decay of the grave but be taken immediately to join her soul, "full of grace."

Motivation: We must love Mary because she is lovable in herself. No one was ever so beautiful in body but especially in soul. (The teacher will bring pictures of Mary into the classroom.)

We must love Mary because God loved her so much. To no other saint did He give such grace; only to Mary could the angel say, "Hail, full of grace." To no other person has God given the great privilege of being conceived immaculately. By God's grace, it was impossible for her to commit even the slightest sin or to be guilty of the slightest fault. Mary was the only purely human being who was ever assumed into heaven.

God wants us to love Mary. At the cross Jesus spoke to His apostle, St. John: "Son, behold thy Mother." St. John was our representative then and Jesus meant that henceforth we must all look up to Mary as our Mother. Then He turned to Mary and told her henceforth to look upon us as her children with the words: "Mother, behold thy son." The Church too seconds this desire of Our Lord by continually reminding us that Mary is our mother.

How can we love Mary? We can do it by just telling her of our love. We can learn many prayers to recite in her honor. We can ask her help for anything we desire as long as it is acceptable to God. Lastly, we can try to become like her.

Organization: Review the story contained in each paragraph.

Reconstruction of Unit Eleven.

MONDAY MORNING CHARACTER TALKS
GRADE II

The caption explains the purpose of these five-minute Talks—fifteen Talks to a semester. The teacher must be wholly guided by circumstances of necessity or appropriateness and will therefore give them in the order she judges best. Some talks have a relation to the progression of catechetical matter; others, marked with an asterisk, refer to feasts or observances of the ecclesiastical year and for best effect these are to be explained when apposite.

The teacher is to enlarge the Talks according to her own ingenuity and ability; for example, where a virtue of a particular saint is extolled, it is well to give a more complete story of that saint's life. A definite effort is to be made towards a practical use. The virtue therein proposed is to furnish, as it were, the particular examen for the pupils during the following week; some little practice should even follow a Talk on a feast day or church observance. The teacher is therefore to remind the pupils of their practice several times during the week. She will devise some method to check on results that does not disclose the negative side of human conscience; that is a matter for the confessional only.

First Semester

1. *To Study My Catechism* (*Unit One*). To learn my religion is a serious duty because I cannot practice the truths of my religion unless I know the Catechism. My soul's salvation depends on the way I use his means of knowing. Ignorance later on will not excuse me, because daily now I am given the opportunity to inform myself. I will therefore memorize the necessary questions; I will study the rest of the matter; I will pay close attention during class hours. I will make good resolutions daily, how to learn my religion in order to practice it better. The resolution is very timely for this first month of the school year.

St. Peter Canisius (June 25) is often called the Father of the Catechism. This great Saint put the truths of the Catholic religion into a form very similar to our own catechism. St. Canisius did great work when the Protestant heresy threatened to sweep over the whole of Europe; it is said that wherever he went, the growth of the heresy was instantly halted. By means of the catechism he instructed the laity and held them fast to the Church. He was the first of his countrymen to enter the Society of Jesus and he later became the first provincial of the Society in Germany. His catechism is still a model for similar texts.

2. *Review All Prayers* (*Unit One*). Each member of the class will be examined in regard to the prayers learned the previous year. The teacher will also suggest a plan of prayers for morning and evening.

St. Jerome Aemelian (July 20), a soldier by profession, had been taken prisoner. While in his dungeon he prayed to the Mother of God for assistance, promising to lead a better life if his request was granted. The Blessed Virgin appeared to him and set him free. The Saint devoted himself to the care of the poor and the unfortunate. He later became the founder of a religious congregation. He became a saint because he prayed.

3. *Work Hard* (*Unit Two*). Hard work, as you will learn more and more frequently is one of the great cure-alls. Idle hands get into mischief. To drive away temptation, work; to overcome a passion, work. To grow up into a useful citizen and a good Christian, you must learn how to work. Try yourself out now with the little tasks in the home and in the classroom. Later on your very existence will depend upon how well you learned to work. Miracles can be performed through work.

St. Thomas Aquinas (March 7) called himself the dumb ox because he did not consider himself sufficiently talented. Whenever he opened his desk he saw that sign "Dumb Ox" which he had made for himself and thus he always was driven to work harder. He later became one of the most brilliant doctors of the Church through prayer and hard work.

4. *Devotion to the Saints* (*Unit Three, I*). Ever since you started school you have listened to stories of the saints. All children love the saints but each child should have a particular saint under whose protection he places himself; the Blessed Virgin is, of course, the patroness of all, but here the reference is to one of the other saints. Select one this week if you have not one already. Perhaps it will be your namesake; any way you should learn something about the saint whose name you bear. When you have made the selection, add a prayer daily to him and try to imitate him. Tell Sister what particular virtue of this saint appeals to you. Learn something too about the saints whose pictures are in the classroom or in your bedroom.

On November 1, the Church celebrates the Feast of All Saints and makes it a holyday of obligation. There are millions of saints in heaven that no one knows of and the Church wishes all to be honored on this day. You can be sure that some of your friends are in this vast number.

5. *Bow the Head at Mention of the Holy Name* (*Unit Three, II*). You tip your hat to a lady and you bow the head as you greet a male friend. You listen respectfully as the President's name is mentioned and you stand at attention when the national anthem is sung. All these observances are right and due but what is any person or any name in comparison with Jesus and the holy name of "Jesus?" It is a name so sweet and so holy that laity and priests hesitate to use it oftener than necessary even in a devout way. Then you must bow the head at mention of the holy name. To do so is a sign of respect, is a profession of faith, is a gesture of love, is even a silent prayer.

St. Bernardine of Siena (May 20) was known for his great love of the Holy Name. The Saint had given up all his possessions to become a humble Franciscan. Gifted as an orator he was commissioned to revive the love of Jesus Christ. He performed his task successfully through the aid of the holy name. He used it frequently in his sermons while his face glowed with love. The listening crowds were so edified by his love of Jesus that they were converted in large numbers. The holy name emblazoned on a tablet was always before him on the pulpit.

6. *Attend Mass Devoutly* (*Unit Three, III*). You can gain great merit from the recitation of prayers but the greatest act of religion is the holy Mass. The greater your devotion, the greater is the fruit you draw therefrom. In the Mass your prayers are more powerful than at any other time because you pray with Christ and Christ prays with you. You recall how Mother used to say the night and morning prayers with you, and how you always felt that those were very powerful prayers. But, here Our Lord Himself prays with you to God, the Father. Then pray devoutly because you are in heavenly company. Be sure to have the right posture, fold your hands and keep away all distractions.

We read of many holy people who went to great sacrifices to attend Mass daily. These persons prayed well because they realized that in the Mass they prayed with Christ. St. Elizabeth, the Queen of Hungary (July 9), attended Mass daily. It was that which made her a saint. Very often she received Holy Communion too, always preparing herself with great austerities and long prayers. This lover of the Mass is today the model of charity to the poor. Jesus in the Mass instructed her on charity.

7. *Be Obedient to Your Parents (Unit Four, I).* The teacher will detail the multiple instances when this virtue can be practiced by her pupils. It deals not only with commands but with prohibitions. To lend a willing ear to either constitutes a good work which again increases sanctifying grace and adds new luster to the soul. Our guardian angel makes a report daily of the acts of obedience which will be presented to God on the day of our judgment.

St. Joseph will naturally be the patron saint of the week. His humble obedience to God should be emphasized. His life in brief follows.

In obedience to her parents the Blessed Virgin who was to become the Mother of God, became betrothed to Saint Joseph. A few months later the time came for Joseph and Mary to go up to Bethlehem, to be enrolled according to the decree issued by Caesar Augustus, Emperor of Rome. The journey brought a new cause of anxiety to Joseph, for there was no room for them in the inn. We can only guess what must have been the thoughts of the holy man at the Nativity, the adoration of the shepherds and Magi, at the Presentation.

New trials followed. The news that a king of the Jews had been born, aroused the jealousy of the bloody tyrant, Herod. An angel of the Lord appeared to warn Joseph to flee to Egypt with Child and Mother. After some time the summons came to return and the Holy Family settled again at Nazareth.

St. Joseph's life was henceforth simple and uneventful like that of a humble carpenter, supporting himself and his family by his work, and faithfully performing the religious practices commanded by the Law. The only noteworthy incident is the loss of, and the anxious quest for Jesus, then twelve years old, when He remained in the Temple following the yearly pilgrimage to the Holy City. This is the last we hear of St. Joseph and we may well believe he died before the beginning of the Saviour's public life. Probably he was buried at Nazareth.

8. *Obedience to Your Superiors (Unit Four, I).* Superiors are your parents, your pastor, your bishop, your teacher and others of whom you will learn later. Obedience is the subject of the fourth commandment. In the complete form, God attaches a promise to

its observance, the only commandment so amplified, saying that you will be long-lived on earth. Obedient children are indeed more blessed than others in many ways. Look at it only from this angle today. You need and want more blessings for your body and soul, want to succeed in your studies, want to be loved by your friends, want continual graces that will bring you the greatest blessing of all, namely heaven. Then obey in word, act and even in thought.

St. Rose of Lima was the first American saint to be canonized. She had a great sympathy and love for her parents. These were very poor so the Saint obtained work that she might assist them. St. Rose did not have to go to foreign lands as a missionary to become a saint. She spent her whole life at home proving that it is possible to achieve sanctity by the practice of home virtues—and chief of these is obedience.

9. *Control of the Tongue* (*Unit Four, II*). The classroom affords the best opportunity by the observance of silence during class hours. Control of the tongue is very necessary if one would avoid sin. Of all the sins to be explained, it is surprising how many are committed in whole or in part by the tongue. St. James said that if a man did not sin with his tongue, he was a perfect man. Wise men have said that no man is entitled to speak who has not first learned how to be silent. Trouble is, we say too many things without thought. God placed our teeth like two fences to check our tongue, but the tongue leaps over the fences too frequently.

We must not include too much in this practice. It would indeed be enough just to cover silence in the classroom. But the teacher must not put the practice before the pupils as something negative, something not to do, as that is always irksome. She must explain rather, that an hour of silence is a positive good deed which will be listed by the guardian angel.

Give a more complete story of St. Francis of Assisi (October 4). Great as the Saint was, there is much in his life which appeals to children. He talked much of the love of God, of the Providence of God that watches even over the little birds. Tell them of the Saint's sermon to the birds and of how at his command they sang the praises of God. St. Francis used his tongue for the purpose for which God created it. Dwell upon the kindness and gentleness of St. Francis. The pupils must learn about these great saints who helped to shape the history of the Church as St. Francis did by his establishment of the Franciscan order.

Grade II   **First Semester**

10. *Learn This Prayer* (*Unit Four, III*). "My Queen, My Mother, remember I am thine own. Keep me, guard me as thy property and possession." This is a short and beautiful little prayer which is to be used in the moment of temptation against purity. Perhaps there is time this week also to learn the "Hail, Holy Queen."

On July 16, 1251, the Blessed Virgin appeared to St. Simon Stock and showed him the habit the Carmelite Order was to wear. She promised to protect all who were so clothed, even those who joined the lay organization of Our Lady of Mount Carmel. For the lay organization the habit is abbreviated to the scapular, now called the brown scapular or the scapular of Mt. Carmel. Children are enrolled in this society of the scapular on the day of their First Communion.

11. *Care of Others' Property* (*Unit Four, IV*). Here is meant caring for property loaned to you, and having respect for the holdings of another. You might borrow a pencil, a book, a ball, a doll, any plaything or any tool. The lawful possession of anything by you or another is approved by Almighty God and He wants all to respect articles owned by you or by another. Be just: take good care of articles loaned to you; have the proper respect for those owned by others. Do not waste or destroy. Even the articles and the clothing given you by parents come under this head. It is just; it is fair. "Do unto others as you would have them do unto you."

St. Paschal Baylon (May 17). He left his flock to graze one day while he went to the church to pray. During his absence the sheep broke through a neighbor's fence and destroyed some grain. Next day the Saint went to that farmer and paid him for the damaged grain.

12. *Be Truthful* (*Unit Four, V*). A truthful boy or girl is noble, is brave. It shows great uprightness of character always to speak the truth as it often demands considerable courage. There was a boy who risked expulsion from college by telling the truth about his escapade but the President so admired the boy's spirit of truth that he would not inflict the full penalty and allowed him to remain; the boy was noble and later became a very prominent business man. Always remember, to speak the truth is one more good deed added to your treasury for the Judgment Day.

St. Sophia and her three daughters (August 1) were taken before the judge and questioned about their Faith. With great courage all four declared the truth that they were Christians. Though offered a handsome reward to deny their Faith, they remained steadfast and suffered martyrdom for the truth.

13. *Be Kind to Others* (*Unit Four, V*). Our Lord spoke continually of the great commandment of love. It was the theme of his beautiful sermon at the Last Supper, just as if He wanted to give you a final grand commission before He died. Are you kind to others? Do you talk kindly with them, help them wherever you can?

St. Camillus (July 18) had once been very careless but he made up for his neglect by founding a congregation that gave all its time to the care of the sick and unfortunate. No one was more assiduous in this work than the Saint himself as he went from bed to bed ministering kindly to the sick and consoling them with kind words.

14. *Be Contented* (*Unit Four, VII*). God knows why He gives this one more and that one less. Only on Judgment Day will you fully understand why and how wisely God apportioned physical and spiritual blessings. Perhaps more, perhaps less would cause the loss of your soul. Use well what has been given and you will positively save your soul. Perhaps this boy is more talented; perhaps that girl is clothed better. Be contented. You may strive lawfully for success and advancement but whether it is given or not, be contented.

St. Vincent de Paul (July 19) did not consider it necessary to possess much worldly goods, for he gave what he had to the poor and thereby earned his eternal crown. He explained to the less fortunate how they could achieve salvation by being contented with their lot.

15.* *A Spiritual Bouquet for the Poor Souls* (All Souls' Day). All Catholics have a great devotion to the Poor Souls. On the Commemoration of All Souls, priests offer up thousands of Masses and the faithful, millions of prayers for them. Even little children can offer a bouquet of prayers for them on the day and during the following week.

Our Lord once said to St. Gertrude (November 15), "God accepts every soul you set free, as if you had redeemed it from captivity, and will reward you in a fitting time for the benefit you have conferred."

St. Malachi (November 2) had said many Masses for his deceased sister but once he made a pause of thirty days without remembering her. She appeared to him then to complain that she had not tasted food for thirty days. He resumed his Masses and shortly afterwards was given assurance that she was now in heaven.

Second Semester

16.* *Prepare for Christmas* (Advent). The Church gives you the example for preparation by its season of Advent. You too must prepare by being a better boy or girl. You can do little acts of penance in reparation for sins committed; you can recite special prayers of longing for the Infant. You can say prayers for those poor who will not have so much for Christmas.

It is the pleasant duty of the teacher to prepare minds and hearts by pictures, posters and a crib in the classroom. She will tell the pupils the story of St. Nicholas (December 6) from whom the name Santa Claus is derived.

St. Francis of Assisi (October 4) is said to have built the first crib. When he acted as deacon of the Christmas Mass in that church for which he had built the crib, the Infant appeared to him and nestled in his arms.

17.* *A Gift for the Infant* (Christmas). At Christmas time all people give and receive gifts. But, the principal One Who so richly deserves a gift must not be forgotten, namely, the Infant Himself. Already now you should get ready some gift for Him, a little act of self-denial or a gift of loving prayers which you will offer the Infant on Christmas Day.

The teacher will tell the story of the gifts of the three Wise Men. Perhaps the pupils can learn one or two stanzas of "A Little Child at the Crib" by Leonard Feeney, S.J.

18. *Courage* (*Unit Five*). This quality is not just a physical one whereby one can defend himself against aggression. It is too a quality of a heart whereby the Catholic bravely says the right thing and does the right thing in spite of all obstacles. It can even be practiced in the daily tasks of a child, for fortitude is one of the cardinal virtues which means that it underlies every thought and word. Can you get up in time? Can you study your lessons at night? Can you correct an erring friend? Can you perform your church duties when others fail to follow you? Can you observe the rule of silence when others in the classroom are whispering?

The two great leaders of the Church, SS. Peter and Paul (June 29) suffered martyrdom on the same day. And what a courage they had exhibited in their long battle with Roman paganism!

They courageously went to their death. St. Peter was crucified and St. Paul was beheaded.

19. *Be Prompt* (*Unit Six*). Begin each exercise on the second and finish same on the second, even stopping in the middle of a word. Likewise, on the playground, cease playing the very instant the bell rings.

Promptness begets decisiveness of character, a very useful habit when repelling temptations; also a good trait for the business world, enabling one quickly to utilize good opportunities. All great characters in the Church and the world were prompt. There is little use in learning about good works unless we cultivate a habit of promptness to do them when the occasion presents itself; good works and promptness are linked inseparably.

Each child must even now try to acquire those good habits which will make him useful in later life. The tree which today reaches high into the sky, was one that grew right and grew straight when it was a sapling. Little children are now like the saplings. They can direct their future by growing right and straight now. Promptness is an effective habit in this regard.

St. Anthony of Padua (June 13) belonged to the Franciscan Order where, as in every order, practically every exercise of the day is regulated by the clock. He was a faithful friar and so you can conclude that he began and ended every exercise promptly on the second.

20. *Say Your Prayers Well* (*Unit Seven*). There is an old adage, "Whatever is worth doing, is worth doing well." This has a particular application to prayer which is a most worthwhile occupation. When you pray, you either get heavenly wages for your effort or you get no wages at all. If you pray carelessly, you get nothing. A bad prayer is a downright waste of time; it would be more profitable to do something else.

When you see a picture of St. Anne (July 26) and the Blessed Virgin, you generally see the mother instructing her child in prayer. Indeed this must have been one of the most delightful tasks of St. Anne. You always see how intent the child, Mary, is during these instructions. St. Anne taught not only that there were words but that the words must be said devoutly.

21.* *St. Valentine's Day.* The children hear much of St. Valentine (February 14) and we therefore select him as the patron for his own week. We wish to acquaint them with the origin of "Valentines" and to turn the present-day practice to something more worthwhile.

St. Valentine was a kindly priest who was imprisoned for teaching the Faith to the people. Here however he did not forget his friends but sent them messages in all manner of ways, sometimes even tying them about the necks of pigeons. This constituted the origin of "valentines." The practice began in a holy way but later on became rather silly. The children can perhaps make booklets of beautiful holy pictures for this day and send them to little friends who are sick at home or in a hospital. St. Valentine always wanted to make other people happy.

22. *Learn the Angelus* (*Unit Seven*). The teacher will tell the story of the Annunciation and the meaning of the three versicles. The class will not yet be able to learn the concluding prayer. From now on, this prayer will be a part of the class prayer.

23. *Examine Your Conscience Nightly* (*Unit Eight*). A good business man goes over his accounts every night to learn how he can succeed better on the following day. You cannot do better until you learn what mistakes you generally make and you cannot find out the mistakes unless you hunt for them. It is the purpose of the evening examination to prepare you for a better day tomorrow. Then look into your conscience nightly in order first to correct the mistakes of the past. You cannot drive your auto out of the lane until you remove the boulders. You are given each day that you may do better tomorrow.

How did Mary Magdalen (July 22) become a saint? Answer, she first found out that she was a sinner. When the hour of grace came, she must have locked herself in her room to examine the mistakes of the past. Then only was she ready to resolve that tomorrow she would correct them, throw herself at the feet of Jesus and go to become a saint.

24.* *Prayer before a Crucifix* (Lent). During the Lenten season the pupils are to be urged to kneel before the large crucifix in church and recite a little prayer of contrition before the Crucified. The Lenten period is given over to a consideration of the sufferings of Our Lord and children can easily be led to exercise the spirit of the devotion.

St. Andrew the Apostle (November 30), loved the cross of his Master. When he was condemned to be crucified he held out his hands in greeting to the cross saying, "O good cross, receive me into your arms." St. Paul used to say he only knew "Christ and Him Crucified."

25. *Be Patient* (Lent). Examples for patience: The hours in the classroom seem to pass too slowly; persevere to the last second. Home work becomes dull; stick to it. Little brothers and sisters annoy you; do not mind them. Tasks about the house get wearisome; remain cheerful. A tooth hurts or you have a headache; do not cry, but suffer patiently.

To be patient is a kind of suffering. Offer it in union with your suffering Saviour. Acts of patience erase sin and increase your merit for heaven. Most saints achieved sanctity through heroic patience in trial and suffering.

St. Peter Balsam (January 6) loved suffering. When tortured with hooks, he only called joyfully on the name of the Lord. When he was condemned to be crucified, he replied: "You have given me the desire of my heart."

26. *A Visit to the Blessed Sacrament* (*Unit Nine*). Go through life with Jesus. There He is right next door waiting to give you light and courage for your daily tasks. You need Him even with your little daily tasks for much depends on them in later years. A visit is an act of the love of God, very meritorious in His sight. After each visit the soul is more beautiful than before. By a visit you can erase venial sins from your soul.

When the Saracens attacked the convent of St. Clare, the Saint called upon her Lord in the Blessed Sacrament. He replied: "My protection will never fail you." When the enemy tried to enter the convent, St. Clare held up the ciborium and put them to flight.

> Jesus, Jesus, come to me.
> Oh how much I long for Thee!

Perhaps the pupils can learn the first two stanzas of Father Ryan's poem:

> I wish I were the little key
> That locks Love's Captive in,
> And lets Him out to go and free
> A sinful heart from sin.
>
> I wish I were the little bell
> That tinkles for the Host,
> When God comes down each day to dwell
> With hearts He loves the most.

A Protestant minister brought his little girl into a Catholic church in London. She wanted to know the meaning of the sanctuary lamp. The father explained: "That signifies that Jesus is here." Brought to a Protestant church she inquired why there was no sanctuary lamp. "Because Jesus is not here," said the Father. She was never again satisfied to be in a Protestant Church, saying always, "I want to go where Jesus is." The words made a deep impression on the minister and some time afterwards he and his family became Catholics, "to be where Jesus is."

27. *To Practice Clean Speech* (*Unit Ten*). Negatively, this consists in an avoidance of taking God's name in vain, coarse slang, and smutty speech. Positively, it implies speaking reverently of holy things, practicing politeness in speech by following all the conventions of refined address. The latter can be practiced at table or in company. The child should learn this month when to say "Thank you," "Please," "Excuse me," etc. Refined speech and mannerly address are an offset and preventive of coarse language.

St. James (July 25) was one of the three apostles whom Our Lord favored with a more intimate association. You often read, "He took with Him Peter, James and John." This great apostle preached clean speech. He said that a man is perfect if he does not offend in speech. Now you know a way how to become perfect—practice clean speech.

28. *Love of Mary* (*Unit Ten*). This practice fits in with the month of October or May, or the week of the Immaculate Conception. This week you will review all your prayers to the Blessed Virgin and perhaps even add one like the rosary. Many great saints have said that it is impossible to be saved without Mary. You certainly wish to be saved; then see to it that no day passes without some prayer to Mary. Learn to love her next to her divine Son and go to her in all your trouble.

The Church has appointed some thirty feasts in honor of Mary, two as holydays of obligation, the Assumption and the Immaculate Conception. Her greatest feast is the latter (December 8). On this day the Church commemorates her glorious privilege, that of all human beings, she was the only one to be conceived free of original sin. Say often, "O Mary, conceived without sin, pray for us who have recourse to thee!"

29.* *To Receive Holy Communion Often during Vacation* (*Before Vacation*). Will you be a better or a worse child at the end of your vacation? Sister will not be there to guide you and you will see Father less often, so, you may get careless. Take Jesus for your Guide and Comforter during those days for He is the best one of all. In other words, receive Him often and get renewed strength from the great sacrament.

Study the life of St. Aloysius (June 21). The saint is the special patron for boys but being a saint he can for this month also be the patron for the girls. In many parishes the first communicants carry out the practice of receiving the Holy Eucharist in honor of the Saint on the six Sundays following their first communion. The Church blesses such a devotion in that she grants a plenary indulgence under the usual conditions to those who spend some time in meditation or prayer or perform some other exercise of devotion in honor of St. Aloysius on six consecutive Sundays preceding his feast or on any six consecutive Sundays at any time. Too often our biographers have made a kind of celluloid saint of Aloysius. He was human as any boy and girl and it will be the obligation of the teacher so to portray him. The pupils can pray to this admirable Jesuit saint to keep them from bad companions during vacation.

30. *Stay on the Right Road.* And now you go into vacation. You have learned much during the year, what to do, what not to do. What you have learned, must be used, not just kept in your head. Some day, that is, the day of your death you must undergo the Particular Judgment and Jesus Who will be your Judge, will ask you, "Did you do the good deeds you were taught to do; did you avoid the evils you were warned against?" No, you cannot escape that Judgment; no man has ever escaped it. If the eternal Judge should find mortal sin for which you had not repented, a terrible fate awaits you, to be forever locked out of heaven and to be punished in hell forever. Oh, pray daily to the Blessed Mother that such a sentence will never be passed on you. If the great Judge finds some venial sins and many good deeds, He will sentence you to purgatory where you must suffer until those sins are erased, for nothing unclean can enter heaven. Pray too that you will always have the strength to avoid those many deliberate venial sins because purgatory is painful. Do not tell lies during vacation; do not disobey your parents. Pray daily that you will get to heaven where you will live forever with all the wonderful saints about whom you have heard this year. The greatest joy will be to live forever and ever with the all-holy, the all-good, the all-beautiful God. Work for heaven during these vacation months.

BIBLIOGRAPHY

Anger, Joseph, *The Doctrine of the Mystical Body of Christ,* tr. from the French by J. J. Burke, C.S.P. New York: Benziger Brothers, Inc., 1931.
Aurelia, Sister Mary, *Practical Aids to Catholic Teachers,* jointly with F. M. Kirsch, 3 vols. New York: Benziger Brothers, Inc., 1928-1935.
Baierl, Joseph J., *The Holy Sacrifice of the Mass.* Rochester, N. Y.: published by the author, 1913 (8th ed. 1929).
Bandas, Rudolph G., *Catechetical Methods.* New York: Joseph Wagner, 1929.
—— *Practical Problems in Religion.* Milwaukee: Bruce Publishing Co., 1934.
—— *Religion Teaching and Practice.* New York: Joseph Wagner, 1935.
Bowden, Henry S., *Miniature Lives of the Saints for every day of the year,* 2 vols. London: Burns, Oates and Washbourne, 1922.
Callan, Charles J., jointly with J. A. McHugh, *Catechism of the Council of Trent.* New York: Joseph Wagner, 1923.
Christopher, Joseph Patrick and Spence, Charles E., *The Raccolta.* New York: Benziger Brothers, Inc., 1943.
Delany, Selden Peabody, *Married Saints.* New York: Longmans, Green & Co., 1935.
Dowd, Edward F., *Conspectus of Modern Catholic thought on the essence of the Eucharistic Sacrifice.* Washington: Catholic University of America, 1937.
Drinkwater, Francis Harold, *Religion in School Again.* London: Burns, Oates and Washbourne, 1935.
—— *Teaching the Catechism.* London: Burns, Oates and Washbourne, 1924.
—— *Catechism Stories.* London: Burns, Oates and Washbourne, 1939.
Dunney, Joseph A., *The Parish School.* New York: Macmillan, 1921.
Durand, Alfred, S.J., *Catholic Ceremonies and Explanation of the Ecclesiastical Year.* New York: Benziger Brothers, 1896.
Dwight, Walter, S.J., *Our Daily Bread.* New York: Apostleship of Prayer, 1911.
Esser, Franz Xavier, S.J., *The Silent Anchorite in the Tabernacle,* translated from the German by Kathleen Jackson. St. Louis: B. Herder Book Co., 1927.
Fonck, Leopold, S.J., *Parables of the Gospel,* 3rd English edition, translated from the German by E. Leahy. St. Louis: B. Herder Book Co., 1915.
Fortescue, Adrian, *The Ceremonies of the Roman Rite,* new ed. revised by John B. O'Connell. London: Burns, Oates and Washbourne, 1930.
Fuerst, Anthony B., S.T.D., *Systematic Teaching of Religion,* vol. 1. New York: Benziger Brothers, Inc., 1939.
Gasparri, Peter (Cardinal), *Catholic Catechism,* translated from the Italian by H. Pope. New York: P. J. Kenedy and Sons, 1932.
Gigot, Francis Ernest Charles, S.S., *General Introduction to the Study of the Scriptures.* New York: Benziger Brothers, Inc., 1900.
—— *Outlines of Jewish History.* New York: Benziger Brothers, Inc., 1905.
—— *Outlines of New Testament History.* New York: Benziger Brothers, Inc., 1898.
Goodier, Alban, S.J., (Archbishop), *Passion and Death of our Lord, Jesus Christ.* New York: P. J. Kenedy and Sons, 1933.
—— *Public Life of our Lord, Jesus Christ,* 2nd ed. New York: P. J. Kenedy and Sons, 1933.
Grisar, Hartmann, S. J., *Luther,* tr. from the German ed., by Frank J. Eble. St. Louis: B. Herder Book Co., 1931.

Bibliography

Guggenberger, Anthony, *General History of the Christian era*, 3 vols. 17th ed. St. Louis: B. Herder Book Co., 1931.
Haering, Otto, O.S.B., *Living with the Church*, tr. from the German by Rembert Bularzik. New York: Benziger Brothers, Inc., 1930.
Herbst, Winfrid, S.D.S., *Follow the Saints*. New York: Benziger Brothers, Inc., 1933.
Houck, Frederick Alphonse, *Our Palace Wonderful*. New York: Frederick Pustet & Co., 1936.
Johnson, George W., with J. D. Hannan and Sister Mary Dominica, *Bible History*. New York: Benziger Brothers, Inc., 1931.
—— *The Bible Story*. New York: Benziger Brothers, Inc., 1931.
—— *Story of the Church*. New York: Benziger Brothers, Inc., 1935.
Kane, Robert, S. J., *Sermon on the Sea*. New York: Longmans, Green & Co., 1911.
Kirsch, Felix M., O.M.Cap., with Sister Mary Aurelia, *Practical Aids for Catholic Teachers*, 3 vols. New York: Benziger Brothers, Inc., 1928-1935.
Lahey, Thomas Aquinas, C.S.C., *God's Heroes*. South Bend, Ind.: Ave Maria Press, 1936.
—— *God's Wonder-World*. South Bend, Ind.: Ave Maria Press, 1938.
MacEachen, Roderick Aloysius, *The Teaching of Religion*. New York: Macmillan & Co., 1921.
McHugh, John Ambrose, jointly with C. J. Callan, *Catechism of the Council of Trent*. New York: Joseph Wagner, 1923.
Martin, Charles Alfred, *Catholic Religion*. St. Louis: B. Herder Book Co., 1927.
Mueller, John Baptist, *Handbook of Ceremonies*, 9th English ed. St. Louis: B. Herder Book Co., 1936.
Pallen, Conde Benoist, *The New Catholic Dictionary*, jointly with John J. Wynne, S.J.
Parsch, Pius, O.S.B., *Liturgy of the Mass*, tr. from the German by Frederick C. Eckhoff. St. Louis: B. Herder Book Co., 1937.
Petz, Andreas, *The Ecclesiastical Year for Catholic Schools and Institutions*. Milwaukee: George F. Zander, 1903.
Sharp, John K., *Aims and Methods in Teaching Religion*. New York: Benziger Brothers, Inc., 1929.
Spence, Charles E., and Christopher, Joseph Patrick, *The Raccolta*. New York: Benziger Brothers, Inc., 1943.
Spirago, Francis, *Anecdotes and Examples Illustrating the Catholic Catechism*, tr. from the German by J. J. Baxter. New York: Benziger Brothers, Inc., 1904.
—— *The Catechism Explained*, edited by Richard F. Clarke, S.J. New York: Benziger Brothers, Inc., 1927.
Sullivan, John Francis, *Externals of the Catholic Church*. New York: P. J. Kenedy & Sons, 1918.
Tanquerey, Adolph, S.S., *Synopsis Theologiæ Dogmaticæ*, vol. I.
—— *The Spiritual Life*, tr. from the French by Herman Branderis, 2nd rev. ed. Baltimore: St. Mary's Seminary, 1930.
Vaughan, John S., *Thoughts for All Times*, 13th Amer. ed. Philadelphia: Central Association of the Miraculous Medal, 1899.
Zulueta, Francis M. de, S.J., *Letters on Christian Doctrine*, 3 vols. London: Burns, Oates and Washbourne, 1905.

N.B. Wherever grants of indulgences are referred to in this book, the respective information is taken from *The Raccolta*. New York: Benziger Brothers, Inc., 1943.

BIBLE HISTORY INDEX

GRADE ONE

Abraham, the patriarch, 46
Adam and Eve, creation of, 37; sin of, 39
Adoration of the Magi, 54
Agony in the Garden, 76
Ain-Karem, 49
Angels, Creation of the, 26; Fall of some, 29; Bad and Good, 30
Annas, Jewish priest, 78
Annunciation of the B.V.M., 47
Ascension of Jesus, 86

Baptism of Jesus, 64
Birth of Jesus, 49

Cain kills Abel, 45
Cana, Marriage Feast at, 68
Commandments, the Ten, 64
Creation of the Angels, 26; of Man, 37; of the World, 33
Crucifixion of Jesus, 80

Egypt, Flight into, 56; Return from, 58
Eucharist, Institution of, 103

Fall of Adam and Eve, 39; of some Angels, 29
Finding of Jesus in the Temple, 62
Flight into Egypt, 56
Flood, The great, 46

Garden, Agony in the, 76

Jesus, Birth of, 49; Presentation of, in the Temple, 53; Baptism of, 64; gave us the Mass, priests and Holy Communion, 75; Passion and Death of, 76-81; before the Rulers, 78; rises from the dead, 83; appears to Mary Magdalen, 84; institutes the sacrament of Penance, 95; heals two blind men, 99; heals ten lepers, 101; institutes the Holy Eucharist, 103; visits Martha and Mary, 108

John, St., the Baptist, 64, 66

Last Supper, The, 75
Loaves, Multiplication of the, 106

Magi, Adoration of the, 54
Marriage Feast at Cana, 68
Mass, Jesus gave us the, 75
Martha and Mary visited by Jesus, 108
Mary Magdalen, Jesus appears to, 84
Moses, Found in the basket, 5; receives Ten Commandments, 63
Multiplication of Loaves, 106

Peter, temptation of St., 78
Presentation of the Child Jesus in the Temple, 53
Prodigal Son, The, 97
Promise of a Redeemer, 49

Resurrection of Jesus, 83; after the, 95
Return from Egypt, 58
Rulers, Jesus before the, 78

Sacrament of Eucharist, institution of the, 103
— of Penance, institution of the, 95
Simeon, 53
Son, The Prodigal, 97
Sufferings of Jesus, 71, 91
Supper, The Last, 75

Temple, Finding of the Child Jesus in, 62
Ten Commandments, The, 64
Three Wise Men, 54

Visitation, The, 48

Wise Men, Three, 54

GRADE TWO

Adam and Eve, Sin of, 142
Annunciation of B. V. M., 259
Assumption of B. V. M., 262

Bethlehem, Journey to, 260
Birth of Our Lady, 258
Birth of the Saviour, 260
Brothers, Joseph and his, 178

Calf, The golden, 155
Child in the Temple, 258
Commandments, The Ten, 150

David and Goliath, 208

Esau sells his Birthright, 195
Eucharist, Institution of the, 244
Egypt, Flight into, 261; Return from, 261

Fall of First Parents, 142
Feed My Lambs, Feed My Sheep, 199
Flight into Egypt, 261
Finding of the Child Jesus in the Temple, 261

Golden calf, The, 155
Goliath, David and, 208

Hidden life of Jesus, 261
Herod, King, 181

Jacob and Esau, 195
Jesus: institutes the sacrament of Penance, 229-230; quiets the storm, 240; institutes the sacrament of the Holy Eucharist, 244; Birth of, 260; in the Hidden Life, 261; in the Public Life, 262; in His Passion, 262; after the Resurrection, 262; with St. John, 262
Joseph and Mary, 258
Joseph; sold into Egypt, 172; made governor of Egypt, 176; and his brothers, 178
Journey to Bethlehem, 260; to Egypt, 261

Kings, The three, 260

Lepers, the ten, 229

Mary and Joseph, 258
Mary Magdalen is forgiven, 238
Moses, Found in the Basket, 155

Passion of Jesus, 262
Pharisee in the Temple, 207
Presentation of Jesus in the Temple, The, 260
Prodigal Son, The, 234
Public Life of Jesus, 262

Quiets the Storm, Jesus, 240

Resurrection, Jesus after the, 262
Return from Egypt, 261

Son, The Prodigal, 234
St. John, Jesus with, 262

Ten Lepers, The, 229
Temple, The Child Jesus in the, 258

Visitation, The, 259

INDEX OF QUESTIONS AND ANSWERS
from the First Communion Catechism

This Index Shows the Location of the Questions and Answers for Study in Grade I and in Grade II

QUESTION	GRADE I PAGE	GRADE II PAGE	QUESTION	GRADE I PAGE	GRADE II PAGE
1	3, 37		28	65	143
2	35		29	65	143
3	5, 42	140	30	66	143
4	7, 42	141	31	67	144
5	19	136	32	67	144
6	17	137	33	67	144
7	20	139	34	69	145
8	13	139	35	70	146
9	14	139	36		146
10	22	134	37		224
11	24	134	38		225
12	24	134	39	91	220
13	24	134	40		225
14	48		41		226
15	48		42		227
16	50		43		227
17	49		44	96	229
18	50		45	100	237
19	73		46	101	240
20	81		47	102	241
21	88		48	104	246
22	30	142	49	104	245
23	30	142	50		247
24	39	142	51	105	247
25	40	143	52	106	251
26	41	143	53	109	252
27	41	143	54	110	253

GENERAL INDEX

(*The numbers indicate pages*)

Abel killed by Cain, 45
Abraham waited for the Saviour, 46; and Lot, 46; tried to save the people of Sodom, 46
Abstinence, Law of, 204
Act of Faith, 123; of Hope, 124; of Love, 125; of Contrition, brief form, 125
Adam and Eve, 37; sin of, 39; waited for the Saviour, 45
Agatha, St., 158-159
Agony in the Garden, 76
Ain-Karem, 49
All Saints, feast of, 115
All Souls' Day, 270
Aloysius, St., 126, 161
Andrew St., Apostle, 113, 273
Andrew Corsini, St., 66
Angels, Creation of the, 26; sin of some, 29, 141; Bad and Good, 30; Guardian, 31; Many loved God, some hated God, 141
Anne, St., feast of, 272; Mother of Blessed Virgin Mary, 47
Annunciation, 47
Anthony of Padua, St., feast of, 272
Apparitions of the Risen Jesus, 85, 95
Ascension of Our Lord, 86

Bad Language, sin of, 163—164
Baptism, Sacrament of, 225
Baptist, St., John the, 64, 66
Bernard, St., 38
Bernadette of Lourdes, St., 120, 184
Bernardine of Siena, St., feast of, 266
Bethlehem, 49
Blessed Virgin Mary: never sinned, 15; Immaculate Conception of, 41, 45; is our Mother, 42; Birth of, 47, 258; Annunciation, 47, 259; Visitation, 48, 259; Apparition to St. Bernadette, 120; Purity of, 182; Betrothed to St. Joseph, 259
Bridget, St., feast of, 115

Cain and Abel, 45
Camillus, St., feast of, 270
Cana, Marriage feast at, 68; an example of Our Lady's power, 68
Candle, The Paschal, 86
Carmelite Order, 269
Catholic Church, prayer for the, 59; institution and membership of, 85, 87
Cecilia, St., feast of, 189
Chastity, 182
Christ, meaning anointed, consecrated, 53
Christmas, 50
Commandments of God, Ten, 63, 64, 151
Communion, Holy, what It is, 103, 246-247; what It does for us, 106, 247; effects of a worthy, 106; how to prepare for It, 108, 250; what to do before receiving, 108, 109, 251, 252; how to receive, 251; what to do after, 110, 253

General Index

Confession, 98 ff; what to do before, 98, 237; what to do in, 101, 238, **241**; Formula of, 101, 240; what to do after, 102, 241; Table of sins for, 99, **197**; of mortal sins, 238; of venial sins, 239
Confirmation, Sacrament of, 226
Conscience, Examination of, 99, 126, 197
Consecration, a principal part of the Mass, 76
Corsini, St. Andrew, 66
Creation of the Angels, 26; of the world, 33, 138; of man, 37
Crucifixion of Our Lord, 80

David and Goliath, 208
Duties toward God, 7, 140, 154

Easter Sunday, 83, 84
Egypt, Flight into, 261; return from, 261
Elizabeth of Hungary, St., 117, 266
Esau and Jacob, 195
Eucharist: What It is, 103, 245, 246; What It does for us, 106, 248; **The** Holy Sacrament of, 243; Institution, 244

False Witness, 191
Father, God is your, 1; is our Father, 3; God the, 4
Felicitas St., and her seven sons, martyrs, feast of, 122
First Communion, 103, 109
First Parents, Our, 37; sin of, 39
Frances of Rome, St., 32
Francis of Assisi, St., 8, 15, 117, 123, **271**
Francis of Sales, St., feast of, 121
Friday abstinence, 204

Garden, Agony in the, 76
Garden of Paradise, 136, 142
Gertrude, St., feast of, 270
Ghost, The Holy—see *Holy Ghost*
God: Father of all, 1; is a Spirit, 11, 132; a great Spirit, 12; Perfections of, 12-20, 135; had no beginning, 13, 139; will always be, 14, 139; is all-good and all-powerful, 15, 19; is everywhere and knows everything, 16, 19, 133-136; Unity of, 21; Trinity of, 23, 133; Three Persons in One, 24, 134; made the angels, the world and man, 26, 137-139
Golden Calf, 155
Good Friday, recalls Our Lord's death, 81
Grace, 89 ff; makes us holy, 91, 220; how it comes, 93, 217; kinds of, **219**; using, 221
Gregory Thaumaturgus, St., 20
Guardian Angels, 31, 32; feast of, 32

Heaven, 30, 59, 60, 73; closed by Adam's sin, 73; opened by Our Lord's sufferings, 74
Hell, 30
Herman Joseph, Blessed, feast of, 124
Holy Communion, see *Communion*
Holy Eucharist, see *Eucharist*
Holy Ghost, the, 23, 24, 97, 161, 162, 218, 227
Holy Thursday, 76
Holydays of Obligation, 202
Home, God's, 3

General Index

Honoring our parents, 173
Honesty, 186
Hóss, Blessed Mary, 160

Injury to others, 180; to ourselves, 180
Immaculate Conception, 41, 45; feast of, **118**
Imelda, Blessed, 161, 251
Incarnation, 48

Jerome Aemelian, St., feast of 265
Jesus: Name of the Son of God made man, 48; birth of, 50; means Saviour, 53; presentation in the Temple, 53; baptism of, 64; tempted by the devil, 66; sufferings of, 71; Passion of, 71; became man to redeem all sinners, 73; and the Last Supper, 75; gave us priests and the Mass, 75; rose from the dead, 83; apparitions of the Risen, 85; Ascension of, 86
John, St., the Baptist, 64, 66
Joseph, St., 49, 56, 58; feast of, 125
Joseph and his brethren, 178, 186
Judgment, The particular, 152

Last Supper, recalled on Holy Thursday, 76; what happened at the, 245
Laws of God, see *Commandments*
Little Flower, The, 110, 114, 183
Lucifer, 29

Magi, 54, 119
Malachi, St., feast of 270
Margaret, St., Queen of Scotland, 127
Marriage Feast at Cana, 68
Mass: obligation to attend on Sundays, 76, 167, 201; on holydays, 76, 202; has three principal parts, 76; Our Lord's 254; the Priest's, 256
Martin of Tours, St., 116

Mary Magdalen, St., 85; 237-239; feast of, 273
Michael, St., Archangel, 29
Morning Offering, brief form, 116
Moses, 5, 155

Nazareth, 49
Nicholas, St., feast of, 118, 271
Noe, 46
Neighbor, who is our, 171

Obedience to parents, teachers and others, 175; Jesus, example of, 177
Occupations allowed on Sunday and holydays, 168; prohibited on Sunday and holydays, 168
Offering, The Morning, brief form, 116
Offertory, a principal part of the Mass, 76
Original Sin, 41

Paradise, 37
Paschal Baylon, St., 126, 188; feast of, 126
Passion of Our Lord, see *Jesus*
Patrick, St., 21, 124; and the Trinity, 23, 124
Paul, St., and St. Peter, feast of, 271
Penance, Sacrament of, 95; what it brings and does, 96-98; what to do to receive it, 237

General Index

Peter, St., 77, 78, 125, 199; feast of, 125; and St. Paul, 271
Peter Balsam, St., feast of, 274
Peter Canisius, St., feast of, 264
Pharisee praying in Temple, 53, 207
Pilate, 80-81
Politeness toward parents and teachers, 172
Pope Pius X and First Communion, 103
Prayer, what it is, 52; why we should pray, 56; how, 56; for whom, 58; its necessity, 60
Prayers: Morning, Evening, and Table, 210; missing them not sinful, 157; for special needs, 212
Presentation of the Child Jesus in the Temple, 53
Prodigal Son, The, 97, 238
Purity, 182

Righting a wrong, 188
Redeemer, Jesus Christ called, 162
Resurrection of Our Lord, 83
Rosary, The Holy, feast of, 114
Rose of Lima, St., 268

Sacrament: what it is, 224; of Baptism, 225; Confirmation, 226; Penance, 228
Samaritan, The Good, 53
Santa Claus, 118, 271
Saviour, Promise of a, 44; Mother of the, 47; Birth of, 49; Name of Jesus, 53
Scapular of Our Lady of Mt. Carmel, 269
Sign of the Cross, 24, 113
Simeon, 53
Simon Stock, St., 269
Sin: what it is, 64, 142, 234, 235; original sin, 64, 143; actual sin, 64, 143; kinds of, 66, 143; mortal, 67, 144; effects of mortal sin, 67, 144; effects of venial sin, 68, 69, 145-146; harms us, 69; offends God, 141.
Sophia, St., and her daughters, feast of, 269
Spirit, God is a, 11, **132**
Stanislaus Kostka, St., 193
Stealing, Sin of, 186
Stephen of Hungary, St., 200
Sunday Mass, 165
Sunday, the Lord's day, 165, 166, **167**

Tarcisius, St., 251
Thomas Aquinas, St., feast of, 265
Three Kings, The, 119
Three Wise Men, Adoration of the, 54, 119
Trinity, The Blessed, 133; and St. Patrick, 23, **124**
Truthfulness, 189

Ursula, St., feast of, 116

Valentine, St., feast of, 120, 272
Vincent de Paul, St., feast of, 270
Visitation, Feast of the, 259

Wolsey, 17

www.ingramcontent.com/pod-product-compliance
Lightning Source LLC
Chambersburg PA
CBHW071427070526
44578CB00001B/26